THE MEANING OF THE CONSTITUTION

An Interdisciplinary Study of Legal Theory

Gary C. Leedes

National University Publications
ASSOCIATED FACULTY PRESS, INC.
Millwood, N.Y. • New York City • London

New Studies on Law and Society

Kushner, *Apartheid in America*
Rubinstein & Fry, *Of A Homosexual Teacher*
Smith, *Genetics, Ethics and the Law*
Riga, *Right to Die or Right to Live?*
Rosenfield, *Labor Protection Provisions in Airline Mergers*
Gordon, *Crime and Criminal Law*
Smith, *Ethical, Legal and Social Challenges to a Brave New World (2 volumes)*
Munro, *Grievance Arbitration Procedure*
Riga, *Human Rights as Human and Christian Realities*
Buetow, *The Scabbardless Sword*
Smith, *Medical Legal Aspects of Cryonics*
Leedes, *The Meaning of the Constitution*
Malia, *Maritime Law*
Schoenfeld, *Psychoanalysis Applied To The Law*

Manufactured in the United States of America

Published by
Associated Faculty Press, Inc.
Millwood, N.Y.

The paper in this book meets the guidelines for permanence and durability of the Committee on Production Guidelines for Book Longevity of the Council on Library Resources.

Library of Congress Cataloging in Publication Data

Leedes, Gary C., 1934-
    The meaning of the Constitution.

    (New studies on law and society)
    Includes index.
    1. United States—Constitutional law—Interpretation
and construction. 2. Judicial process—United States.
I. Title. II. Series.
KF4550.L39   **1986**   342.73   83-12297
ISBN 0-86733-038-4   347.302

For Carol and John
Their patient heroism far surpassed my reasonable expectations

ACKNOWLEDGMENTS

The author wishes to thank his secretaries Gloria Sapp and Ann Robinson for typing, and retyping numerous early drafts. The author also gratefully acknowledges the assistance of several brilliant students who checked the footnotes and corrected his mistakes: Stephen Johnson of the University of Richmond Law School, John Power, and Louis Goldberg of Washington University Law School. The author also expresses appreciation for financial support from the National Endowment of the Humanities, Santa Clara University School of Law, Washington University School of Law, and the University of Richmond. Finally and most important the author wants to praise the Lord for His help.

*   *   *   *   *   *

A portion of this book appeared previously, in different form, as an article in the **Santa Clara Law Review,** copyright 1983. It is incorporated within the text here with permission of that journal, for which the author expresses his gratitude.

ABOUT THE AUTHOR

Gary Charles Leedes is a Professor of Constitutional Law who has taught at Loyola Law School in Los Angeles, Santa Clara University Law School, University of Richmond Law School and at Washington University School of Law in St. Louis. He is the author of many law review articles. He has numerous law degrees, including an S.J.D. from Harvard Law School. For ten years, Professor Leedes was an active trial lawyer, but he has devoted full time to teaching and research since 1972.

Contents

Preface

The meaning of the Constitution is a social fact that is found by a human being who brings to bear his own perspectives and state of mind. To this extent, the Constitution's interpreters lack objectivity. Judicial objectivity is a misunderstood shorthand reference for a judge who is governed by law, the resultant case ruling that is authoritatively established by an acceptable method, and the values that exist independently of a particular judge's private notions of morality, politics, and justice. While so-called objectivity is demanded by the public, we disqualify a judge for legal bias, which is not the exact antonym for judicial objectivity.

In this book, I describe the authoritativeness of the Constitution, but the values underlying the basic norm obviously do not emanate solely from the parchment, or the word symbols impressed upon the written text. The values, coinciding with the ethos of the nation, are filtered by the judge's mind, and transform his mind as he transforms the values and the mode by which they are expressed. A process is at work as judges attuned to the public's social conscience preserve the Constitution's first principles of civic virtue while new developments of law are generated. By means of this process, the impartial judge seeks the true meaning of the Constitution, but his prejudices, often reflecting truth, are the energies that constitute his mind. Thus, the resultant case ruling is neither solely objective nor subjective, but is authoritative, if certain institutionalized technical requirements are met. The judge, faithful to the law's calling, is an acceptable mediator of the Constitution's antinomies because he is a servant of the valid balance the Constitution strikes at the moment of his decision, which is but a point on a line of growth.

Introduction

Slogans about judicial restraint, judicial activism, and the Supreme Court's role in a political democracy do not decide hard cases. Judges do. A fair-minded judge will carefully evaluate the competing interests of groups and individuals, assigning weights to privileges, liberties, fundamental rights, duties, and governmental goals. These difficult judgments about priorities entail judicial discretion, which is considered a worrisome variable in constitutional cases.

According to the claims of pundits, judges should never decide cases subjectively. The pundits' claim, however trite, is not self-explanatory; indeed, the concepts of objectivity and subjectivity are often used rhetorically; they have become nonedifying slogans that serve in lieu of a descriptively accurate theory of constitutional law. Judges are not critically aware of all their preconceptions, nor can all their biases be corrected. However, to say that a judge's exercise of power is either subjective or objective is to mistake the elements of the court's judgment for the alloy.

This is a book of essays about conventional theory which explains the interaction between several dependent variables, including the beliefs of law-abiding citizens and the content of case law. Conventional theory is distinguishable from radical or skeptical schools of thought. Some radicals advocate axioms of substantive justice that are incompatible with existing understandings about the content of the Constitution. Skeptics often prefer judicial restraint, even when politically accountable officials behave outrageously. Radicals and skeptics, alike, doubt the competence of the Supreme Court to interpret the Constitution impartially. In contrast, the conventional specialist in constitutional law considers the Court adequately competent to decide cases in accordance with the legal system's basic norm.

Some contemporary scholars disparage the legal system's basic norm as an empty symbol;[1] I explain, however, how the basic symbol (that is, the written Constitution) represents definable limits on power, which officials respect. To preserve the rule of law against despotism, judges cite and enforce the Constitution, but the basic norm adapts, within reason, to society's evolving basic values. In fact, widely shared understandings about reasonable expectations have become substantive constitutional rights. This is a natural process, which enables an ancient text to serve as a successful medium for communicating and preserving enduring norms derived from first principles.

In hard cases, the Court's responsibility is to "mediate, to accommodate, to cushion"[2] the controversy that is presented by an aggrieved litigant's challenge to governmental action. The Court decides whether the harm done to *an individual*'s reasonable expectations is disproportionate to the government's pursuit of public purposes.[3] In performing its mediating functions, the Supreme Court lacks the authorization to effectuate a revolutionary social transformation, and rarely imposes socially unacceptable change. Conventional theory accordingly analyzes the steadying factors of the American legal system. These steadying factors help judges transcend the dualism of subjectivity and objectivity.

Principles of constitutional law are occasionally reformulated by judges, but as Professor N. MacCormick writes:

> A person appointed to be a judge takes up a position within a fairly well-defined institution, "a Court," and as a consequence of his appointment he incurs a duty to resolve disputes coming before him in accordance with law — not just to arbitrate according to the equity of an individual case (whatever that might be supposed to mean) nor to conciliate or procure compromises.[4]

MacCormick's statement is sound, but needs to be clarified when the government enacts, or is unable to repeal, oppressive laws. For example, during several generations, state-mandated racial segregation in public schools was not unconstitutional; now it is.[5] The Constitution is capable of absorbing inchoate principles of law when they are ripe for recognition because of changing social perceptions about the balance to be struck among competing interests. In short, important and substantial reformulations of the Constitution's meaning have occurred because the Constitution's more indeterminate principles are capable of growth.

A summary of the series of essays comprising this book follows: Part I discusses the general characteristics of social theory, and points out some limitations of legal theory. The second chapter of Part I evaluates theories for interpreting the evocative text of the Constitution. I analyze the authoritative status of the Constitution, its philosophical underpinnings with normative force, and the relevance of the framers' intent. The Fathers' horizon of thought simultaneously opens and delimits each succeeding generation's own horizon of thought about law.

Part II discusses the framers' world of ideas including those of two great thinkers of the Scottish Enlightenment, Francis Hutcheson and Thomas Reid. Inexplicably, most American legal historians have neglected Reid and Hutcheson, though their views influenced many of the Founding Fathers. The Founders were encouraged by Hutcheson's views on civic virtue, which suggested that self-seeking individuals are capable of self-government if there is an impartial arbiter who is able to resolve factional controversies. Reid was concerned with a rational method for persuading persons with different conceptions of morality to adhere to self-evident first principles. Reid and Hutcheson were pragmatic empiricists who avoided the relativism of the skeptics, and the dogma of the rationalists. The spontaneous evolution of law, which satisfies a citizen's reasonable expectations, was conceivable in the eighteenth century owing, in part, to their profound contributions to liberal thought.

Part III introduces a theory that explains how a judge can interpret a text impartially even though he reads it with his own preconceptions. This hermeneutic approach also explains how the irradiant meaning of an ancient text can be brought forward into a contemporary horizon of thought. In Part III, several critiques of conventional legal theory are presented. I argue, the critiques notwithstanding, that the Court's substantive due process doctrine is appropriate in a political democracy.

The final chapters of Part III identify, describe, and justify a legitimate political agenda for the Supreme Court of the United States. I elaborate upon the following conventional thesis: activism on behalf of litigants in constitutional cases is warranted when politically accountable officials, at the behest of a majority, violate their duty to respect limits on governmental power. Limits on official power stem, in part, from understandings among people about tolerance, mutual forbearance, and reasonable expectations generating constitutional rights. When the dimensions of constitutional rights are uncertain, and impartial forum determines whether the challenged action violates the balance our civil society strikes between individualistic and utilitarian preferences — a balance that varies from generation to generation. During a process of dialogue and dialectic, the meaning of the Constitution becomes revealed as judges try to extract the unsaid, and work out the inconsistencies and anachronisms of the case law. Each case, therefore, presents an opportunity to let the Constitution speak. In other words, understanding the Constitution is a progressive of its universal meaning — a progression that is always underway as concrete cases continue to be adjudicated.

It is difficult to generalize about the process of interpreting the Constitution, and equally difficult to explain the interdependence of legal principles, and the pragmatic policies of people governed by legal principles. Nevertheless, this book develops a theory of constitutional law that is based upon the authoritative status of the Constitution, which, as interpreted, is ever approaching socially acceptable legal answers to ultimate questions about freedom, equality and fairness. This theory mirrors American law's complexity as courts cautiously grope their way towards the satisfaction of a pluralistic society's needs and ideals.

Part I   Theories
Chapter 1   General Characteristics of Theories

A. The Limited Perspective of Legal Theory

Social theorists tend to be interested in the ultimate questions: universal truths, the fundamental traits of human nature, the ideal government, and the progress of civilization; they aspire to transcend traditional conceptual boundaries and some particular time period.[6] Such aspirations were once thought realistic. The *philosophes* of the Enlightenment worked toward a comprehensive theory of law, morals, and politics, one that described how the elements of legal and political systems can harmoniously interact with persons and groups in society. One comprehensive social theory has more power to organize norms and facts than an uncoordinated group of partial theories. However, lacking such a social theory, we lack the greater comprehension of the universal ideal that justifies particular theories of law.[7]

In jurisprudential theory, the law, typically, is depicted as a constellation of reasons for actions that are taken, permitted, prohibited, recognized, and enforced by authoritative law-making and law-applying institutions.[8] The reasons that are dispositive in court are those recognized in the legal system as valid. *Validity* is a technical term. A law can be technically valid, unpopular, and disgusting at the same time.The legal system,however, is not an autonomous discipline. Its apparent independence is illusory because it is "bound up with the existence and identity of the political system of which it is a part."[9] Since the boundaries of the legal system are ultimately dependent upon the reverberations of the larger political system,[10] judges might not have the final word when boundaries are drawn between the two systems. A legal system is a transitory phenomenon with just a "momentary"[11] existence when compared with the span of history. Similarly, of course, theories of constitutional law are transient.

A theory of constitutional law provides limited but useful perspectives because the Constitution and the body of norms which it generates and justifies would be disconnected and groundless if it were not for the organizing principles of theory. A useful theory has a structure that is grounded on verifiable data; its concepts are sufficiently abstract to give the structure a capacity to handle a wide range of normative data, and a capacity to assimilate many explanations of the theory's subject matter.

A structural theory of constitutional law conveys the impression of order and coherence when it unifies diverse and apparently discrete phenomena through its explanation of various normative and institutiona¹ relationships

1

that would otherwise be unclear. For example, John Ely's influential theory of judicial review [12] serves this purpose, as it discloses otherwise unnoticed relationships among the Warren Court's decisions, some early Marshall Court decisions, historical data, and other diverse data including footnotes [13] in judicial opinions. Ely's theory, however, recognizes no judicially protected domain of substantive human rights. The theory goes to the verge of adopting the premise that the individual in a broadly participatory democracy may be subjected to the arbitrary actions of the government, so long as the purity of the political process is maintained.

Ely's coherent theory is technically sound, and it is plausibly based on the institutional limitations that constrain courts in a democratic society. His theory of judicial review is a classic example of the limited perspective of constitutional theory because it prescribes a set of technical doctrines that do not necessarily satisfy society's reasonable expectations. Moreover, Ely's theory does not try to describe the current methodology of the Supreme Court.

No theory of law attempts to provide a complete picture of social reality. There are "pure" theories of law;[14] analytical theories of jurisprudence;[15] process-oriented theories of constitutional law;[16] and inquiries into the legitimacy of constitutional policy-making by the judiciary.[17] We have theories of legal reasoning;[18] theories of politics which focus either on groups, elites, or power;[19] functionalism;[20] formalism,[21] psychology[22], and theories of democracy.[23] These different and discrete theories clarify our thoughts and enable us to view the law and politics, but each perspective, although useful, restricts peripheral vision. Several different theories can be combined; nonetheless, we are compelled to settle for less than total vision.

Talcott Parsons wrote that "a general theory of the processes of change in the social system is not possible in the present state of knowledge."[24] That statement, written several decades ago, still holds true. Even in the physical sciences, contemporary theorists are primarily concerned not with ultimate questions about reality, but with "systematically ordering and relating the elements of human experience so that further experiences can be anticipated (under stipulated conditions) and past experiences can be explained, made to seem reasonable in the light of relationships already established."[25] A theory of constitutional law with practical value is also concerned with ordering the elements of law into some coherent pattern, so that further developments can be anticipated under stipulated conditions, and past developments can be explained and evaluated in light of the explanatory power of the theory. I suspect, however, that constitutional theory, if it is to have credible explanatory force, has to beg the ultimate questions of justice,[26] and be tempered by "the sense of [accomplishing] what is feasible, what is possible, and what is correct here and now."[27]

Theory is defined as "a system of assumptions, accepted principles, and rules of procedure devised to analyze, predict, or otherwise explain the nature of a specified set of phenomena."[28] If a theory of constitutional law were exhaustive and complete, not to mention boring, it would (1) identify sources of law that generate or justify legal norms, and explain their relevance, value, and legitimacy; (2) facilitate informed predictions about the resolution of specified legal issues; (3) facilitate informed estimates about the utility of proposed formal and instrumental theories of adjudication and interpretation (and explain how they contribute to specified objectives); (4) indicate various options for interpreting the text of constitutional provisions, historical materials, precedent, and other materials which are relied upon by interpreters; (5) describe and analyze various techniques of adjudication and interpretation that are actually in use (and indicate the probable consequences of adhering to various methods of adjudication and interpretation); (6) describe and analyze the degree to which various methods of adjudication and interpretation conform to, or deviate from, the reasonable expectations of various specified groups in society; (7) identify and analyze various interests of individuals and groups and indicate the degree of contemporary national consensus, if any; (8) indicate, with respect to various modes or levels of judicial scrutiny, the probable consequences for specified objectives and interest groups; (9) indicate the possible, actual, and acceptable range of judicial discretion in specified cases, the factors that judges take into consideration, the various rules of judicial administration (for instance, presumptions and canons of self-restraint), the choices that are foreclosed, and the courses of actions and options that will be open or closed if conditions change in specified ways; (10) indicate the degree to which judge-made law adapts to the emerging needs of society and compare, in various specified respects, judge-made law with law made by other officials in society; (11) specify the extent of the judicial branch's power (de facto and *de jure*) to decide political issues; (12) indicate the relative competence of judges to contribute to the attainment of certain carefully specified objectives of social justice; (13) identify modes of relief that are available when judges make mistakes of law or fact; (14) define and assess the impact of judicial decisions and mistakes on society; (15) indicate the options open to the governed when there is dissatisfaction with judicial review; and (16) identify, generate, and make available additional data to improve the theorist's ability to analyze the preceding elements of a complete theory of law.

Many elements essential to a complete theory of constitutional law are not listed, and a comprehensive theory of justice based on constitutional law does not exist. There are several heuristic "limited function" theories in constitutional law, some of which will be identified in the following section.

B. Limited Function Theories

An "example [of a limited function theory] is a factor theory, . . . that explains by stipulating the necessary and/or sufficient conditions for the generation of a particular phenomenon."[29] The generalizations are related through, and dependent upon, the phenomenon they describe and explain. The form of factor theory can be symbolized as follows: If there is A, B, and C, there is X, or unless there is A, B, and C, there is no X.[30] For example, if we assume that X is a coherent body of constitutional law, a factor theory describes and explains the necessary conditions for coherence and consistency.[31] Such a factor theory would have only limited usefulness; for example, the unpredictable psychological factor in judging, the number of judges with different views, and the social consequences of producing X, suggest that a perfectly coherent body of constitutional law, consistently applied, is not only impossible but socially undesirable in some respects. A factor theory therefore falls far short of a complete theory of law.

Other partial theories include "genetic" theories,[32] which trace the development of constitutional law or its concepts through successive states. Although the value of "genetic" theories is limited, they deepen insights and they can supplement a normative theory of interpretation. There are also "teleological explanations" which make use of the concept of purpose or goal as an explanatory device";[33] thus, the "idea of progress" can be the objective for a theory that is useful for constitutional law specialists[34] who advocate social change (usually at an accelerated pace).

Another partial theory is the functionalist explanation.[35] Functionalist theories "refer to the contribution of some element in a system [such as judicial review] to the maintenance of the system in a given state."[36] A functional approach to judicial review describes the effects of judicial activism on parts of the political system, including for example, the legislature, the executive branch, other institutions, groups of people, and individuals.[37] Still another theory of law is based on the psychological argument.[38] Many writers claim that judges have a temperament that equips them to resolve certain issues more sensitively, impartially, or reflectively than electorally accountable officials.[39]

Theories can also be classified according to their logical form. There are theories based on deductively related generalizations, and inductive theories based on the probabilistic form of generalizations.[40] The latter takes the form of a tendency statement ("Some A is B") or an arithmetic ratio ("N percent of A is B").[41] A deductive relationship, on the other hand, refers to universal propositions (either "all A is B," or "not B, then not A") that are formally deduced from a set of prime axioms,[42] or what are variously called first principles, self-evident truths, or symbolic generalizations.[43]

Strictly speaking, legal theory cannot take the form of deductively related generalizations that explain the impact of law on society.[44] Although it might be possible to derive a logically "right" answer to social problems from preexisting principles of law,[45] the logical answer's future impact on the society can be described only by the probabilistic or tendency forms of generalization.

Concerning the general impact of judicial review on society, the reliability of probabilistic forms of generalizations[46] varies depending on the quality or quantity of available information. For example, if we estimate that judicial review generally is likely to eliminate impurities from the political process, the accuracy of our assessment depends partly on our ability to specify all the factors that facilitate or interfere with a courts' efficient performance of this function. Since the relevant evidence is never complete, for we are tracking a developing, somewhat unpredictable, social process, we must do the best we can — make educated guesses.

Models[47] are not theories but rather parts of theories. A model has heuristic value, but it is not an adequate substitute for a theory that explains the subject matter represented by the model.[48] A model characteristically consists of a set of elements whose interaction is governed by stipulated rules.[49]

Models can be constructed to symbolize the law's elements and their interaction. For example, the logical model of positivism defines an exhaustive set of elements (valid laws), distinguishes this set of elements from elements which do not count as law, and stipulates the rules that govern the manipulation of these elements by legal organs.[50] "Models are always partial and approximate"; "there will be properties of observed reality not duplicated in the model", and the model often has "properties that are not duplicated in the empirical world."[51] A model, like a map, a blueprint, an analogy, or a metaphor, is "useful for suggesting expectations about empirical phenomena."[52] Each model, however, has certain built-in assumptions that are presumed to be true, and only a theory can explain whether the model's built-in assumptions are actually true.

There is no general agreement about criteria for evaluating the formal models incorporated into legal theory.[53] Therefore, any analytical model's built-in assumptions can be challenged. For example, Professor Dworkin challenges the assumption built into Professor Hart's model of positivism that presumes the existence of social pressures that channel judicial discretion. Dworkin claims that Hart's model has no counterpart in the empirical world.[54] Hart's model, however, whatever its alleged shortcomings, facilitates an explanation of the concept of law because it reduces empirical questions to formal, logical terms.

The typologies (elements classified conceptually in order to make analytical distinctions) of a model can provide new insights for viewing subject matter.[55] A model's typologies can also distort reality. The most common errors of models, and of theories which uncritically incorporate models, are (1) attributing to reality what are only the properties and built-in assumptions of the model, (2) reading into the model a basis for unwarranted predictions, and (3) failing to ascertain the degree of congruence between the model and reality.[56]

Theorists who do not use models, as such, may fall into the same traps. For example, John Ely's theory of judicial review[57] consists of typologies (for instance, the technical distinction between substantive and political participation values) that trigger rules of choice which govern judicial discretion. The rules of choice in Ely's theory disallow aggressive judicial review in most substantive rights cases. The unsupported assumption is that representative government is benefited by judicial review only when political process values are protected actively by courts. The more typical premise is that judicial review of substantive political outcomes is beneficial. Which premise is supported by reliable data?

C. The Inadequate Data Base of Constitutional Theory

Ely's theory of judicial review is useful for evaluating the state of the art in constitutional theory. In the words of one critic, Ely comes close to perfecting process-oriented theory,[58] yet he fails to "ground his descriptions of our present political process in data."[59] For example, Ely assumes that the attempts of certain minority groups to become part of protective coalitions "prove recurrently unavailing,"[60] but he offers no study of coalitions; moreover, it has been pointed out that "the study of coalitions in congress . . . may be quite useless for the study of decision-making in congressional committees."[61] To the extent that a theorists's normative judgments are made on the basis of unverifiable factual assumptions, it is quite difficult to evaluate how much bias or error is built into his conceptual scheme.

Ely refers to a representation-reinforcing kind of judicial review, which requires courts to correct political malfunctions that violate the underlying assumptions of representative government.[62] Can political malfunctions be remedied by courts? With what degree of success? At what cost? How different would the political system be if Ely's theory were adopted? What are the psychological consequences? These are questions that obviously cannot be answered by the normative component of a partial theory unsupported by empirical data.

The common failing of constitutional theory is its inadequate data base. We just do not know, for example, when and how often judges are best equipped to make political decisions, nor do we know what the consequences of their actions will be. The kinds of questions that legal scholars ask, and the kinds of theories that they develop, are often determined by the methods of research that they employ. Many theorists, primarily interested in the advocacy of normative doctrines, are not interested in careful social science research.[63] They often merely react to each other's work. Some theorists treat the existence of substantive values and political process values as a suprafactual dichotomy. This venerable practice often disguises a factually unsupported evaluational statements.[64] Dichotomous distinctions like the construct between substantive and process values are interesting, but their "content must be discovered by observing then in application to the data they are meant to elucidate."[65]

Ely's theory has a strong functionalist emphasis — that is, it explains the phenomenon of judicial review; it explains the political system in which the phenomenon occurs; and it stipulates the consequences of judicial review for the system. The theory refers to the harmful and beneficial consequences to the democratic process, which will occur if one mode of interpreting the Constitution is adopted in preference to another. The democratic process, however, is a complex, stratified, differentiated, interacting bevy of public and private power centers that cannot easily be captured by any analytic definition.[66] Functional explanations amount to little more than propaganda when the dynamics of the political system cannot be stipulated clearly enough to provide a reference point for demonstrating the consequences of active judicial review in some cases and passive judicial review in others.

Ely explains that the judicial role should be passive "out of a respect for the democratic process,"[67] and suggests that the Supreme Court's role should be restricted to process values that reinforce the quality of representation in the political system. It is difficult to establish the correspondence between obscure concepts (for example, quality of representation, political malfunction, virtual representation, and representation-reinforcing) and "empirical data that are wholly unambiguous and testable."[68] When measured by the scientific criterion of testability, any functionalist explanation of judicial review — not just Ely's — is weak.

Functionalists face a difficult boundary problem when they refer generally to the democratic system or the political system. "An unbounded system is not a system; systems exist only by virtue of being distinguished from the [total] environment which contains several systems."[69] Even when the theorist defines a system analytically, and distinguishes between system, structure, and function, there is the danger of forcing the facts into a pattern of unacceptable postulates such as (1) every part in the system is related to every other part; (2) only one part (for instance, the courts) can perform certain functions; and (3) every part in the system has a function. Moreover, there is the tendency to equate functional necessity with the phenomenon that is explained.[70] Furthermore, the assumption that the system *"works well enough as it is,* and it is given (only) to rather *discrete* sorts of malfunction"[71] is typical of functional explanations.[72] This assumption is implicit in Ely's explanation.[73] When a theory of constitutional law attempts to explain too much phenomena without empirical support, it is, obviously, suspect.[74]

D. Conventional Theory

Conventional theory describes and explains constitutional law in light of its historical development with a view toward its future development. It analyzes techniques for interpreting the Constitution's meaning, and it provides a basis for predicting trends and the probable outcomes of cases. Since conventional theory describes the techniques that actually are used by judges, it corresponds to events that occur daily in courts.

Conventional theory also prescribes a safe, sound, and stable method of deciding constitutional cases. Therefore, it is concerned with each individual's reasonable expectations, which are protected or generated by the Constitution. When the reasonable expectations are unknown, owing to the absence of reliable data, conventional theory presumes the absence of reasonable expectations with constitutional significance. Thus the reasonable expectations standard has a double barreled normative component since it constrains judges as they determine what constitutionally significant limits constrain the power of legislatures and other officials of the government.

The reasonable expectations standard enables the law to change in ways that are compatible with society's basic values. Judges are affected by this direction-giving, dynamic standard in different ways, and not all judges realize or express how they are affected. Obviously, countless variables are involved when courts flesh out and apply this multi-faceted criterion. The essays that follow deal with many of these variables.

Chapter 2. The Possibility of a Theory of Ultimate Interpretation

A. The Problem of the Constitution's Indeterminate Provisions

The Constitution is widely accepted as the basic source of valid law in the United States, but its indeterminacy is a problem for its interpreters. Some provisions appear to be empty vessels. The inscrutable Ninth Amendment immediately comes to mind,[75] and there are others.[76] The equal protection clause[77] has perhaps an uncontested core meaning, but its evocative peripheral meaning lacks discernible limits. The due process clauses have stimulated heated controversy, and some of the Supreme Court's best and worst opinions involve substantive due process doctrine.

Each indeterminate constitutional provision requires intermediate premises to connect the written text with events, past, present, and anticipated.[78] As intermediate premises are introduced, inevitably the meaning of the written provisions changes, which creates new areas of uncertainty. The development of new mediating abstractions is a creative enterprise since judges alter the meaning of textual provisions in accordance with their own understanding of constitutional law.

Interpreters of the Constitution disagree about methods for its interpretation. Interesting questions concerning the proper methods of interpretation are provoking many responses, but no widely accepted theory. The difficulties have not changed the fact that the Constitution is still the center of gravity for the system of law making.[79] It is, however, becoming less unusual for critical scholars to claim that the Constitution is no longer *the* basic norm that specifies the criteria of legal validity. Theories, however, are far more transitory than the Constitution, which they describe.

Some of yesterday's theories of interpretation, for example, "strict intentionalism"[80] and "literalism"[81] are no longer credible. Discernment of the framers' actual intent is difficult since the light that reveals the authentic original meaning of the Constitution is dimmed by the mist of time. When we try to reconstruct the framers' intent, the available materials permit us to take only "samples" and "soundings."[82] The voices of those who adopted the Constitution are virtually inaudible owing to the huge "unrecorded hum of implication."[83]

The Supreme Court of course has successfully asserted its power to interpret the Constitution. Official action is said to be invalid when it is repugnant to the Court's interpretation of the Constitution in "cases or controversies."[84] Owing to the doctrine of judicial supremacy,[85] jurists and scholars take turns attacking and defending the legitimacy of constitutional policymaking by the judiciary.[86] Some of the participants in the debate have developed theories of constitutional law,[87] but their theories generate serious differences of opinion.[88] Among the theorists, there are interpretivists,[89] noninterpretivists,[90] and other rival groups, which have split into sects with diverse views. Some believe that judges should take the lead in the movement for moral growth.[91] Others are apostles of judicial restraint;[92] still others advocate the process-oriented approach.[93] Furthermore, there are commentators who are content to let the Court do its own thing because it always has and always will.[94] As a result there are many fragments of theory; the Court itself is eclectic when it adopts ideas. Because the Court remains somewhat unpredictable, there is a basis to conclude that the current crop of theories is not descriptively accurate. Despite endless academic brainstorming, there is still a need for, but an absence of, a reliable descriptive theory of constitutional law.

Different judges have different theories,[95] and therefore demands for consistency and coherence, if pressed too far, are "forms of utopian argument."[96] It is not utopian, however, to expect continuity rather than disconnected points of law. Alexander Bickel wrote, "[C]ontinuity is a chief concern of the Court, as it is the main reason for the Court's place in the hearts of its countrymen."[97] If a theory that stressed continuity could be developed, a judicial decision consistent with the theory would be perceived as theoretically sound instead of result oriented.

Two pitfalls have trapped certain theorists: incurable romantic speculation and pedantry. Political scientists, with good reason, mistrust "the incurable romanticism of the speculative theorist who requires no evidence beyond his own intuitions, and ... the compulsive earnestness of the quantitative technician who accepts nothing that cannot be expressed in numbers and everything that can."[98] The fussy interpretivists who would keep the Constitution in the straitjacket of the framers' specific intentions stumble into both pitfalls. For numbers, they substitute snippets from the historical record, and for inferences, they lean heavily on their own dogmatic preconceptions. Fortunately, this type of interpretivism is on the decline. All interpretivists, however, are under attack because disciplined adherence to original sources of constitutional law is perceived, by some revisionists, to be inimical to moral progress[99] or some other fashionable objective.[100] But if the Constitution's text, structure, and history are no longer the only foundations for a theory of constitutional interpretation, then what else is acceptable?

One method, frequently used by theorists to overcome the indeterminate provisions of the Constitution, is to single out a supreme principle of political morality as the premise from which all elaboration follows. For example, it is tempting to identify the concept "equal concern and respect"[101] (or "the duty of representation that lies at the core of our system")[102] as *the* fundamental first principle that supports the entire body of constitutional law. The case has not yet been proven that the Constitution rests solely upon one or two identifiable underpinnings. This building block method frequently ignores the Supreme Court's case rulings. A better theory is required to explain the cases that elaborate authoritatively upon the Constitution's indeterminate provisions.

There is reason to believe that the framers left to their posterity the development of many provisions in the Consitution.[103] Dean Ely's notion of "ultimate interpretivism"[104] implies that a vital presupposition of the Constitution is the authentic consent of the governed. This presupposition is a standard usually adhered to by the Constitution's interpreters, a fact which suggests that the Constitution can be viewed as a "disciplinary matrix"[105] — disciplinary because it refers to norms that obligate "the practitioners of a particular discipline; 'matrix' because it is composed of ordered elements of various sorts, each requiring further specification."[106]

The ultimate interpretivism paradigm requires a clarification of the conception "framers' intent" and a reexamination of their first principles and our conception of a first principle. Each first principle reexamined and perhaps reformulated should be verified as authentic, but as T. Kuhn writes "[V]erification is like natural selection; it picks out the most viable among the actual alternatives in a particular historical situation."[107] The most viable alternatives are those that appear to have a historical pedigree, or those with the power to connect the present with the past in accordance with the objectives of a theory of law that stresses continuity.

References to history, of course, can lead to unwarranted assumptions. Trustworthy inductive generalizations about the framers' intent might be unavailable. Moreover, there is not necessarily only one right answer to a question of social science.[108] Prescriptive theories of interpretation, therefore, should be offered tentatively. The Constitution has a chameleonlike quality that takes its color from its surroundings and from its interpreter's preconceptions.

B. The Continuum Between Interpretivist and Noninterpretivist Extremes

The debate between interpretivists and noninterpretivists is a sequel to the nineteenth-century jurisprudential debate about positive law. According to one side of the older debate, law evolves spontaneously within a society, and the search for the origins of law is the search for custom.[109] Law in other words has its own vitality, and the language of law is a medium indicating the customary norms of behavior that are enforced by the state. Under John Austin's different view, law is not merely the recognition of custom; the image invoked is that of a powerful authority that stands above the society and issues commands.[110] Similarly, contemporary interpretivists supposedly look only to the electorally accountable officials who issue laws, unless a more authoritative generator of norms, the Constitution, clearly prohibits the official action. Noninterpretivists, on the other hand, supposedly look to the observed customs of society, tradition, consensus, and the developing insights of advanced thinkers.

Some references to interpretivism and noninterpretivism are manifestations of stereotypical thinking, and the dichotomy is somewhat misleading. Now and in bygone eras, both "ideal types" describe only part of the truth. The cases disclose that judge-made constitutional law is partially the embodiment into law of reasonable expectations and partially the product of the positive law that is more or less spelled out in the Constitution's specific provisions.

Thinkers, usually classified as interpretivists, are motivated by objectives that relate to concerns about representative democracy, the value of continuity in the law, the value of a safe and sound approach that respects the written positive law, and the advantages of a legal system that consists of a coherent body of norms that are derived from the basic positive law norm. They stress the importance of having the legislature transform popular will into law, the disanalogies between law and morality, and potential abuses of judicial review. Interpretivists mistrust natural law because of fears that it will lead to radical social transformation. Of course these concerns and objectives are not obvious deductions from the text,[111] and many so-called noninterpretivists share these same concerns.

The "interpretivist" label supposedly depicts a positive law orientation[112] that allows interpreters of the Constitution little leeway in the expansion and contraction of principles with constitutional dimensions. Because of the objectives, principles, and policies which motivate interpretivists, their demand for the strict construction of the Constitution mainly applies to the judicial branch. Contemporary interpretivists permit the electorally accountable officials substantial leeway. The Congress can interpret the Tenth Amendment[113] and the necessary and proper clause[114] virtually as it pleases. The point can be overstated; Justice William Rehnquist's resurrection of the Tenth Amendment comes to mind.[115] But in the area of individual rights, the so-called interpretivists, by and large, presume that the legislature has virtually unfettered discretion unless there is a specific prohibition on their powers.

Most specialists in legal theory realize that the Constitution is respected as *the* basic norm by the Supreme Court; indeed, the Court's respect for constitutionalism is a virtue that earns it respect, although some opinions cheat.[116] Noninterpretivism is not necessarily at odds with the values of constitutionalism. This is not to say that all noninterpretivists who adhere to constitutionalism reject the ideals of natural law. In fact, the positive law versus natural law debate in the United States is somewhat unusual. The power of judicial review enables judges to incorporate into the Constitution those natural law principles logically compatible with its meaning. Therefore, technically, all judge-made law is positive law since courts are duly established legal organs with the power to prohibit, authorize, and permit official behavior.

In sum, the differences of opinions between the interpretivists and the noninterpretivists run along a continuum. Nearly everyone, except those who prefer banging on the table as opposed to describing the cases, respects the value of precedent, standard modes of legal reasoning, and plausible interpretations of language. Few question the value of constitutionalism, which imposes some limits on all branches of government — federal, state, and local.

If we must generalize, it is more likely that noninterpretivists want to improve or change the system; they tend to emphasize human rights and look for the answers to the ultimate questions of social justice. Interpretivists generally tend to be more conservative when judge-made law is discussed; it is more likely that they want to preserve the status quo while they look for authentic principles and sources of positive law with pedigrees.

The danger is that the foregoing generalizations tend to degenerate into a conceptualism, which ignores the real line-drawing problem; namely, the line between permissible discretion and the kind of discretion that is prohibited by the doctrines of constitutionalism and the rule of law. The problem of unfettered discretion becomes intolerable when courts impose unacceptable values on fair-minded people. The solution is to confine the judges' discretion, no easy trick, but extremists miss the legitimate middle ground along the continuum between "will-o'-the-wisp," noninterpretivism, and the strict canons of fussy intepretivism. They are imprisoned by conceptualism.

C. Ultimate Intepretivism

The distance between interpretivism and noninterpretivism is bridged by the Supreme Court since it sometimes uses one method and sometimes the other. There is, however, a need to build a better bridge, for as Justice Rehnquist has written, "Constitutional building blocks have been piled on top of one another so that the connection between the original provision in the Constitution and its application in a particular case is all but incomprehensible."[117] This "tottering tower"[118] image suggests the need for a constitutional theory with several underpinnings, so that when one line of cases is rejected, the integrity of the entire structure of constitutionalism is not undermined.

The theory that builds from the paradigm of ultimate interpretivism describes a structure of legal norms that has both a steadying and dynamic quality. Although law, at times, is "the outcome of interactions among a chaotic set of contingent forces,"[119] the object of a conventional theory of ultimate interpretivism is to classify a multitude of data and to arrange it so that the data can be comprehended as a cosmos instead of chaos. The steadying factors described by a conventional theory of ultimate interpretivism are also prescriptive, because the theory advocates adherence to patterns of judicial behavior that are regular and predictable.

Conventional theory identifies rules for constitutional adjudication that permit the expansion and contraction of principles at a rate, and on a scale, which ensures stability in the law. The principles of the law are the primary sources of the justifications for the case law. As MacCormick writes:

> when we ask what gives a principle *legal* quality we must give the answer in terms of its actual or potential explanatory and justificatory function in relation to law already established, that is, in relation to established rules of law as identified by reference to criteria of recognition.[120]

A conventional theory of ultimate interpretivism, accordingly, presupposes that the Constitution itself, and not the theory which explains it,[121] is the basic norm. Although the basic norm has several philosophical underpinnings, the theory that builds upon this structure might be invalid. Although theories can be discarded by judges, the basic norm may not be disregarded.

D. The Legal Code and the Framers' Intent Justification

Ultimate interpretivism is a paradigm that can support a descriptive theory that explains what the courts are doing but its notion of ascribing the framers' intent is accepted reluctantly by many lawyers and judges. Judge R. Neely, for example, writes:

> Lawyers . . . who take seriously recent U.S. Supreme Court historical scholarship as applied to the Constitution also probably believe in the Tooth Fairy and the Easter Bunny. The truth of the matter is that judges do not say these things with a straight face; they are talking in code which most of the bar understands.[122]

What is the code that most of the bar understands, and how devious a code is it?

The legal profession understands that the framers' intent is a powerful justification for a case ruling. No lawyer who can show that the original understanding of a constitutional provision is consistent with his client's cause will fail to call that fact to a court's attention. The framers' intent may be a reification,[123] but as Dean Sandalow notes, it is comforting to the public; and "it seems to support the institutional arrangements we have established for giving contemporary meaning to the Constitution. . . ."[124] Just as no lawyer will ignore the framers' intent in a hard case, no judge will hesitate to cite the original understanding if it supports his case ruling. Even if the framers' intent is nothing more than an *ostensibly* justifying reason for a decision,[125] there are strong pressures on judges to give reasons for their decisions which appear to be authoritative.[126] Attributing responsibility for the decision to the "wise men we call the framers" gives comfort to the public and a sense of repose to the profession.[127]

Judges are expected to be the impartial determiners of disputes that are brought to court, and the law reviews and newspaper editors will righteously criticize the judge who does not appear impartial. When Smith sues Jones, a decision in favor of Smith is not, according to neurotics, impartial because there is a winner and a loser. The applicable law obviously favors some interests over others, but if the law can be traced back to principles compatible with the framers' intent, there is an objective (impersonal) justification for the judge's decision. Of course, it would be absurd to contend that the framers wanted Smith to win and Jones to lose; every decision at the most concrete level of particularity goes beyond the framers' intent.

Judge Neely writes, "[F]ocusing on the purported intention of the geniuses in 1789 is like looking at one frame in the middle of a motion picture film."[128] The entire moving picture, however, would capture the whole course of relevant history, including the antecedents of the contested constitutional provision and its line of growth. If I were to name the motion picture, I would call it ultimate interpretivism to distinguish it from the X-rated film, known as illegitimate noninterpretivism, and the cartoon known as literal interpretivism. But I do not want to wander from my purpose, which is to decipher the code used by lawyers and judges when *they* interpret the Constitution.

The lawyer for Smith who cites *The Federalist Essays* or selected snippets from Max Farrand's *Records of the Federal Convention of 1787* is more than likely earning a fee. He might want to win the case in order to justify the amount, but he need not bring this fact to a court's attention. The judge who decides the case for Smith does so perhaps because he has a political philosophy, which happens to be quite different from the philosophy of James Madison, yet in his opinion, there are numerous references to Madison. Why does the judge not make his opinion more candid and cite his own philosophy, which is based on the complete works of Mark Twain? Because a decision based on the framers' intent is considered a better reason for the judgment of a court. What actually prompts a judge to decide for Smith "is quite a different matter from the question whether there are . . . good justifying reasons"[129] that connect his decision to the Constitution. The code is the medium for communicating the ostensibly justifying reasons; we call it the legal code. It is the law. What the judge had for breakfast may prompt him to rule in favor of Smith, but his breakfast, even if agreeable, is an extralegal irrelevancy.[130]

There is a tendency to leap to the conclusion that the process that I have just described is hypocritical, but it is not a dereliction of duty if the judge has conscientiously developed certain habits which satisfy the public's demands for impartiality. In my Smith versus Jones example, there was obviously some hidden motivation on the part of the judge, as well as the lawyer, but the hidden motivation reveals that "[t]hose who work within [the] system persuade precisely by convincing the relevant audience that there are reasons of overriding weight why X *ought* to be done...."[131] Justice Hugo Black, for example, would not be regarded by the legal profession as a hypocrite if his private papers were published revealing that all his decisions were consistent with some political philosophy that was his own peculiar synthesis of John Locke, Madison, the ancient Greek historian Thucydides, and Tom Watson. Justice Black might cite Madison for obvious reasons, but Tom Watson — no way. Black was perceived as an interpretivist, but he was not naive in attributing his value choices to the Founding Fathers. If not completely candid, his opinions reveal what is expected of the Court. "The way an institution advertises tells you what it thinks its customers demand."[132]

E. Salvaging Remnants of the Framers' Intent Justification

Never has conventional legal theory been under attack from so many quarters.[133] A new generation of academicians is not satisfied with codes and fictions that disguise existing unjust power relationships. Clearly, the preceding self-congratulatory and complacent description of the usefulness of the framers' intent code as a justification for these relationships will no longer satisfy all critical legal scholars. It is tempting to abandon the framers' intent personification and speak, as Learned Hand did, of the "proliferation of purpose."[134] But even that euphemism will no longer suffice, because critical scholars want to know the *real* meaning of the case ruling. Thus, Justice Peckham's decision in *Lochner* v. *New York*[135] is attributed to its alleged *real* meaning: the development of industrialism and the untamed urges within the truculent capitalist order, which could no longer be denied.[136]

Some critics of conventional theory imply that Justice Black distorted the real meaning of the First Amendment.[137] Criticism, which focuses solely on the *real meaning,* overlooks a pertinent distinction: "Believing is a mental activity which may be distinguished . . . from that which is believed — sometimes called . . . the *content* of the believing."[138] Justice Black probably did believe that he was interpreting the framers' intent, however unreal his belief may appear to the sophisticated historian of ideas. Surely Justice Black sometimes had doubts, but it is not unconscionable when a judge keeps private his doubts. Indeed, if a judge's understanding of the Constitution is ascribed to the framers in an opinion, he is following a traditional practice that has not been abandoned.

It is frequently useful to ascertain which principles were important to the people who reached the original compromises. When reliable historical materials are accessible, evidence that the (eighteenth-century) rival factions shared some fundamental principles that shed light on the meaning of the Constitution (and on the methods for its interpretation) is always relevant to a court.

Maintaining the continuity of law and being true to oneself are the arduous duties of a judge, whose calling requires impartiality and fidelity to established law. The framers' intent is a source of law that helps a judge who is looking for the steadying factors. Yet, those who want to abandon the practice of bringing forward the framers' intentions write, "[N]o amount of looking into the minds of the framers . . . can render the text less authoritative."[139] This misses the point. *Reynolds* v. *Sims*[140] would have been a much easier case if there were evidence showing that the framers desired a "one-person, one-vote" formula.

When counsel cites the framers' intent, a responsive court reads the relevant evidence to test the representation. Although a court may rely on trustworthy evidence, sometimes it is misled. A corporation was held to be a person within the meaning of the Fourteenth Amendment in 1886[141] partly because counsel, four years earlier, had indulged in deliberate deception.[142] On the other hand, suppose counsel had been telling the truth about the framers' intent — is a court supposed to put the evidence out of its mind? If not, and they rely upon trustworthy information, it is an appropriate justification for the case ruling. The framers' intent perhaps is elusive[143] (and even somewhat mystical on occasion), but the problems created by its relevancy will not go away by wishing they would disappear.

Some commentators argue that the framers' intent justification should be used only when there is adequate historical evidence to support it.[144] A distinction should be made (as a concession to this point of view) between *finding* the framers' intent and *ascribing* intent to the framers. A theory of ultimate interpretivism would *find* the framers' intent on the basis of evidence disclosing that influential participants in the Convention's debates intended specifically to constitutionalize a particular conception. The framers' intent justification would then be unquestionably relevant when used as direct evidence or used by way of analogy. Suppose the evidence discloses that the framers intended only to constitutionalize broad concepts and aspirations. Under these circumstances, intent may still be *ascribed*. It is extravagant to maintain that all ascriptions of the framers' intent are illegitimate. The judge who ascribes intent to the framers is bridging the historical distance between their minds and ours.

The commentator who finds "wholly lacking"[145] the evidence indicating that the framers intended to constitutionalize broad concepts, overlooks Madison's thirty-seventh essay in *The Federalist*.[146] Madison wrote that "all new laws"[147] are obscure until their meaning is clarified, and that one method of ascertaining their meaning is a "series of . . . adjudications."[148] Madison added, referring to the failure of the framers to be more specific: "Experience has instructed us that no skill in the science of government has yet been able to discriminate and define, with sufficient certainty, its three great provinces — the legislative, executive, and judiciary; or even the privileges and powers of the different legislative branches."[149] Madison expected the different branches to check each other,[150] but he did not suggest limits which would prevent each branch from "liquidat[ing]"[151] the meaning of the Constitution's "equivocal"[152] provisions.

Madison wrote that "no language is so copious as to supply words and phrases [for the framers] for every complex idea, or so correct as not to include many equivocally denoting different ideas."[153] He added that language was by its nature "dim and doubtful"[154] and was susceptible to "vague and incorrect definitions"[155] because of "indistinctness of object," "imperfection of the organ of conception," and "inadequateness of the vehicle of ideas."[156] A judge with a hermeneutic perspective might or might not draw the inference that Madison was authorizing all three branches of government to particularize broad concepts as future experience dictated. There is, however, ample evidence in *The Federalist* to provide a rational basis for such an inference.

Madison doubtless was aware that once a particular principle is discerned within a broad concept, the principle expands and contracts in unpredictable ways. He referred to "the common law"[157] of Great Britain as the exemplar.[158] This is not to say that a court has power to ignore the admittedly imperfect work of the Convention and to adopt covertly an improved Constitution submitted by an "ingenious theorist"[159] who designs "a Constitution planned in his closet or in his imagination."[160] On this score, Alexander Hamilton agreed, but wrote that, over time, the courts can particularize the meaning of the Constitition's various provisions "and can adjust them to each other in a harmonious and consistent WHOLE."[161] The Scottish Enlightenment philosophy that was influential in the United States during the late eighteenth century also stressed the difference between a concept and a conception and the need for those educated in the law to clarify and particularize concepts.[162]

According to Professor Michael Perry, the judge who ascribes intent to the framers lacks candor.[163] This is true on occasion. However, ascribing intent to authors of texts is part of the art of judging. Learned Hand wrote, "[N]obody does this exactly right; great judges do it better than the rest of us."[164] Hand was not suggesting, however, that the greater the judge, the less the candor. Learned Hand himself was unable to perceive the words of the Constitution as anything other than "empty vessels."[165] As a result, he deferred, perhaps excessively, to the electorally accountable officials. This "hands-off" pattern characterizes the Supreme Court's work product between 1937 and 1973, and it persists to a substantial extent.

Deference is surely one legitimate option when the judge throws up his arms in despair because he cannot find a principle grounded in the Constitution that justifies careful judicial review. Deference to electorally accountable officials is, however, but one underpinning of the Constitution. There are others — deference to the plain meaning of the text, to precedent, to the rule of law, to the doctrine of constitutionalism, to the reasonable expectations of the American people, and to the demonstrably perceptible yearnings of the framers. The art of judging, however, cannot be explained by any theory of constitutional law that completely ignores the art of ascribing intent to the framers.

Any legitimate technique of interpretation that requires both personal detachment and creative imagination can be abused; however, it is clearly premature to abandon the practice of ascription. In constitutional law, as in other fields, complete "retooling is an extravagance to be reserved for the occasion that demands it."[166] The abuse of the practice of ascribing intent to the framers has hardly reached the crisis stage. It is still helpful; when "so very few ways of seeing will do . . . the ones that have withstood the tests of group use are worth transmitting from generation to generation."[167] This does not mean that the nature of the framers' intent paradigm must remain static. As a paradigm, "the balance between [its] inseparable legislative and definitional force shifts over time."[168] Only after the nature of a change is appreciated "is normal puzzle-solving research possible."[169]

The recent scholarly attack on the practice of ascribing intent to the framers is so relentless that citation of the Constitution is in some quarters already regarded as a mere "linguistic convention."[170] The irony is that some modern commentators construe the framers' intent very strictly, yet they would have the courts engage in what, on occasion, is illegitimate policy-making, a practice which they justify by means of functionalist considerations. For example, Professor Perry's effective argument for judicial activism is "informed and guided by a developing sensitivity to the moral and political plight of society's 'marginal' persons."[171] His justification for judicial intervention is the prophetic competence of the courts to discern developing moral insights.[172] Equating a court's ability to discern moral progress with its legal power is a more worrisome approach than the practice of relying plausibly upon the framers' intent.

Is the ascription of the framers' intent pseudohistory? Judge Neely writes:

> What the courts are really saying when they engage in this pseudohistory is that if the Founding Fathers had grown up in the twentieth century, had had all of our experiences, and perceived the problems from our vantage point, they would decide the case the way the court writing the opinion is deciding it. That is an interesting, but hardly reassuring, approach to applying the mandates of a *written* constitutional document.[173]

A cure for pseudohistory is better research. But if another cure for the infection of pseudohistory is a speculative functional justification that does not depend on authentic sources of law, one might justly wish to retain the disease.

Some ascriptions of the framers' intent are dubious; for example, Chief Justice Warren, who wrote the Court's *Reynolds* v. *Sims*[174] opinion, cited Abraham Lincoln's Gettysburg Address for authority.[175] That kind of embellishment is hardly reassuring. Dean Ely, on the other hand, delivers a more powerful argument in defense of Warren Court reapportionment decisions.[176] It is not my intention to discuss whether *Reynolds* v. *Sims* was a mistake of law, or whether Ely's approach is ultimately convincing. I do think, however, that Ely's approach points us in the right direction toward a theory of ultimate interpretivism, which is more credible than pseudohistory.

It is unrealistic to expect Ely, or some other ultimate interpretivist to deliver a "knockdown" argument that dispels all doubts about the framers' intent. In most, if not all cases, the historical materials do not yield absolute inductive generalizations. Those who demand knockdown arguments are demanding the impossible, which is a tactical device that is useful for those advocates who urge the courts to hasten our moral evolution. Any resemblance, for example, between constitutionalism and the principles of morality cited by Professor Perry in his argument for Supreme Court activism is purely coincidental.[177] It is this type of runaway noninterpretivism, which urges courts to rush pell-mell to judgment, that stiffens the resolve of the conventional theorist to fight back.

One astute commentator who is fighting back is Professor Henry Monaghan, who stresses the following points:[178] (1) "No convincing reason appears why purpose may not be ascertained from any relevant source, including . . . 'legislative history.' "[179] (2) Original intent "is . . . a way of thinking about constitutional 'meaning' that follows from the basic concepts that legitimate judicial review itself."[180] (3) Many of those opposed to the limitations of a framers' intent restriction view those restrictions as an impediment to their political goals.[181] (4) Many law professors in the present generation have little interest in history. They "are problem solvers by training."[182] (5) "Currently the most fashionable formula is that the constitutional language is best understood simply as an open-ended delegation to future interpreters to resolve problems in accordance with the framers' 'concepts,' but not with their specific 'conceptions.' "[183] Professor Monaghan concludes by reiterating his well-argued position that it is "wrong to believe that one can ascertain the meaning of the Constitution by asking: 'Is this what America stands for'?"[184]

I am less rigid than Professor Monaghan. There does come a time when one must concede that a precedent is solidly entrenched. At some point, a precedent like *Reynolds* v. *Sims*,[185] which perhaps was mistakenly introduced into the law, becomes legitimate. For technical reasons, a case ruling is deemed valid until overruled, and its very existence over a period of time as a valid norm gives it legitimacy. A case ruling is legitimate when it "is rightful . . . in the eyes of those subject to it."[186] At first, the public might not actually consent to the precedent; there is, however, a half-conscious acquiescence induced by the charisma of the Supreme Court of the United States. Over time an authoritative ruling becomes not only legitimate, but a tradition and a basis for new case rulings that are generated by reasoned elaboration from seminal precedent.[187] A line of principled case law development will likely take the courts beyond the framers' horizon of thought.

It is perhaps time to substitute Professor Dworkin's "concept of constitutional intention"[188] for the practice of ascribing intent to the framers, a practice which tends to stir controversy. A theory of descriptive ultimate interpretivism, however, would retain the method of ascribing intent because it is occasionally a convenient and plausible justification for a court's ruling and the law's line of growth. Those who claim that the framers' intent is not binding should have the burden of persuasion to show, in each case, that the original understanding has become absurdly anachronistic.

F. A Critique of Pseudointerpretivism

A judge who imposes his "instinctive preferences and inarticulate convictions,"[189] has the duty of "ensuring the unbroken continuance of law and preserving the tradition of the legal idea."[190] To borrow an image from Heidegger, the interpreter might have to jump outside of, and beyond, the shadow of the original and partially hidden meaning of the Constitution. But how? The judge often relies on relevant history, traditions, precedent, enduring principles of law, the framers' intent, and other materials that look backward in time. Thus, a judge is empowered, under certain circumstances, to deviate from the framers' particular concrete intentions.[191] Professor Perry claims, however, that the framers did not authorize any judge to write his own conceptions of individual rights into the Constitution.[192]

Contrary to Perry's position, there is circumstantial evidence that the framers authorized interpreters of the Constitution to make value judgments that are not necessarily analogous to the framers' own particular value judgements. For example, the framers knew the Magna Carta lay dormant for four hundred years until it was revived in the early seventeenth century to serve as the foundation of a natural law edifice which would support English subjects' demands for greater participation in government and for improved guarantees of their civil and economic rights."[193] Thus they knew that "those seeking dramatic change in the order of society were able to allege that [the Magna Carta] has always been the law."[194] Is it not rational to assume that the Founders contemplated that their posterity would also employ the same venerable technique of adding gloss to an authoritative document beyond that which was contemplated by its authors?

The Founding Fathers were apprehensive but realistic about indeterminate provisions, "for whenever we leave principles and clear and positive law," John Adams observed, "and wander after Constructions, one Construction or consequence is piled upon another until we get an immense distance from Fact, Truth, and Nature."[195] Eighteenth-century Americans were quite familiar with the English common law which kept pace with custom including "the reforming work of Lord Mansfield in England who convinced many Americans that judges could not be depended upon merely to apply existing law."[196]

The influential common sense philosophy of Thomas Reid,[197] although neglected by contemporary American legal historians, distinguished between a general concept and a particular conception. According to Reid, a popular conception of a word's meaning is the shared meaning of the word, and the interpretation of a general concept of law depends on the conceptions of interpreters who understand the law.[198] Reid, whose writing was well-known in eighteenth-century North America, made it clear that the meaning of words and concepts change as shared conceptions of meaning change.

The evidence also supports a plausible argument that the framers were sophisticated enough to understand that an interpreter of the law has the discretion to expound the particular meaning of the general principles in the Constitution. Carl Friedrich wrote that in the eighteenth century "[N]orms generally seemed to these times and their representative thinkers to be the more important and valuable, the more general they were."[199] The general norms were the principles: the content, left to posterity, was simply policy.

The framers of the Fourteenth Amendment also adopted broad language, knowing full well that the Court's previous interpretations of the Constitution's broad provisions were often creative. The concept "privileges and immunities"[200] is so broad that Justice Bushrod Washington in *Corfield* v. *Coryell*[201] was unable to enumerate all the rights that are comprehended by Article IV, § 2. The concept is also dynamic since the evolving common law drops and adds privileges and immunities as it keeps pace with custom. Although the privileges and immunities clause of the Fourteenth Amendment has its roots in article IV, § 2,[202] it was intended specifically to consitutionalize the few rights that were identified in the Civil Rights Act of 1866.[203] The phrase *privileges and immunities* was chosen for several reasons. First, Congress wanted to reserve the power to enact additional legislation to secure adequate racial equality.[204] The words were also chosen to encourage a latitudinarian construction of the Fourteenth Amendment by the courts that would decide whether the Civil Rights Act of 1866 is constitutional. Moreover, the generality of the language [205] was designed to attract support from all — radicals, moderates, and conservatives — who subscribed to the abstract ideal of equal civil rights,[206] even if many persons had doubts about interpretations that might occur long after the Fourteenth Amendment was added to the Constitution.[207]

When the proposed Fourteenth Amendment was debated, a full measure of equal rights for the emancipated slaves was not contemplated for the immediate future. The freedmen were not yet economically self-reliant; as a group, they were not yet perceived to be fully prepared for freedom and as a result, when the Fourteenth Amendment was ratified, blacks in some respects were simultaneously regarded as citizens and wards of the government.[208] The urgent problem during the early phase of Reconstruction was the coercive state codes that prevented emancipated blacks from enjoying the civil rights of free persons.[209] The school segregation problem was not a high priority item on the agenda of the Congress. There was virtually no public education provided for blacks in the South.[210] Moreover state-mandated, systematic segregation in public places in the South was less of a problem in the late 1860s than it was in the late 1890s and early 1900s.[211]

Congress in 1867 actually had nothing that resembled a comprehensive plan for racial equality; it is not surprising, therefore, that the dominant coalition that was in charge of Reconstruction kept open many options. The federal government had adequate military and police powers to protect its most immediately pressing interests,[212] but no one was sure what other particular measures would be appropriate so as to ensure racial equality. In short, most of the nation adopted a "wait and see" attitude.[213]

Although Congress feared that the Court might be too sympathetic toward the states' rights point of view,[214] a few Supreme Court decisions had generously construed the Constitution in favor of human rights, and this sporadic judicial activism added gloss to the Constitution.[215] Thus, in the 1860s, the nation was aware that the framers' specific intentions do not always count, particularly when they are unclear. The loose language of the Fourteenth Amendment was a standing invitation for innovative interpretation. The text is passive; its meaning has to be extracted wherever what is stated is not immediately intelligible

The burning question, by the 1870s, was the scope of the Fourteenth Amendment's protection for blacks. As Charles Fairman writes, "A form of words had been made supreme law."[216] The developments that eventually determined the content of the Fourteenth Amendment's "form of words" can be briefly summarized. Several of the common law's substantive privileges and immunities became rights that were protected by the Court's conception of substantive due process.[217] Although the Court strictly construed Congress's Fourteenth-Amendment enforcement powers,[218] in several cases, [219] the Court took the position that what is implied in the Constitution "is as much a part of the instrument as what is expressed."[220] Justice Joseph Bradley pointed out that the language of the Fourteenth Amendment was "general embracing all citizens, and . . . [that] it was purposely so expressed."[221] Thus, there was a built-in need for courts to discern the underlying aspirations of the amendment's supporters.

Justice Bradley's generous interpretation of the Fourteenth Amendment was consistent with a shift in the balance of power between the federal government and the states, which was desired by most of the framers. In Justice Bradley's view, the judiciary is empowered to define the scope of the Fourteenth Amendment, and he wrote:

> [T]the amendment was an attempt to give voice to the strong national yearning for that . . . condition of things, in which . . . every citizen of the United States might stand erect in every portion of its soil, in the full enjoyment of every right and privilege belonging to a freeman. . . .[222]

Charles Fairman suggests that Justice Bradley's understanding of the "national yearning" is in accord with what members of Congress, hazily and hopefully, had seemed to be saying when they supported the amendment.[223] This kind of ultimate interpretivism is not a novel twentieth-century doctrine. In the *Dartmouth College* case,[224] Chief Justice Marshall explained that the underlying reason for a constitutional provision governs situations, unanticipated when the text was framed.[225] This is a solution to the problem of awakening the meaning that could be concealed by words. Concepts endowed with a forward-directed rationality have a built-in incomplete quality, and aggressive courts seize the opportunity presented by the controversy that asks hard questions of the authoritative text.

By 1954, interests that were labeled "social rights" as late as 1883[226] were labeled "civil rights" — even by racists who fought desegregation. It became obvious during the twentieth century that blacks had become, once again, victimized by a system that prevented them from enjoying the civil rights of free persons. In the *Slaughter-House* cases,[227] the Court had warned the states that they are to protect blacks from racially motivated "bad men" who would deprive them of the rights of emancipated men.[228] The oblique warning went unheeded, and it was not until the 1950s that the accumulated case precedent clearly justified the Court's wholesale invalidation of state-mandated segregation laws.[229]

Was *Brown* v. *Board of Education*[230] an incremental step in a long line of growth, or was the decision, as Perry suggests, an example of unauthorized, extraconstitutional policymaking by the Court? Although Professor Perry points out that "segregated golf courses are not simply an analogue"[231] of a practice specifically banned by the framers, segregation was actually a greater evil than many of the practices that were specifically banned by the Civil Rights Act of 1866. The combative, comprehensive, ruthlessly destructive, rigid system of segregation which prevented blacks from mingling with whites at golf courses, picture houses, auditoriums, bus terminals, ball parks, lunch counters, washrooms, schools, parks, neighborhoods, homes for the deaf, and penal institutions operated to push blacks farther down the ladder leading to equality and progress.[232] One insulting ordinance required a circus and tent show to have separate entrances, exits, ticket windows, and ticket sellers kept at least twenty-five feet apart.[233] Is it really crucial whether the framers banned this particular manifestation of an oppressive system?

It was the *system* of segregation that deprived the blacks of their enjoyment of civil rights and liberties. Given the long-standing aspirations for equal civil rights, regardless of race, did it any longer make sense for the Court to condone systematic racial segregation in public facilities? After a long process of tentative gropings, the Court acted forcefully in the 1950s. If *Brown* is "extraconstitutional," then *MacPherson* v. *Buick Motor Co.*[234] is extralegal. Both cases were the culminations of lines of growth in case law,[235] and were incremental by-products of an acceptable and traditional common law theory of adjudication.[236]

In *Brown,* the Court took account of the absence of any original specific understanding about school segregation, but it was aware of the reasonable expectations inspired by the Fourteenth Amendment. Although the Court defined afresh the normative scope of the equal protection clause, *Brown* was not a radical break with accumulating precedent. In legal hermeneutics, "[T]he judge who adopts the transmitted [Constitutional] law to the needs of the present is undoubtedly seeking to perform a practical task, but his interpretation of the law is by no means on that account an arbitrary reinterpretation."[237] Not only are the antecedents of a constitutional provision legally significant, but its line of growth is taken into account by the interpreter. The valid meaning of a constitutional provision is correctly understood "by seeing the past in its continuity with the present."[238]

Reliable descriptive theories of law recognize the force of case precedent, which creates reasonable expectations and civil rights. "To avoid an arbitrary discretion in the courts," Alexander Hamilton wrote in *The Federalist,* "it is indispensable that they should be bound down by strict rules and precedents, which serve to define and point out their duty in every particular case that comes before them. . . ."[239] The framers *intended* the courts to follow precedent.[240] They knew that "precedent gives to the legal system that rigidity which it must have if it is to possess a definite body of principles, and the flexibility which it must have if it is to adapt itself to the needs of a changing society."[241] Hamilton envisioned a system of judicial review that required the Court to adopt a theory of adjudication that was modeled on a doctrine of precedent in force in the courts of Great Britain. Therefore, a case ruling consistent with a binding precedent and compatible with the reasonable expectations of fair-minded people is valid. Since *Brown* is consistent with a line of judicial precedent and with the underlying values of the Fourteenth Amendment, it is not an example of illegitimate noninterpretivism. Perry, however, believes that *Brown* is extraconstitutional, unauthorized, and yet still justifiable because of the Court's comparative competence to discover "right answers — to fundamental political-moral problems."[242]

The unusual facet of Perry's thesis is his belief that the Court can make policy decisions that are based on extraconstitutional points of law. Perry anticipated correctly that his critics would argue that "extraconstitutional policymaking is a contraconstitutional practice."[243] In my view, absent a justifying valid principle that is generated and justified by the basic values of society, which are inchoate in the Constitution's text, structure and history including its presuppositions and its elaborations in precedent, a case ruling that is extraconstitutional is a contraconstitutional exercise of judicial power.

I run the risk of belaboring an obvious technical point, but a legal norm that is a legally *valid* norm is a part of a system of legally valid norms. A norm that is logically incompatible with any norm, which has superior validity, is not a valid norm. The basic norm, which always has superior validity is the Constitution which "is in fact, and must be regarded by the judges, as a fundamental law."[244] It is repugnant to traditional canons of legal reasoning and constitutionalism when a Court, exercising the power of judicial review, uses the pretext of extraconstitutionality "to substitute their own pleasure to the constitutional intentions. . . ."[245]

Validity is an epistemological, organizing concept that is devoid of substantive political content,[246] but it provides the basis for the logical possibility of a legal system that has intelligible form and structure. Indeed, validity is the technical attribute that gives a norm its obligatory character, and it is the obligatory character of a norm which distinguishes extraconstitutional norms from the authorized norms that qualify as law in the legal order.[247] Perry's theory ignores the concept of validity and is, for that reason, a political theory in search of validation. Absent validation, his argument lacks the quality of a legal theory.

Professor Perry claims that Americans, if they "fully understood the issues . . . would . . . accept . . . noninterpretive review in human rights cases."[248] It is sheer speculation, however, for a theorist to suggest that the public would accept unauthorized extraconstitutional policymaking by a Court simply because Congress allows the Court to grab power. Perry concedes that some of his theoretically important assumptions "are not susceptible of empirical demonstration."[249] More specifically, Perry concedes that he cannot demonstrate that his alleged "functional justification"[250] for extraconstitutional policymaking by courts will "enable us to keep a rough faith"[251] with our dualistic commitment to (1) "ongoing moral revaluation and moral growth,"[252] and (2) "the principle of electorally accountable, policymaking."[253] He nevertheless claims that extraconstitutional judicial policymaking is justified by the significant control by Congress over federal Court jurisdiction (which, he supposes, will contribute to an ongoing national moral dialogue). This controversial claim would give Congress unreviewable power to negate Supreme Court case rulings that are compatible with precedent and with society's evolving basic values.

There are several objections to Professor Perry's approach which encourages Congress to second-guess the Court's decisions that are not modern analogues to specific practices that were banned by the framers. *First,* sponsors of Court-stripping bills can exploit Perry's idea for illegitimate purposes that are designed to end the ongoing moral dialogue in courts.

Second, when the courts are free to exercise their virtually unfettered discretion, a sophisticated litigant will ask whether there is valid reason that requires him to obey a case ruling. Clearly, non-litigants will be less likely to obey the Court's decree voluntarily. *Third,* the executive branch can honestly take the position that it is not authorized to enforce extraconstitutional norms. The executive branch is not the puppet of the courts. The exercise of the executive power is authorized only by valid norms.[254] Perry, by seeking to close the countermajoritarian loophole in constitutional theory, opens Pandora's box. There is no reason, which is based on the Constitution, that suggests why the executive branch ought to obey an extraconstitutional decision; in fact, ordinarily it should not obey an admittedly unauthorized judicial decision.

Fourth, Perry's theory authorizes the Supreme Court to act as an administrative agency with rule-making powers. The public, however, does not have any procedural protections (for example, notice and an opportunity for comment)[255] when the Supreme Court qua Supreme Administrative Agency makes rules. Moreover, when an authorized government agency makes rules and the legislature retains the power to reverse the rule-making agency, the difference between a court and an agency is hard to perceive. Perry himself is ambivalent about the power of Congress to reverse the Supreme Court's case rulings.[256]

In the legal system of the United States, many political actors and scholars grudgingly tolerate the Court's mistakes, particularly when the general public is not aware that a serious mistake of law has been made, or when the decision is perceived by the public as a decision that is consistent with society's reasonable expectations. But few specialists in constitutional law condone or encourage mistakes of law by courts. Professor Perry's approach condones and, in some cases, encourages mistakes of constitutional law. Is not that its greatest danger? The stakes are indeed high when the Court is encouraged to make mistakes of law — deliberately.

Perry's theory encourages a judge to select any *"particular* political-moral criteria that are, in [his] view, authoritative."[257] The judge is also free to select the less fragmented "developing insights of moral philosophy and theology."[258] There is no stipulation in Perry's theory that the extraconstitutional principles selected by the judge have to be established or inchoate in the law. There is no requirement that the particular criterion selected must explain and justify previously decided case rulings in addition to the case at the bar. There is no admonition about deciding like cases alike. Perry, who encourages the judges to be "candidly clear."[259] also writes, "[s]urely there is no harm in maintaining *the linguistic convention* of saying the action violates the Constitution. . . ."[260] This approach which gives the prophetic judge unusual discretion to decide cases (intuitively) based upon his inclinations, is clearly at odds with contemporary and traditional expositions of the rule of law concept — depending of course on the judge's inclinations, and how often he changes his mind.

John Rawls refers to the rule of law as "justice as regularity,"[261] and writes, "If deviations from justice as regularity are too pervasive, a serious question may arise whether a system of law exists as opposed to a collection of particular orders designed to advance the interests of a dictator or the ideal of a benevolent despot."[262] Inspired by Professor Perry's theory, a judge could change his particular political-moral criteria as often as he develops new insights. His new insights, however benevolently intended, "would not [belong to] a legal system since they would not serve to organize social behavior by providing a basis for legitimate expectations."[263] Perry, however, rejects the framers' intent and tradition as not "much help"[264] to the judge, and Perry apparently would often sacrifice stability in the law for progress.

A judge who develops a "principled ground"[265] for his human rights doctrine, can overcome some problems that destabilize the legal system. But suppose his developing insights of moral progress are incompatible with the general principles of the Constitution. The judge, according to Perry, may nonetheless attribute his case rulings to the Constitution — without a credible discussion that discloses why.[266] Contrary to Perry, the Supreme Court of the United States is expected to justify its case rulings on the basis of principles that appear genuinely attributable to the Constitution. The public demands this safeguard because "[t]here is, to many men, something frightening and uncontrollable about an individual who insists upon taking his own reasoned judgment as the final authority for his actions."[267]

Perry, as noted, seeks to overcome these familiar objections to the activism of an electorally unaccountable Supreme Court by a functional justification for judicial review. His justification, which contemplates congressional supervision of illegitimate judicial policymaking is weak: he admits, "the burden of legislative inertia"[268] prevents Congress "from serving as a source of political control over noninterpretive review"[269] and "serves to enhance"[270] the Court's political power. When Madison devised the Constitution's system of representation, he counted on the ambition of officials to check the power of other officials;[271] he did not count on the kind of inertia that Perry seems to have in mind.

The politically ambitious members of Congress who presently want to strip the Court of jurisdiction are catering, sometimes excessively, to single-issue groups, the very kind of factions who, in Madison's day were interfering with the government's ability to promote an acceptable conception of civic virtue and the *general* welfare.[272] Professor Perry claims, however, that an educational nationwide dialogue will be beneficial, because "[t]he moral sensibilities of the pluralistic American polity typically lag behind, and are more fragmented than the developing insights"[273] of prophetic moralists. Perry's functional justification is not, strictly speaking, a legal justification, and it has the weakness of any functional approach that utilizes obscure concepts (more indeterminate than many he rejects on grounds of indeterminacy) that are not grounded on testable empirical data. The judge is expected to have a valid basis for selecting one developing insight over another, but Perry's theory leaves courts at large, without valid criteria.

Perry notes that a very great jurist, Justice Cardozo, knew when one competing interest outweighs another by consulting sources external to the law: "from experience and study and reflection; in brief, from life itself."[274] Justice Cardozo, however, did not have a theory of law that empowered judges to ignore clearly applicable legal principles. He did believe that judges had the discretion to fill in the gaps — the unanswered questions — in the Constitution. Rights, not specifically mentioned in the written Constitution, can be incorporated on the basis of the traditional, reasonable expectations of individuals in a self-governing republic. These rights, peripheral to the Constitution, are derived from trustworthy evidence that indicates whether particular liberties are sufficiently cherished, widely shared, and enduring enough to have special constitutional significance. Justice Cardozo was careful to justify his own judgments upon the values "so rooted in the traditions and conscience of our people as to be ranked as fundamental."[275]

Justice Cardozo did not impose a system of authoritarian ethics upon an unconsenting republic. Such a despotic exercise of power was contrary to his conception of the Court's role. Thus, when Professor Perry cites, with approval, the judge's own values as the authoritative source and justification of the law, he abstracts a part of constitutional interpretation from the whole. The part should be recognized as such and not mistaken for the whole.

Part II   The Framers of the Constitution, and Their World of Ideas
Chapter 3   Moral Sense

A. The Enlightenment: Its Indirect Influence on the Framers

A conventional theory of constitutional law notes that the judge may not legally impose his willful preferences without a justification that is compatible with the consent of the governed and with the first principles of the Constitution. There is a story about Georgi Plekhanov, perhaps apocryphal, that discloses the frightening potential of a small, well-intentioned elite group that acts as if it is above the law.

In 1903, at the conference of the Russian Social Democratic Party, there was a discussion about party discipline, and the anticipated benevolent social transformation that would ensue. A comrade asked whether the absolute authority that was exercised by the party's revolutionary nucleus was incompatible with the basic liberties that protected the inviolability of the person. Plekhanov, a venerated scholar and a warm, humane, and morally sensitive leader, informed the party that "if the revolution demanded it, everything — democracy, liberty, the rights of the individual — must be sacrified to it."[1] The so-called benevolent social transformation, in other words, "could not be carried through by men obsessed by scrupulous regard for the principles of *bourgeois* liberals."[2]

Plekhanov's deviation from first principles is not, needless to say, an appropriate model for a judge. He absolutely may not — it is simply impossible to avoid evoking the Platonic Guardian image at this point — seek to save the people from their own reasonable expectations because they hold "morally incorrect" values. He may not intrusively interrupt the ongoing democratic dialogue, however morally flawed, by fiat; nor may he employ the justifications that he knows better what the people really want. Moreover, a Court is not an impartial arbiter when it adopts the position of the Grand Inquisitor in *The Brothers Karamazov:*

[He] said that what men dreaded most was freedom of choice, to be left alone to grope their way in the dark; and the Church by lifting the responsibility from their shoulders made them willing, grateful, and happy slaves. The Grand Inquisitor stood for the dogmatic organization of the life of the spirit: Bazerov for its theoretical opposite — free scientific inquiry, the facing of the "hard" facts, the acceptance of the truth however [socially unjust].[3]

Modern scholarly advocates, generally, are more subtle than Plekhanov, or the Grand Inquisitor. Michael Perry, for example, writes that noninterpretive judicial review enables us as a people "to see beyond, and then to live beyond, the imperfections of whatever happens at the moment to be the established moral conventions."[4]

The Court would not impose right answers; it would generate a dialogue that leads to moral progress toward right answers. Perry's Court generates the moral dialogue perhaps before the time is ripe for an enlightening national debate. Yet, the Court is said to be an institution that looks "ahead to emergent principles in terms of which fragments of a new moral order can be forged."[5] Perry points out that the current political morality on certain issues within the competence of courts is "a stagnant or even regressive morality."[6] In short, the pluralistic American polity "typically lags behind" those who have better insights.[7]

It is one thing for a theorist to point out the moral flaws in the American people; it is quite another when he presumes that they would consent to a prophetic role for the Court. The judge is expected to be an intermediary between the people and their representatives; a court is not an institution that is in charge of society's spiritual development.

The world view of the Age of Enlightenment was not that of Plekhanov or the Grand Inquisitor; many *philosophes* believed that

Man is, in principle at least, everywhere and in every condition, able, if he wills it, to discover and apply rational solutions to his problems. And these solutions, because they are rational, cannot clash with one another, and will ultimately form a harmonious system in which the truth will prevail, and freedom, happiness, and unlimited opportunity for untrammeled self-development will be open to all.[8]

The late eighteenth-century *philosophe* knew nothing of dialectical materialism, the power of the irrational forces in civilized societies, the unconscious, relativity, natural selection, and the reported death of God. It was an optimistic era with ideas perhaps quaint by our standards. In many forms, however, eighteenth-century liberal values have survived in the United States, and since those values inspired the Founding Fathers, it is relevant to study their enlightening world of ideas.

It was the business of the Philadelphia Convention to strengthen the league of states pursuant to a theory of government in which "there exists a latent order that has a *legitimate claim*"[9] on the enduring respect of the governed. "This [latent] order once recognized is both a reassuring fact and a goal for constructive striving."[10] The Convention's challenge was to accommodate the needs of individuals and society, and to delineate their respective powers, rights, duties, privileges, and immunities. The delegates, encouraged by Newton's success, were influenced by Montesquieu's "purely empirical and inductive treatment of political and legal institutions."[11] There is, according to Montesquieu, "no universally applicable solution"[12] to social science problems, "only types of solutions" for concrete problems. The Founding Fathers believed that striking a balance between civic virtue and the demands of individuals for freedom was the great unresolvable puzzle. The puzzle remains, and so does the Constitution, which opens up the realm of ideas, out of which tentative solutions can be supplied.

The Constitution was inspired, in part, by the framers' belief that man is responsible for himself, for his self-development, and, by extension, for the welfare of his fellow man. A winner-take-all republican system of government, however, can be unjust, because civic virtue is a variable in the social equation; there is no guarantee that the winner of an election will put society's resources to work in order to secure fairly the happiness of mankind. A constitution cannot guarantee everyone's happiness; it facilitates the pursuit of happiness under law. The Constitution, however, was and is designed to rule out certain destructive tendencies (for example, destabilization and despotism) as it accommodates man's natural strivings. This undertaking, however, was difficult and delicate in a world where self-government on such a large scale was unprecedented.

Tolerance and mutuality of forbearance became virtues during the age of Enlightenment; each person was entitled to decent responsiveness from the authorities. Robust, unpleasantly vehement debate, however, was not a vice; indeed, the Founding Fathers traded off some tranquility for greater freedom.

Trade-offs were not uncommon in an age of reason in revolt against ultra-rationalism.[13] The *philosophes'* expectations were moderate, and perfect justice was considered an immoderate expectation.[14] The Founding Fathers recognized the limits of their own intellectual powers as well as the limits on the government's power. In the Constitution, therefore, space was left for the future expansion of rights and duties.

President George Washington was apologetic about the imprecision of the Constitution. He explained to Congress that the share of liberty for each individual is unspecified because "[t]he magnitude of the sacrifice must depend . . . on situation and circumstances as [well as] on the object to be obtained."[15] The object to be attained was "the consolidation of our Union, in which is involved our prosperity, felicity, safety, perhaps our national existence."[16] The Constitution, although imprecise, provided a compass for factions that were going in different directions. It could serve as an objective standard useful for resolving disputes.

An authoritative criterion of law, even if incomplete and variable, was imperative since many framers embraced Francis Hutcheson's doctrine that the moral sense of each individual is subjective.[17] Inescapably, each person feels a certain way, and he *knows* when he feels that a certain course of action is virtuous.[18] When he is opposed by a party who feels just as surely that he is wicked, the law does not necessarily have the right moral answer; it only provides an authoritative answer.

The Constitution obligates persons with different views of social justice. When Mr. Justice Holmes was told that the legal system was unjust, he replied: "I hate justice . . . when I hear a man appealing to that, I expect to find it an apology for not playing the game according to the rules — dodging some settled principle without articulate discrimination."[19] The point stated with less acerbity, is that the Constitution serves as a surrogate for an objective norm of justice, because it is recognized, by and large, as the most practical way to settle irresolvable moral disagreements. So long as the rules that control the judge's discretion point him to the authoritative Constitution,[20] the subjective component of his decision need not lead to a relativism that is arbitrary (invalid).

Were the eighteenth-century *philosophes* familiar with these jurisprudential notions? My investigation reveals that "their habits of mind and their feelings [were not unlike] ours."[21] On the one hand, these were natural scientists who believed that each person's moral sense answers questions of morality. On the other hand, however, the so-called common sense school of natural scientists was concerned with criteria for demonstrating the objective validity of moral principles.[22] The common sense school held that one could not be persuaded that a moral principle was right unless he could be persuaded that it was truly consistent with first principles[23] disclosing the duties of individuals[24] in society.

After observing the psychology of man and society, the common sense school led by Thomas Reid noted that a person must have the means of knowing his obligation.[25] However, since first principles are abstract, indistinct, and wavering generalities (for example, a person ought "to pursue what is good upon the whole, and to avoid what is ill upon the whole"),[26] Reid wrote that "our reasoning from these axioms to any duty that is not self-evident, can very rarely be demonstrative."[27] But he adds, "To act against what appears *most probable* in a matter of duty is as real a trespass against the first principles of morality, as to act against demonstration. ..."[28]

Like Reid, the Founding Fathers, for the most part, did not believe that man achieves mastery over his surroundings mainly through a priori premises and untested logical deductions. Like Reid, they believed that man rationally pursues his ends by relying on the evidence that experience discloses. Reid's common sense bolstered the framers' confidence that indeterminate concepts in constitutions can have permanency in controlling behavior. The framers were also reassured by Reid's message that rational man had the intellectual capacity to understand that it was in his prudent self-interest to exercise disciplined control over his actions and to obey rules. In short, citizens with free will are capable of disciplined self-government.

Francis Hutcheson is a relevant figure in the eighteenth-century's world of ideas because of his important indirect influence on the framers. Hutcheson's doctrine, like Reid's, bolstered the framers' confidence that the lot of mankind would be improved by self-government. His moral sense notion relieved the anxiety of those who believed that the subjectivity of values inevitably leads to antisocial behavior. He claimed that each person's self-interest inclined him toward the higher pleasures of civic virtue. His conception of virtue stressed man's obligation to produce the greatest happiness for the greatest number.[29] Hutcheson, Adam Smith's professor in moral philosophy,[30] anticipated the English jurist and philosopher, Jeremy Bentham,[31] and his confidence that ordinary people were virtuous encouraged the Americans to experiment with a republican form of government.

Hutcheson admitted that the moral sense can malfunction due to ignorance, mistaken belief, prejudice, and the like. An informed person, however, can avoid adopting arbitrary policies that impair social cohesion if he acts impartially pursuant to general rules consistently applied.[32] Hutcheson stressed the virtue of compromise since a socialized individual's moral sense is pleased when the system as a whole is operating more efficiently than any feasible substitute system.[33] Hutcheson believed that the best institutions evolve gradually, through trial and error — "a slow half-conscious growth."[34] He was a forerunner of those who later developed more elaborate doctrines of legal evolution.[35] His emphasis on institutions that are not planned by rationalists reminds us that the Supreme Court was not a prepackaged, ready-to-go institution emplaced in a closed system of law by ingenious system builders.[36]

Reid and Hutcheson are still relevant thinkers since a modern theory of law, accurately describing the American legal system, cannot ignore the antecedents of a constitutional provision and its line of growth.[37] The following discussion attempts to grasp the moral and epistemological antecedents of our constitutionalism.

B. The Heart of Francis Hutcheson's Theory

In 1900, Francis Hutcheson's biographer wrote that he "is an interesting . . . figure in the History of Modern Thought," but there is "uncertainty, when any attempt is made to specify his exact spere of influence."[38] J.R. Pole, in one of his two passing references, notes that Hutcheson's philosophy of benevolence "contained the seeds of a more systematic equality,"[39] but Hutcheson's name is mentioned only once by Bernard Bailyn, who groups Hutcheson with a hymnologist.[40] Page Smith in his recent book[41] does not mention him at all, and neither does F.A. Hayek[42] nor John Ely.[43] The contributors to the American Historical Association's collection of papers for the sesquicentennial of the Constitution[44] do not recognize his existence. In his paper, "European Doctrines and the Constitution," the usually meticulous R.M. MacIver writes:

> The seminal works of the age were English and French, those of Montesquieu, the Physiocrats, and Jean Jacques Rousseau on the one hand, and those of Locke, [James] Harrington, [Sir William] Blackstone, [David] Hume, Adam Smith, Algernon Sidney, and Tom Paine on the other. But Locke came nearer to *the heart of the case.*[45]

The "heart of the case" is the case for the Revolution. Hutcheson's works do not make for fiery propaganda pamphlets or soapbox speeches, which helps explain why he is a mysteriously neglected figure in accounts of the Revolution. Hutcheson believed that all men were naturally virtuous. His works became more pertinent when the incendiary phase of the Revolution passed, and it became necessary to lay the foundation for a new order. The social contract concept has a different function at this stage.[46] Locke's vision of the people delegating all sovereign power to the legislature appeared attractive, but when this idea was carried out in practice, state legislatures were captured by factions.[47] As a result, Locke's axiom that the legislature reigned supreme over both the executive and the courts, was rejected, "and in the rejection lay one essential difference between the emergent political system of America and that of England."[48]

Locke believed that property rights were natural, unalienable, and reserved by the people,[49] yet he also believed that the "very end and function of government" was to preserve an individual's natural rights.[50] Since Locke believed that the legislature could not be impartial in disputes over property between society and an individual, his social contract theory, which stresses individual rights but also stresses the absolute power of a legislature lacking in neutrality, is "hopelessly confused."[51] Revolution, Locke's way out of this paradox obviously, is an undesirable option when leaders are laying the foundation for a peaceful new social order. Another option is found in Hutcheson's moral sense doctrine, which directs rulers and ruled alike to pursue the general welfare.[52] Hutcheson's philosophy was more relevant than Locke's after the American Revolution, for he showed Americans that some portions of their liberty should be voluntarily sacrificed, since natural rights yielding personal advantages entail civic duties.

The gamble that civic virtue would triumph explains in part why the Constitution did not spell out the details for reconciling the legislature's police powers with the doctrine of vested rights. The details could be worked out later only after experience with the new system provided more data. It was said at the federal convention: "Experience must be our only guide. Reason may mislead us."[53] This empirical-inductive approach was also the approach of Francis Hutcheson.

In 1787, the principle that all men are "created equal" was no longer quite self-evident. The burning question no longer was the equal rights of "a whole people as a unity."[54] The quest was for a principle of equality that applies to a national community composed of individuals unequal in several material respects. In Hutcheson's depiction of the state of nature, "we are under *natural* bonds of beneficence and humanity toward all. . . ."[55] Hutcheson believed that a natural right arises "when a man's acting, possessing, or obtaining from another . . . tends to the good of Society."[56] Thus, Hutcheson's perspective of natural law is consistent with a stable republican government. This perspective tended to make Americans more confident in a skeletal Constitution that divided power: one that deliberately left the details for securing equality and the "Blessings of Liberty" to experience and to "[P]osterity."[57]

This survey of Hutcheson's philosophy is not a claim that the Constitution captures and memorializes his thoughts. Hutcheson was well-known in America, but the Constitution is not the product of any one philosopher, or some composite drawn from a list of great thinkers. Doubtless, it was a manifestation of the spirit of the time in which it was written. However, the contribution of Hutcheson has been given short shrift by most scholars. Although his moral sense doctrine obviously is not *the* underpinning of the Constitution, it is *an* underpinning which clarifies some contemporary misconceptions about the unity of liberal thought.

Roberto Unger, for example, refers to the "unity of classic liberal doctrine"[58] and assumes that there is an inescapable "antinomy in our conception of the relation between reason and desire in the moral life."[59] A partial antidote for Unger's generalization is Hutcheson's works. Hutcheson was a pioneer in recognizing that the connection between knowledge and political theory is intimate. Desire motivates individuals who think they know what civic virtue requires, but reason[60] enhances the probability of social cohesion. Although Hutcheson did not conceive of society as a whole that is greater than the sum of its individual parts, civic virtue is attainable because individuals are motivated to pursue the greatest happiness of the greatest number.[61] Thus, reason and desire, individualism and social utility, are brought into harmony.

In the sections that follow, after discussing how Hutcheson's contributions were introduced into the colonies,[62] there will be a description of the moral sense doctrine,[63] the auxiliary role of reason,[64] the implications of Hutcheson's ideas,[65] and the relevance of his ideas.[66]

1. The Influence of Francis Hutcheson

Francis Hutcheson was a professor of moral philosophy at the University of Glasgow[67] from 1730 to 1746, the year of his death.[68] He taught that the principle underlying the concept of moral goodness is not simply a revelation from God.[69] He also taught that a self-evident truth, however reassuring in the realm of epistemology, is neither moral nor immoral. Whether it is moral depends on the perceptions and approval of one's internal moral sense.[70] Hutcheson may be grouped with Lord Shaftesbury who influenced him, and with David Hume, whom he influenced profoundly.[71] Hume acknowledged his indebtedness,[72] but Jeremy Bentham did not realize that the maxim, "the greatest happiness of the greatest number," was introduced into British thought by Hutcheson.[73] Francis Hutcheson also had a great influence on his student, Adam Smith, who later modified his teacher's views on economics.[74] Hutcheson's influence in North America has not been underestimated by Garry Wills[75] and Morton White.[76] His moral sense doctrine was a strong rival of the rational intuitionism of both John Locke and Thomas Reid.[77] W.K. Frankena argues that Hutcheson is perhaps the first noncognitivist in the history of English-speaking ethical theory "who is at all clear and thorough."[78]

The starting point for Hutcheson is that "a sentiment or moral sense, not reason, is the foundation of morals."[79] Jefferson, a careful reader of Hutcheson, seemed to embrace the idea when he wrote, "Morals were too essential to the happiness of man to be risked on the uncertain combinations of the heart. [Their foundation is] therefore in sentiment, not in science."[80] Hutcheson's immediate influence in North America is evident in Jonathan Edwards's treatise entitled *The Nature of True Virtue.*[81] Edwards agreed that the language of morals is primarily an expression of moral sentiments.[82]

Hutcheson's empirical-inductive approach to moral philosophy insisted that the laws of nature relevant to morality could be formulated on the basis of human experience. He disagreed with system builders who maintained that valid moral distinctions are made on the basis of our knowledge of unchanging and unchangeable laws. Hutcheson also believed that rationalists do not explain morality when they find a synonym for it. Their tautologies were rejected by him.

Several future leaders of the United States were literally taught how to think when, as students, they were confronted with the views of the rationalists who attacked Hutcheson, and the empiricists who enthusiastically defended him. His ideas were carefully studied as part of the curriculum at Princeton, the College of Philadelphia, Kings College in New York, and William and Mary in Virginia.[83] His influence became even stronger, indirectly, after his views had been taken into account by others including David Hume, Adam Smith, the Scottish philosopher Adam Ferguson, Thomas Jefferson, James Madison, and John Adams. It may be that Hutcheson's influence on the succeeding generation of great thinkers actually obscures his own reputation, but his contemporaries in Great Britain, in

Europe, and in North America understood and appreciated[84] his "central role in the rich development of British moral philosophy in the eighteenth century."[85]

The very unsystematic character of Hutcheson's thought, when compared to the great system makers — René Descartes, Nicholas Malabranche, Baruch Spinoza, Gottfried Leibniz — "was precisely his strength in his own day."[86] Neither Great Britain (nor its colonies) were "ripe for a thoroughly consistent and coherent system."[87] His primary objective was to create enthusiasm[88] for civic virtue. The well-educated person and even the masses[89] were familiar with Hutcheson's works, which paved the way for declining importance of natural law, the partial separation of law from morals, and the need for a stronger central government that fosters economic growth. His liberalizing influence, his optimism, and his message that the virtuous have more pleasure, if not more fun, was just what many Americans wanted to hear.

2. The Mechanics and Function of the Moral Sense

Hutcheson rejected reason as the ultimate source of morality. Although reason may take one logically from premise to premise, it does not explain how the moral quality of an act is evaluated by the mind as virtuous. The rationalists explain that when A helps B, reason deems the act virtuous because it exhibits benevolence. But Hutcheson pointed out that the rationalists argue in a circle that does not illustrate.[90] Hutcheson asked why benevolence is a criterion for virtue; he was not satisfied with the rationalists' answer that it is self-evident. The rationalists explain that it is fitting for one human being to help another. Again, Hutcheson pointed out that this explanation does not account for the moral quality of the relationship between A and B when A helps B. Reason fails to explain anything other than that a relationship exists or that an act has occurred. Reasoning, standing alone, does not establish that the act or relationship is virtuous. Since reason· is inadequate, the only discriminating sense which can apprehend the moral quality of the act is a moral sense.[91]

Hutcheson compares the moral sense with a sense of beauty. An individual may be delighted with order, harmony, or grandeur. The human appetite gratified lies in some separate internal faculty of the mind that operates independently of the five senses. An aesthetic sense approves of beauty because of the pleasure felt when beauty is perceived; it is motivated to share the beauty with others unselfishly. The moral sense is delighted with benevolence in a similar way.[92]

Hutcheson explains that when A helps B, the moral sense of A is pleased. This pleasure motivates A to seek benevolence, and it causes A to approve of benevolence. The moral sense works simply because it has an appetite for pleasure, or, in less hedonistic terms, it is pleased with benevolence much as our aesthetic appetite is pleased with beauty.[93] This feeling "of peculiarly moral pleasure"[94] is the drive of sociability, a natural law which determines human behavior. It is a natural law because ordinarily a man-made rule cannot be formulated without relation to some proposed end, and "no [worthwhile] end can be proposed without presupposing natural instincts, affections, or a moral sense"[95] that motivate people to be sociable.

Language describes the motives and tendencies of the moral sense, but the tenor of language, approving of such motives and tendencies, is normative. When A helps B, the language of approval is: 'A' s act is virtuous." The moral sense helps explain the intuited connection between the "is" and "ought." The link is simply our felt pleasure when the moral sense tells us that the "is" conforms with the "ought." Thus, the moral sense "provides the basis for the transition from descriptive . . . to normative terminology."[96]

Hutcheson concedes that one reaches a state in which one can only cite a desire as a reason for an action. The moral sense functions, at this stage, as the *gründnorm,* the stopping point, which avoids an infinite regress of "logical" reasons that justify desires, actions, or policies.[97] Thus, the *ultimate* justifying reason is the statement, "Here is where I stand." As Hume would later say, it is "absurd" to ask for a further reason beyond the moral sense.[98] Similarly, Hutcheson writes, "Why do we approve concurring with divine ends? This reason is given: He is our benefactor; but then, for what reason do we approve concurrence with a benefactor? Here we must recur to a sense."[99] Hutcheson admits that the moral sense cannot explain why its tendency to pursue the public good is right.[100] Obviously, "a chain of proofs must have their commencement somewhere."[101]

Hutcheson's work points out that "there are a great many good reasons for recognizing [benevolence]"[102] as the fundamental moral principle. His attempt to demonstrate that benevolence is better for society than an alternative course of action is his "pragmatic vindication" of benevolence.[103] Hutcheson resorts to a pragmatic balancing of interests because, in all his writings, there is no concession that the statement, "Virtue is benevolence," is self-evident.[104] Hutcheson, however, insists that civic virtue, is a human commitment,[105] which appeals to "the kind of person, all things considered, one wants to be."[106] Man judges what he is and does psychologically by examining his motivations and actions, rather than by examining principles that do not depend on observed experience. The moral sense doctrine, therefore, is not justified by a priori reasoning;[107] indeed Hutcheson's primary objective was not to build a system of morality[108] based on deductive reasoning, but rather to bolster man's self-esteem. In sum, Hutcheson "was the sworn foe of every . . . degrading estimate of human nature. . . ."[109] and his moral sense doctrine enabled others to bet on the future of man's capacity to be virtuous.

3. The Role of Reason

Hutcheson subordinates the role of reason to the guidance of the moral sense because he rejected the idea that there are objective moral norms that are constituent parts of the universe, discoverable by rational intuition. The rationalists treated "normal discourse as if it were . . . descriptive of moral qualities . . . which exist 'in the nature of things.' "[110] Moral knowledge for some opponents of Hutcheson meant knowledge of values (existing independently of the percipient) which are the basis for valid moral judgments. The rationalists assumed that the mind, intuitively, is capable of a direct and immediate awareness of the nature of things, including the objective values that are part of a universal fabric. For example, the eighteenth-century rationalist Samuel Clarke held that

these eternal and necessary differences of things make it *fit and reasonable* for creatures so to act . . . even separate from the consideration of these rules being the *positive will* or *command of God;* and also antecedent to any respect or regard, expectation, or apprehension, of any *particular private and personal advantage or disadvantage.* . . .[111]

Objectivism about values undoubtedly had a hold on ordinary thought in the eighteenth century, as it does to a lesser extent in the twentieth.[112] The moral sense theorist, however, maintains that reason enables us to determine truth, and it "may discover means to ends, but it cannot set ends . . . [or] motivate or oblige us to pursue them."[113] According to Hutcheson, there are no moral values, characteristics, or relations that exist in the nature of things; at least, the rationalists provide inadequate evidence that such moral qualities exist independently of the feelings and attitudes generated by the moral sense.[114] Hutcheson's epistemology "assumes that all ideas are sense-given and that moral ideas are therefore the work of a moral sense,"[115] not reason.

Reasoning has a role in Hutcheson's doctrine of the moral sense.[116] Hutcheson admitted that the moral sense can malfunction when it is "interfered with by ignorance, mistaken belief, prejudice, or the like."[117] The role of reason is to remove these elements, thus allowing a healthy moral sense to function normally.[118] Just as eyeglasses correct myopia, reason corrects an errant or erratic moral sense by putting the available information into proper focus. Cognitive and noncognitive elements are subtly blended, but the moral sense remains the fundamental source of morality.[119] The views of Hutcheson "on the role of reason . . . provide a place for objectivity and validity in his general theory. . . ."[120] In short, reason prevents the moral sense that malfunctions from becoming vicious and arbitrary.

Arbitrariness can be avoided by a moral sense that follows rules of action based on adequate "knowledge, impartiality, consistency, and generality."[121] Without knowledge of the facts, moral judgments which depend upon facts cannot be made with reasonable certainty. Impartiality is also a quality that enables the individual's moral sense to consider the relevant competing points of view. Consistency facilitates the formal recognition of the appropriate normative principles that govern various sets of circumstances. The requirement of generality makes it less likely that an individual's approval or disapproval of a political action will be based on narrow prejudice. The four requirements of a healthy moral sense facilitate social cohesion by making general agreements among individuals more likely. Although the moral sense itself determines what agreements, actions, or principles are virtuous, the four formal conditions enable an individual's moral sense to reject policies incompatible with civic virtue.[122]

4. Implications of Hutcheson's Views on the Nature of Man

In Thomas Hobbes's depiction of a brutal state of nature, individuals exercise "arbitrary discretion . . . to pursue their ends . . . without regard to the impact of their actions on others."[123] Each man's freedom has to be curbed by a strong autocratic government. For Hobbes, democracy is not a desirable form of government.

John Locke expressed "the liberal . . . ideas of the seventeenth century"[124] which paved the way for democratic government. But Locke's analysis of political theory, like Hobbes's, focuses on the atomistic individual "assuming that his preservation, his liberty to exercise his talents, and his right to be governed by a regime to which he consented [are] fundamental."[125] Locke's depiction of a state of nature is far less brutish than Hobbes's, but the individual remains as "an owner of himself"[126] rather than as an integral part of a larger social whole. The individual owes society nothing for his capacities and his acquisitions.[127] This focuses on individualism, condones self-seeking, competitive drives and highlights many areas of human life beyond government control. Locke's views have had an influence on leaders in the United States from its beginnings.[128] The Fathers, however, also took into account a different view of the nature of man, a view that is consistent with a commitment to republican principles of civic virtue: Hutcheson's view.

Hutcheson explains social behavior in terms of the attitudes of an individual motivated by his moral sense.[129] The natural desires of such an individual do not conflict with his natural duties and obligations to his community. Hutcheson's explanation implies that social institutions arise from natural inclinations, not from the fear of natural inclinations.[130] Indeed, "the surest way [for an individual] to promote his private happiness [is] to do publicly useful actions."[131]

Hutcheson wrote extensively about economics, noting "that we are indebted for comforts and conveniences of life 'to the friendly aids of our fellows.' "[132] He stressed the need for a cooperative division of labor. The Fathers favoring the consolidation of the American confederacy, owing to its economic problems were, perhaps, reassured by Hutcheson's view that

[l]arger associations may further enlarge our means of enjoyment, and give more extensive and delightful exercise to our powers of every kind. The inventions, experience, and arts of multitudes are communicated, knowledge is increased, and social affections more diffused. Larger societies have force to execute greater designs of more lasting and extensive advantage.[133]

Hutcheson gave the Fathers grounds for optimism that the objectives of security of person and property could be met by a republic of limited powers which governed a large expanse of territory. John Ely refers to the republic our forebears envisioned as "not some 'winner-take-all' system in which the government pursued the interests of a privileged few . . . but rather . . . one in which the representatives would govern in the interest of the whole people."[134] To the extent that Ely captures the spirit of 1787, it is not the outgrowth of a Hobbesian or Lockean psychology.

Hutcheson's views on the nature of man suggest that a viable accommodation between equality and liberty is possible, if liberty were defined as "the opportunity for spontaneous and deliberate self-direction in the formation and accomplishment of one's purposes."[135] The doctrine of moral sense has egalitarian overtones because it stipulates that noble birth, wealth, and intellectual superiority do not provide one with a superior capacity to make moral judgments. This stipulation was encouraging to the Fathers who trusted the "heart" of the ploughman and the common laborer, but who doubted they could become experts in a Lockean "science of deductive ethics."[136] Thus the development of the moral sense doctrine "was a step in the direction of democracy,"[137] since free citizens do not have to be "moral Euclids"[138] in order to be virtuous when they pursue happiness.[139]

Hutcheson identified the natural rights that should be protected by government in a civil society[140] calling them "perfect rights."[141] The right of self-preservation is an example of a perfect right.[142] The government is, therefore, obligated to protect the individual from criminals who threaten his life, and the government itself has a duty not to take the life or limb of an innocent person.[143] The individual's perfect right to life and limb is derived from his moral obligation to stay healthy in order to pursue benevolence.[144]

Hutcheson also distinguished between alienable and unalienable rights.[145] An unalienable right is literally nontransferable, regardless of any social compact; for example, the capacity to believe that one thing or another is a natural attribute of every individual, a power which cannot possibly be transferred to another.[146] Hutcheson also discussed the immorality of alienating certain rights,[147] when transfer serves no useful purpose.[148] The test is whether the public welfare is served when the right is alienated.[149] Thus, again, the right to preserve one's own life and limb is morally unalienable because continued good health is normally a precondition for doing good deeds. An exception applies during wartime when soldiers may transfer their perfect rights (to preserve life) in order to serve their country.[150]

Hutcheson also refers to the right and duty of an individual "to exert his powers, according to his own judgment and inclination . . . in all such industry, labor, or amusements as are not hurtful to others in their persons or goods."[151] Thus, human activity that has beneficial consequences for the public welfare is distinguished from selfish desires. Since Hutcheson believes that whenever there is a duty to act,[152] the individual has a right to act, his approach simultaneously protects individual liberty and the social welfare. This is a view of natural law that focuses on "social drives and interdependence."[153]

Hutcheson classified property as an adventitious, not a natural, right.[154] Property should not be stolen,[155] but it may be regulated. An individual does not have the right to destroy his own property if it is still useful to the community.[156] Hutcheson did recognize that "every man has a perfect right 'to the acquisitions of his honest industry,"[157] but ownership and use of property should be "altered and limited under civil policy, as the good of the state requires."[158] Thus, if "any acquisition is dangerous to the liberty and independency of a neighborhood . . . neighbors have a right to defeat it altogether, or compel the proprietor to give sufficient security for the safety of all around him."[159]

According to Hutcheson, the definition of property, its uses, and rules for its ownership are dependent upon a civil society; legal definition does not precede government.[160] Thomas Jefferson, it has often been noticed, did not put property among the unalienable rights listed in the Declaration of Independence; nor did the Committee of Five comprised of Jefferson, John Adams, Benjamin Franklin, Roger Sherman, and Robert R. Livingston insist upon its inclusion.[161] The American educator, V.L. Parrington, regarded the Declaration's omission of property as "a complete break with the Whiggish doctrine of property rights that Locke had bequeathed to the middle class."[162] Property rights however, are derived from the so-called *secondary* natural law.[163] Even Blackstone recognized that property may be limited by government in a variety of ways.[164] Blackstone is close to Hume in his "manner of conceptualizing and justifying the institution [of property] and the particular rules governing property, and in this they stand in marked contrast to Locke."[165] Hume, following Hutcheson, made "the point that . . . property rights must be precisely defined" by a system of justice pursuant to a standard of social utility.[166]

Hutcheson clarified his views on social utility when he discussed contractual obligations. He writes that "whatever contracts we make, not induced by any fraud or error in the known and professed conditions or unjust violence, we are obliged to observe and fulfill, tho' we have contracted imprudently. . . ."[167] Even if the party with whom we have contracted "is acting against humanity and real justice," we are nevertheless bound.[168] This "law of nature,"[169] as Hutcheson refers to it, admits of an exception when "one has probable knowledge that adhering to the rule will have *extremely* bad results"[170] for society.

James Wilson, jurist and distinguished Associate Justice of the Supreme Court, was influenced by Hutcheson,[171] and wrote that "the happiness of the society is the *first* law of every government."[172] This first law for many of our eighteenth-century forebears was natural law, and to some extent they "derived the concept of natural right from the claims of moral sense."[173] The social contract, therefore, contrary to the perceived Lockean view, is based not solely on property but on the happiness of the society which is the ultimate end set by the moral sense of the individuals who comprise the society.[174] In sum, natural rights entail natural duties to society.[175]

The moral sense doctrine tolerates differences of religious and secular opinion. Tolerance is a sound policy owing to empirical considerations. If the moral sense is ignorant of facts or is misled, it malfunctions. The safeguard against a malfunctioning moral sense is the impartial consideration of each diverse view, which is possible only where there is religious freedom and freedom of speech. The freedoms of expression and worship were listed by Hutcheson as unalienable rights,[176] but he did not fix their meaning or scope.[177] The process of clarifying and delineating individual rights against the state had recently just begun, and, as the *philosophes* of the Enlightenment surely anticipated, the process would continue.

The Enlightenment primed the world for empirical thinking about rights. It was an age in revolt against unchangeable forms and essences. John Adams and Thomas Jefferson were of different political persuasions, but Plato's *Republic* was repugnant to both of them.[178] When Adams and Jefferson took quill in hand and drafted the language identifying a right, it was not a Platonic form. They were part of a liberal movement which did not stop in 1776, 1787, or in 1791 when the ninth state ratified the Constitution. When constitutional rights are viewed from the evolutionary perspective, the Constitution itself is adaptable.

On the occasion of the Constitution's sesquicentennial, Walton Hamilton wrote, "Its flexible provisions yielded to circumstance and necessity. Unwritten usage grew up to temper its command, and novel ideas found lodging within its classic clauses."[179] Few eighteenth-century empiricists would be shocked. Indeed, the Constitution invites innovation because it incorporates the idea that human innovation will continue.

5. Political Implications of Empiricism*

Two traditions of liberty, often mistakenly lumped together, developed during the eighteenth century. One tradition was "empiricism," a relatively unsystematic theory; the other tradition was "rationalism," a more systematic and speculative school of thought.[180] These labels, of course, refer to "complex tendencies of thought, not to static and uniform positions,"[181] although some historians group Hutcheson, David Hume, and Adam Smith together as representative empiricists and classify Jean Jacques Rousseau, Thomas Hobbes, the eighteenth-century Welsh moral and political philosopher, Richard Price, and Thomas Paine as rationalists.[182] The rationalists lost influence in America after the American Revolution, although rationalism retained dominance in France[183] and became more influential in England.[184]

Rationalism is the tendency "to regulate individual and social life in accordance with the principles of reason and to eliminate as far as possible . . ."[185] institutions that spontaneously evolve but that are imperfectly understood.[186] Empiricists are more willing to wait for the future to unfold, while rationalists are more willing to reconstruct society from top to bottom. Dichotomies are usually misleading, but it is helpful to compare the two approaches, and to note that Americans, in the late eighteenth century, tended to follow Hutcheson's antirationalist approach.

The empiricist tradition "finds the essence of freedom in spontaneity and the absence of coercion."[187] Empiricists, like Hutcheson, find goodness and utility in organic growth,[188] which occurs after "trial and error."[189] Rationalists on the other hand, find liberty, equality, and justice for all "in the pursuit and attainment of an absolute collective purpose."[190] They are prepared to follow and impose rigid patterns of behavior, which is a more ideological, if not doctrinaire, approach to government. Many Americans had the instinct that "political order is much less the product of our ordering intelligence"[191] than the rationalists believed. Thus, they were inclined to favor divided power as opposed to the consolidation of political power in a small elitist group. As a result, both liberty and responsibility were in unprecedented degree left to free individuals.

*In this section, I discuss Hutcheson as a representative figure in the tradition of liberty.

The Americans, after their experience with the Articles of Confederation, were painfully aware that there were too many persons lacking in moral virtue. Hutcheson had recognized that "just as some men are born blind, . . . others have defective moral senses."[192] This creates political problems. The immediately pressing problem in 1787 was the enactment of parochial legislation alleged to be harmful to the general welfare.

These empiricists, inspired by the premise that mankind follows the dictates of a benevolent moral sense, learned that elected officials often follow the dictates of factions with interests that are contrary to the general welfare and the rights of individuals. The Convention's task in 1787 was to devise appropriate safeguards for individuals in the light of experience showing which kinds of legislative actions were detrimental. The objective was to improve the traditional institutions; no one suggested starting from scratch. The common law, as illuminated by Blackstone, was understood as an impartial "mediator between abstract state power and abstract individual freedom."[193] Although the British common law was subordinate to the Parliament's will, a written constitution could change "this relationship in a fundamental way. . . ."[194] Moreover, if the legislative power were to be separated from the judiciary, the courts, which traditionally protected citizens from the executive,[195] could mediate the conflicts of interests[196] between representative and their constituents.[197] The legislature, however, could not be crippled, and all the rules of morality, which are the products of reasoning by courts, should not be incorporated into the law.[198] It was necessary to leave room for negotiation, which entails political compromise.

The empiricist tradition never equated liberty with license, and neither the empiricists nor the Fathers ever developed a complete laissez-faire argument.[199] Their quite different argument was that undue governmental interference hinders individual initiative as well as cooperative efforts. Their solution was a central government with limited but sufficient elastic powers to do what is necessary and proper for the public weal. It was typical of the empiricists not to draw lines limiting power too closely; room for change was provided. This was a pragmatic compromise that furthered unity, but accommodated the diverse interests of the American people.

Slavery was an institution in 1787. The "peculiar institution" of slavery was attacked by several Scottish empiricists[200] and by many Americans. The paradox is that the empiricist tradition explains slavery's survival. Its survival supports the empiricists' main argument that "although we must always strive to improve our institutions, we can never aim to remake them as a whole [overnight] and that, in our efforts to improve them, we must take for granted much that we do not understand."[201] It has been noted, more recently, by historians of slavery that "political instability is seldom conducive to long-range plans for reform."[202] In 1787, there was an overriding need for unity to overcome the political instability that plagued the league of states. Antislavery Americans could find hope, if not immediate solace, in the world view of Hutcheson's pupil, Adam Smith, who opposed slavery; in time, slavery would cease to exist because there is "perfect harmony between morality, which arose from our spontaneous inclination to identify ourselves with others; and utility, which was the product of our self-interested decisions as economic men."[203]

Conditions that affect the general welfare vary from place to place over time.[204] This fact of life, documented by Montesquieu, meant that rules to eliminate slavery would have to develop gradually as the result of trial and error responses to a cultural lag in an age of Enlightenment. In short, only experience could teach the lawmakers how to cope with the contradictions between slavery and the moral sense.

I have yet to discuss what appears to be a contradiction between the moral sense doctrine and the empiricists' approach of gradualism. The empiricist tolerates traditions that run counter to the ethical judgments of his moral sense. When a tradition like slavery is tolerated as the result of a deal made after a social struggle between contending interests, the rationalist complains that a liberal moralist should not ratify such an outcome; instead, he should oppose the unjust political decision.[205] The empiricists' apologetic response will not satisfy the impatient rationalist. The empiricist will point to material factors and economic forces beyond any reformer's control; he will cite society's inability to fashion a quick fix for an intractable problem, and he will direct his attention to other constraints and complications. Finally, to avoid the option of hopelessness, revolution, or violence, he will point out that, on balance, the present system, notwithstanding injustice, serves the general welfare.[206] By blaming his impotence on external factors beyond his control, he can condone injustice. It is the willingness to make safe and sound trade-offs that separate the empiricist from the rationalist.

The combination of empiricism and moral sense tends to make natural law less than absolute and more debatable, and as such, it can be applied flexibly to human beings by human beings. This is a characteristic of a natural law that is derived from an optimistic view of mankind. The objective of a view of natural law, such as Hutcheson's, is to bring particular individuals, public officials, and private citizens into harmony with one another and with the whole society. Thus, it is not so much government power versus individual freedom but (1) state power in harmony with freedom, and (2) state power that creates the opportunity for freedom for benevolent individuals.[207] There is an ordering of the social universe which sees rights and duties as near equivalents and which sees individual rights and governmental powers as complementary, not incompatible, concepts.[208] The original Constitution (although much altered by a developing dichotomy between rights and powers) had the *potential* to express yearnings for a natural law of individualism that was consistent with the public welfare. Although Hutcheson had no occasion to discuss majority rule or minority rights, whenever there is a reference in his works to duties, rights, or social policies, his ultimate test for the morality of a course of action is whether it contributes to the public welfare.[209]

Recall that Hutcheson recognized that the moral sense itself could violate the principle of benevolence if it malfunctioned owing to prejudice, lack of information, or some other influence that caused it to become arbitrary.[210] From the same kinds of interference, it follows that a legislature, which is presumed to be benevolent, can become arbitrary. An unfair law enacted by a shortsighted, arbitrary majority is evidence of a malfunctioning political process. Although Hutcheson did not discuss the subject, a court that invalidates arbitrary laws would be viewed by him as an institution with great utility, so long as it observes his conditions for valid rules of action: adequate knowledge of the facts, impartiality, consistency, and adherence to general principles of benevolence.[211]

C. The Present and Past Relevance of Hutcheson's Moral Sense

The spontaneous evolution of the Supreme Court's role in the United States was obviously an innovation that Hutcheson did not address, and it would have surprised, if not appalled, Blackstone. But Blackstone was merely tracing the development of the common law which he admired. He was not looking for a new paradigm;[212] many of the Fathers were. Their object was to promulgate a body of rules and to empower institutions which "prevent the state from going beyond its function of guaranteeing real freedom."[213] The already existing elements of civil society, which had to be patterned into a process,[214] were three in number: "the notion of individual rights, the notion of sovereign powers, and the notion of the rule of law as a mediator between the two that is, as a set of principles harmonizing the interaction of [the first two....]"[215] Although Hutcheson's moreal sense doctrine was not a model adequate for a Constitution, it was a philosophical underpinning for a reformed system of self-government that retained important parts of the existing legal system.

The scientific approach of Francis Hutcheson was part of the spirit of liberal inquiry in the latter half of the eighteenth century. His contemporaries knew "that it was he who first applied the inductive method, developed by the natural scientists . . . in the study of morals."[216] Hutcheson himself believed that principles of morality require an empirical base, and to acquire data, he observed the feelings of man. This psychological approach provoked his rationalist opponents. In the Cartesian system, "[t]he certainty of the facts is subordinated to that of the principles and dependent on the latter."[217] Hutcheson, however, moved in the opposite direction, believing that a moral principle cannot be based on itself, by means of circular reasoning, but it can be based on the observed moral sense of the community.

Hutcheson's empiricism appeared to the framers as safer and sounder than the dogmatic closed systems of the rationalists. The framers' goal was liberty — liberty with order, liberty with safety and security.[218] Professor James MacGregor Burns writes, "They saw themselves — in a word they would never have used — as *pragmatists,* as men thinking their way through a thicket of problems. . . ."[219] The framers "conceived of themselves as engaged in a grand *experiment* — a word they often used. . . ."[220] It was not likely that such men would try to bind their posterity in some tight constitutional straitjacket that did not allow for meeting new contingencies. Indeed, the framers left myriad questions unanswered.[221]

Hutcheson's empiricism suggests that the impartial arbitration of controversies is a process of balancing various interests, adjusting competing claims, and preferring one value over another pursuant to general but evolving standards of dignity, utility, reasonableness, and fairness. This approach had appeal for those framers who realized that the basic problem of a republic is one that has no permanent answer. The basic perennial problem of course is the reconciliation of liberty and equality with the need for maintaining order, stability, and virtue.[222] Hutcheson and other thinkers of the Scottish Enlightenment (Lord Kames, David Hume, and Adam Smith) "suggested that law changes in accordance with changes in society, and that just as society progresses, . . . so the rights and duties prescribed by the law develop in a corresponding way."[223] Thus, paradoxically, even slavery could be simultaneously condemned and condoned by an ambivalent moral sense that malfunctioned owing to ignorance and prejudice.[224]

Hutcheson's views on conventions and customs were underpinnings of the new American Republic because they emphasized the need for unbiased arbitrators in the event of irresolvable moral disagreements among the governed.[225] Political issues were to be resolved on the basis of the "general good of all,"[226] "on the universal goodwill to all,"[229] Thus, he distinguished of all."[228] In short, political issues were to be decided according to the concept of civic virtue.

Hutcheson thought the law should include as many ethical components as possible, but he stressed "the difference between what one ought morally to do and what one can be compelled legally to do."[229] Thus, he distinguished between perfect rights that are enforceable by law and imperfect rights.[230] He left it for lawmakers to supply the "fine tuning"[231] which distinguishes between legal rights and moral obligations. Hutcheson although an "important mediator"[232] in natural law thinking,[233] "in the tradition of [Hugo] Grotius and Baron Samuel von Pufendorf,"[234] de-emphasized the distinction between natural and positive law.[235]

Francis Hutcheson's moral philosophy undermined traditional ways of thinking about natural law in several respects: First, natural law tends to confirm what society feels, as does positive law in a more institutionalized setting. Therefore, natural law can be adopted by positive law in a system that is responsive to a community's reasonable expectations. Second, a system that gives priority to man's feelings and reasonable expectations[236] does not have the certainty of axiomatic thinking. Third, Hutcheson's point that the moral sense is vulnerable to bias, prejudice, and erroneous information, "directed the attention of thinkers away from ideal systems to actual legal systems."[237] Fourth, his insistence on duties as well as individual rights suggested that a more extensive system of public law would be necessary when the growth of commerce and the division of labor required centralized coordination of interdependent economic actors. Hutcheson recognized that "any society which has advanced beyond the primitive state needs . . . [an] effective administration of justice. . . ."[238] His focus on utility and the future consequences of decisions anticipated the increasing importance of legislation. The need for ad hoc legislation that applies prospectively is implicit in his notion that most of society's norms are instrumental rather than eternal. Fifth, since law reflects community feelings, a more systematic way of registering community feelings becomes useful — for example, elections. Sixth, Hutcheson's distinction between man's civil duties and his religious obligations[239] undermined claims that political leaders can rule by divine right or by a natural law that is part of the eternal mind of God. Hutcheson's works enabled others to see more clearly that law is, or reflects, observed social customs, and that law must be justified on the basis of its roots in the community's customs. In sum, the distance between natural law and positive law was diminished.

Hutcheson's view of man was a view through rose-colored glasses. One wonders what he would have thought of the factions that were to worry James Madison and his colleagues. But, who is to say that a powerful group that wants relief from onerous financial obligations lacks virtue? The framers of the Constitution realized that in a free republic, however unpleasant, coalitions comprised of like-minded individuals, are expressing views, and that such expression is the essence of the political process. The power of factions, however, was diluted through various contrivances in the Constitution that are consistent with a representative democracy. Madison's ideas for controlling factions were different from, yet compatible with Hutcheson's emphasis on the "unbiased arbitrators."[240] Even Madison, however, did not anticipate that the impartial arbiter would eventually be the Supreme Court of the United States. The role of the Supreme Court as an impartial arbiter is complex but less so when the word *impartial* is understood to connote the Court's duty to consider the points of view of many people, not just a few. In a nation where the people's collective moral sense doctrine is inadequate, especially judges are called upon to justify their decisions in hard cases on the basis of objective principles. It is, therefore, instructive to study the works of Thomas Reid. He explains how case rulings can be based soundly on the first principles of a political alliance.

Chapter 4 Thomas Reid's Common Sense

A. On Controlling the Effects of Faction: the Need for Common Sense

James Madison and many of his colleagues were concerned about the problem of partisan politics in the young republic. In the Tenth Essay of *The Federalist,* Madison wrote that "the latent causes of faction are . . . sown in the nature of man."[241] A faction is "a majority or minority . . . who are united and actuated by some common impulse of passion or of interest, adverse to the rights of other citizens, or to the permanent and aggregate interests of the community."[242] Madison's worry was that "[m]en of . . . local prejudices, or of sinister designs, may, by intrigue, by corruption, or by other means, first obtain the suffrages, and then betray the interests of the people."[243] He had a basis for his concern. The state legislatures under the Articles of Confederation had demonstrated that "human virtue can bear the temptations of power" only so long.[244]

Madison drew the inference "that the *causes* of faction cannot be removed,"[245] and he reluctantly concluded that corruption, which taints "our public administrations,"[246] cannot be prevented simply by dint of a moral sense. Nevertheless, Madison believed that the scheme of representation outlined in the Constitution[247] would enable the public's sense of civic virtue to "control the violence of faction."[248] The Tenth Essay concludes on this felicific note: "In the extent and proper structure of the Union . . . we behold a republican remedy for the diseases most incident to republican government."[249] *The Federalist* essays by Madison, therefore, indicate the belief that a decent society of virtuous individuals can be protected from corrupted representatives.

Madison's essays do not exhibit the same reliance upon man's innate benevolence that is found in Hutcheson's works. Nevertheless, Madison's world of ideas was "the world of Encyclopedists, of the Scottish social scientists."[250] Despite their differences, many Federalists and anti-Federalists aimed for a politics of decency, a "political order" that would be more "secular, reasonable, humane, pacific, open, and free."[251] The plan for the Constitution "has to be explained, historically, in terms of the Enlightenment, of the code of public virtue espoused without embarrassment by its most distinguished leaders."[252] This reliance upon virtue, however, was reinforced by various safeguards, checks, and balances.

The Constitution, in many respects, was a vague directive to lawmakers and judges. Madison conceded that "no language is so copious as to supply words . . . for every complex idea . . .;"[253] indeed, the words through which the conceptions of the Convention are conveyed render the Constitution's meaning "doubtful."[254] He wrote, "Questions daily occur in the course of practice which puzzle the greatest adepts in political science."[255] Thus, the greatest provisions in the Constitution will remain "more or less obscure and equivocal, until their meaning be . . . ascertained by a series of particular discussions and adjudications."[256] Hamilton concurred and wrote, " 'Tis time only that can mature and perfect so compound a system. . . ."[257] In the Constitution, not every right that guaranteed "personal and private concerns"[258] was set forth in "minute detail,"[259] but Hamilton assured his readers that when the *form* of a government changes, "it is a plain dictate of common sense"[260] that "rights are not lost and obligations are not discharged."[261]

The Constitution consists of various specified procedures, allocations of power, and prohibitions that limit the government's opportunity to exercise arbitrary power. To determine whether official action is arbitrary, there is a need for an impartial judge and a recurrence to fundamental principles. Recurrence to fundamental principles, however, takes us beyond a blind reliance upon moral sense. The impartial judge can no longer look solely to what gives him moral pleasure; he is expected to justify his decisions by valid law.[262]

Hamilton wrote essays in *The Federalist* that describe the power of the courts.[263] It was not claimed that the Supreme Court would impose its moral sense on the people; if that were the case, there would not be a republican form of government. Hamilton referred to judicial review,[264] not judicial supremacy.[265] The process of applying the law does not give courts power "on the pretense of a repugnancy . . . to substitute their own pleasure to the constitutional intentions of the legislature."[266] Thus, the courts are restrained by established and controlling principles.[267] But the question often is: Which principle is controlling? The answer is found in "the plain dictate of common sense."[268] Indeed, as noted, another underpinning of the Constitution, which should be compared and reconciled with the moral sense philosophy of Francis Hutcheson, is the philosophy of Thomas Reid, a seminal thinker who called his investigation of the causes and laws underlying reality common sense.

B. Reid's Rejection of Skepticism

During the second half of the eighteenth century, Thomas Reid's philosophy was a highly respected school of thought, and his essays were greeted with special interest in America. Reid parted company with Francis Hutcheson because of the latter's refusal to accept self-evident principles as the basic source of knowledge and morality. Both the common sense and the moral sense schools of thought attracted Thomas Jefferson,[269] who often expressed the thought that Reid's common sense approach was necessary in a government of laws.[270]

Reid wrote that "there cannot be perceptions without a perceiver (something other than the perceptions themselves), just as there cannot be actions without actors."[271] Reid, however, attempted to give coherence and systematic structure to the self-evident principles that he perceived. His scientific outlook attempted to make epistemology "organized common sense," since he tested his conclusions against the lessons of experience (his sense of the community's traditions, customs, and conventions) before making firm judgments as to the verity or falsity of certain maxims of morality. Unlike Immanuel Kant, with whom Reid is often compared[272] (since both challenged Hume's skepticism), Reid took into account the *sensus communis,*[273] and in that respect his views, more so than Kant's, provide a pertinent underpinning for a government that respects the reasonable expectations of the governed. In short, Reid relied, in part, upon the beliefs of the community, as revealed by experience,[274] to prove the existence of its moral principles.

Reid rejected the assumption that knowledge is the view that the mind has of its own ideas, "which leaves no ground to believe any one thing rather than its contrary."[275] Reid observed sarcastically, "If my mind is indeed what (Hume's) *Treatise of Human Nature* makes it, I find that I have been only in an enchanted castle, when I seemed to be living in a well-ordered universe."[276] Reid wrote, "The theory of ideas, like the Trojan horse, had a specious appearance both of innocence and beauty; but if those philosophers (Descartes, Malabranche, Locke, Berkeley, and Hume) had known that it carried in its belly death and destruction to all science and common sense, they would not have broken down their walls to give it admittance."[277] He added, "This philosophy is like a hobby-horse, which a man in bad health may ride in his closet, without hurting his reputation; but if he should take him abroad with him . . . his heir would immediately call a jury, and seize his estate."[278]

The fundamental skeptical assumption attacked by Reid is "the doctrine that all the objects of our knowledge are ideas in our own minds."[279] Reid attributed this doctrine to Descartes,[280] who had written in his *Third Meditation,* "the things which I perceive and imagine are perhaps nothing at all apart from me. . . ."[281] But it was Locke's theory of ideas that made the separation of mind from matter "current coin"[282] in English thought. Locke compared the mind to a blank sheet of paper, an unmarked tabula rasa that at first is "without any ideas."[283] He wrote, "The mind knows not things immediately, but only by the intervention of the ideas. . . ."[284] In other words, there are no innate ideas.[285]

Locke based part of his theory upon the distinction "first used in antiquity and then revived by Galileo — namely, the distinction between *primary and secondary* qualities of physical objects."[286] The primary qualities are the intrinsic characteristics of matter itself, such as solidity, size, shape, motion, and number.[287] The secondary qualities include the matter's color, taste, smell, sound, and temperature, qualities that obviously are detected by our five senses.[288] But Locke believed that the secondary qualities exist only when sensed and, therefore, exist only in the mind. Locke did not deny that the primary qualities exist in the object itself.[289]

Locke wrote, "All ideas come from sensation or reflection."[290] The senses convey into the mind the primary and secondary qualities of external objects. The mind, however, perceives its own operations. This perception enables us to think, doubt, believe, know, will, and otherwise act.[291] The mind's operations are a "source of ideas [that] every man has wholly in himself."[292] Although this source "might properly enough be called *internal sense,*"[293] Locke called the notice which the mind takes of its own operations reflection.[294] Thus, all our understanding, our "whole stock of ideas"[295] comes into being in one of these two ways,[296] either from *"external objects* (furnishing) the mind with the ideas of sensible qualities,"[297] or from *"the mind* (furnishing) the understanding with ideas of its own operations."[298] All knowledge of facts, therefore, comes from experience which is impressed upon the mind and causes it to reflect; knowledge of facts is not gained from "certain *praecognita*"[299] or from "general propositions."[300] Locke's theory of ideas screens the knower from the object known, and "(w)e cannot see, therefore, what is behind the screen, . . ."[301] since knowledge is "nothing but the perception of the connection of our ideas. . . ."[302]

Bishop George Berkeley (1685-1753) undermined Locke's concession that a material world exists outside of the mind. According to Berkeley, "There is no such thing as matter at all, and . . . the world consists of nothing but minds and their ideas."[303] The universe therefore "is through and through mental,"[304] and "if there are any things that exist independently of us they cannot be the immediate objects of our sensations."[305] But even Berkeley did not maintain that the soul exists only when it is perceived.[306] Hume took bolder steps, and the skeptical doubts created by *A Treatise of Human Nature* motivated Reid to refute Hume's assumptions.

"Hume, a more radical and more consistent empiricist than either Locke or Berkeley [identified] the self with the series of its perceptions."[307] A perception for Hume denoted the "distinct existences"[308] which composed the mind, and he wrote in the *Abstract* to his *Treatise,* "I say, *compose* the mind, not *belong* to it. The mind is not a substance, in which the perceptions inhere."[309] Having concluded that the self must be formed by a composition of particular perceptions, Hume reluctantly embraced skepticism. In his words, "When I turned my reflexion on *myself,* I never can perceive this *self* without some one or more perceptions; nor can I ever perceive anything but the perceptions. 'Tis the composition of these, therefore, which forms the self."[310] He then added (in the Appendix to his *Treatise*) that he could not explain how this composition was effected, and he pleaded the "privilege of a skeptic," confessing "that this difficulty is too hard for my understanding."[311]

Locke's theory, which contained minds, ideas, and matter, is amended by Hume's assertion that there is no mind and no matter apart from the particular "distinct existences" which compose the mind. In short, mind and matter both collapse into perceptions, and we can never know whether what seems to be a fact external to our mind really is a fact. Hume also decided that the search for objective moral principles was in vain.[312] He, like Hutcheson, concluded that when we say "an action [is] virtuous we say nothing but that we feel a pleasing sentiment of approbation in contemplating it. . . ."[313]

Although "the problems that trouble us at the present time are precisely Hume's problems,"[314] Reid proposed a solution.[315] Reid concedes that reasons cannot be given for self-evident principles, moral and otherwise, beyond admitting that "I just cannot help but seeing that it is so." He insisted, however, that the moral principles and legal principles are "also apprehended by reason"[316] and that "the determination of order in human affairs is a matter of reason."[317]

Reid, despising Hume's atoms that "dance about in emptiness,"[318] claimed that we perceive *real* "physical objects and events, and in thus perceiving them we have sufficient evidence for the belief that we have in their existence and nature."[319] When we see an object with our eyes, we may take it as self-evident that there is an object — the one we see — external to our mind. It may, of course, happen that the object a person takes to be a gray cat is not a cat or is not gray;[320] if so, the witness is mistaken. Reid never claimed that common sense is infallible.

Reid rejected Locke's explanation of a mind that operates in some sort of a chronological order, receiving ideas first. Reid clarifies the point in the following way:

[T]he smell of a rose signifies two things. *First,* a sensation which can have no existence but when it is perceived, and can only be in a sentient being or mind. *Secondly,* it signifies some power, quality or virtue, in the rose, or in effluvia proceeding from it, which hath permanent existence, independent of the mind, and which by the constitution of nature, produces the sensation in us. By the original constitution of our nature, we are both led to believe, that there is a permanent cause of the sensation, and prompted to seek after it; and experience determines us to place it in the rose.[321]

Thus, the mind is capable of making a judgment, directly connects the person's perception with the theing perceived. Reid maintained that we do not start by studying the content of our minds left by impressions, and we do not start with simple ideas of sensations.[322] We make a judgment that simultaneously connects the odor we smell from the rose with our conception of the real rose, which is perceived. In other words, perception is a complex process of sensation, conception, and judgment, for immediately and directly we pass from sensations to a belief that a material object exists. So natural is the process, that we may call the beliefs we have acquired in this way self-evident truths.

Reid refutes Hume's argument that there are only particular "distinct existences" which compose the mind. For example, he writes that space is a "necessary concomitant"[323] of the objects perceived by the senses. Therefore, the notion of space is a self-evident "intuitive judgment."[324] Judgments about space are natural judgments "which are no sooner understood than they are believed"[325] owing to the "common sense and reason of mankind."[326] Space perceptions that enable us to make immediate judgments about relationships are not clearly accounted for either by the particular "distinct existences" of Hume or by Locke's ideas of sensation. In this way, Reid attempted a refutation of the skeptical argument "that there is no existence but in the observer's awareness."[327] No longer is the "solid 'objective' world . . . made to melt into the 'subjective' experience of particular streams of consciousness, which between them comprise all there is."[328]

Hilary Putnam captures Reid's argument when he writes, "Reid tries to show that conceptualization requires the use of abstract schemata, which are not identified either with images or with simple abstractions from images."[329] After suggesting that Reid's concern with innate human cognitive structure is closely related to Noam Chomsky's theories,[330] Putnam notes that Reid "trie[d] to show that the concept of extension which we use to interpret both vision and touch,"[331] refers to relationships that exist outside of the mind. Putnam writes, "Any realist wants to maintain that the concepts we employ . . . don't *merely* have a 'use'; he wants to maintain that they *refer*."[332]

When Reid was asked how we acquire common sense, he would either ignore the question as an "idle" one,[333] attribute this faculty of the mind to the "Almighty,"[334] or observe that our capacity to make judgments is "part of that furniture which nature hath given to the human understanding . . ."[335] In other words, he had no answer. He pointed out, however, that when philosophers try to go beyond the limits of what we can comprehend they often wind up with "nothing at all"[336] or the "metaphysical lunacy"[337] of Locke, Berkeley, and Hume. Reid wrote,

All reasoning must be grounded on first principles. This holds in moral reasoning, as in all other kinds. There must, therefore, be in morals, as in all other sciences, first or self-evident principles, on which all moral reasoning is grounded, and on which it ultimately rests. From such self-evident principles, conclusions may be drawn synthetically with regard to the moral conduct of life; and particular duties or virtues may be traced back to such principles, analytically. But, without such principles, we can no more establish any conclusion in morals, than we can build a castle in the air, without any foundation.[338]

Thus, Reid provides us with a theory of reasoning that takes into account a reference to the fundamental first principles, which serve as the ultimate basis for evaluating the conduct of human beings. Reid, who employed the inductive method, "extended the sphere of self-evident truths, and made them the basis for his whole philosophy."[339] Similarly, many eighteenth century political leaders used self-evident truths[340] as the starting premises for a political theory of government. They believed, as did Reid, that fundamental principles of government are not merely in our minds, if there is sufficient evidence to demonstrate their application to the subject matter of government.[341] Thus, when legal judgments about the application of self-evident principles of American society are made by judges, the judgments are verified if supported by trustworthy data disclosing the nation's reasonable expectations concerning adequate representation by officials. Only primitive skepticism insists that such judgments necessarily are mere mirror images of the judge's own psyche.

C. Reid's Distinction Between Feelings and Principles of Morality

Reid did not deny that affections are inherent in the nature of man.[342] We have many affections, which Reid calls "instincts," "appetites,"[343] and "passions;"[344] they could also be called sentiments, predispositions of will, libido, psychic energy, personal preferences and predilections. Reid's term *affections* embraces our biological drives, which precede rationalization.

Reid thought that "the benevolent affections planned in human nature"[345] are "necessary for the preservation of the human species,"[346] since "man may be the most useful or the most hurtful"[347] influence on another. Every man is, in important respects, subject to the power of every other man with whom he associates. It follows that "it would be impossible to live in society, if men were not [benevolently] disposed. . . ."[348] Reid, however, also refers to affections which dispose men toward evil — man's blind desires — the "animal principles of action."[349] Reid distinguishes affections from rational principles of action which direct men to pursue certain ends.

Reid specifically referred to two benevolent ends: "*What is good for us upon the whole,* and *What appears to be our duty.*"[350] Concerning what is good upon the whole, reason counsels us to think twice about our first inclination and to take into account "its consequences, certain or probable, during the whole of our existence."[351] For example, we may be inclined to satisfy the lusts of our flesh, but reason counsels prudence.[352] Reid wrote, "The fundamental maxim of prudence, and of all good moral,"[353] is that "the passions ought, in all cases, to be under the dominion of reason. . . ."[354] In all cases, "to pursue what is good upon the whole . . . is a rational principle of action ground upon our constitution as reasonable creatures."[355]

Reid's common sense is not an "invisible hand,"[356] which enables man unwittingly to serve mankind while pursuing his self-interest. Reid wrote, "A man is prudent when he consults his real interest; but he cannot be virtuous, if he has no regard to duty."[357] If a person showed no concern for his duty, he might be "capable of being trained to certain purposes by discipline, as we see many brute-animals are, but [he] would be altogether incapable of being governed by law."[358] On the other hand, a subject of law with a sense of duty will have an "inducement to obey the law, even when his strongest animal desires draw him the contrary."[359]

"The subject of law must have the conception of a general rule of conduct, which without some degree of reason, he cannot have."[360] If a person happens to conform to a rule without intending to do so, we cannot say that he conforms to duty, or that he is virtuous. In such cases, his inclination fortuitously coincides with the rule. Duty implies an awareness of a relationship between the agent and an "ought" action. However, when the agent has no conception of the rule of conduct which prescribes the "ought," there is no basis to say that he is law-abiding. Reid's common sense point is that an obliged person must have "the means of knowing his obligation."[361] Man's power to conceptualize his duties, and to act pursuant to articulated rational principles is indispensable in a nation that relies on rulers and the ruled alike to abide by the rule of law.

Reid maintained that the meaning of the concept *obligation* refers to a relationship[362] between the agent who acts and an action that conforms to a norm (external to the agent's mind). He could not accept, without qualification, Hutcheson's doctrine of moral sense, or Hume's position that reason is the "servant of the passions."[363] Though a judge's approval of an action is usually associated with an agreeable feeling on the part of the judge, Reid wrote that there is a difference in kind between a judge who states that (1) the actor's conduct gave me an agreeable feeling,[364] and one who makes a judgment that (2) the actor conformed to the law "well and worthily; his conduct is highly approvable."[365] The statement tells us only about the judge's pleasure, which is irrelevant when the judge is supposed to be impartial. The judgment informs us about the actor's action and its conformity with a norm.

Reid held that judgment and pleasure are in their nature different kinds of mental events,[366] and that an expression of mere feeling is an inept expression of judgment.[367] While a judge's desire to comply with his duty is a feeling worthy of commendation, the judge's state of mind cannot be evaluated rationally by others when he does not refer to the conduct which is the object of his judgment, and to a standard that determines whether the conduct is lawful.

Reid's common sense philosophy reinforced the eighteenth-century intuition that indeterminate concepts written into constitutions can have some permanency even as they are adapted to circumstances. Thus, when we speak of a concept like an obligation or a right, its meaning it not merely its use.[368] A judge's use of a concept must be justified. Otherwise, the statement that the controlling law authorizes or prohibits a challenged policy is not necessarily true.[369]

D. Reid's Views on the Formation of Concepts, Language and Judgment

Reid's famous essay on conception[370] discloses how many educated persons in the eighteenth century understood the function of language. Language is the tool for communicating conceptions, and Reid, as previously noted,[371] believed that when a person has a conception, he simultaneously makes a judgment, which, when expressed, is understood as an evaluation of the conception.[372] Thus, according to Reid, a judgment, when expressed, is either true or false,[373] unlike bare conception which "neither affirms nor denies."[374]

Reid wrote, "If we analyze those speeches in which men [evaluate] our conceptions of things, we shall find . . . that there is some . . . judgment implied in what they call conception."[375] For example, if a man sees A strike B, his judgment will affirm or deny the truth of his conception that the act is oppression. The meaning of terms, like oppression, is settled by those who understand the language,[376] and the common meaning attached to the word.[377] When the legal meaning of a word is different from the common meaning, the truth or falsity of a legal judgment depends on the technical meaning attached to conceptions by those who reputedly understand the application of the law's language.[378]

Legal judgment, like other judgments expressed in language, arranges various perceptions into an orderly body of suitable "general rules of conduct."[379] Suitable rules do not depend solely on a single individual's "instinct, habit, appetite, or natural affection,"[380] but upon a society's first principles. When the legal question presented pertains to the content of first principles, frequently the answer refers to society's reasonable expectations about the basic duties and rights of individuals. Since these reasonable expectations vary over time, the rich content of first principles that evoke thought is read in light of the shared conceptions of their diachronic meaning.

Reid did not develop fully the relationships between word and object, and indeed, philosophers still struggle with this subject.[381] Reid's writings, however, disclose that our eighteenth-century forebears were hardly unsophisticated in the uses and misuses of language.[382] They realized that language is used for communicating thoughts about reality,[383] and that these thoughts can be arranged into a legal system that rejects subjectivism, pure and simple,[384] without becoming a closed system beyond the ability of man to revise.[385] In short, language connects the knower with the object known.

E. Political and Jurisprudential Implications of Reid's Common Sense

Reid extols the usefulness of reasoning without becoming a rationalist who thinks "man has achieved mastery of his surroundings mainly through his capacity for logical deduction from explicit premises. . . ."[386] The premises deemed self-evident by common sense are not those which are untested by experience.

Reid recognized that "[m]an is as much a rule-following animal as a purpose-seeking one."[387] He would agree with the statement that

> *Man is a rule-following animal.* His actions are not simply directed towards ends; they also conform to social standards and conventions, and unlike a calculating machine he acts because of his knowledge of rules and objectives. For instance, we ascribe to people *traits* of character like honesty, punctuality, considerateness, and meanness. Such terms do not, like ambition, or hunger, or social desire, indicate the sort of goals that a man tends to pursue; rather they indicate the type of regulations that he imposes on his conduct whatever his goals may be.[388]

Common sense enables man to allow himself to be "governed by rules which have by a process of selection been evolved in the society in which he lives, and which are thus the product of the experience of generations."[389] A man observes the rules because he may be called upon to justify his actions. Certainly no less is expected of an impartial judge. The power to reason also enables man to understand why it is his duty and to his benefit to conform to such rules.

The legal mind is attracted by Reid's rational principles of action. "Without them human life would be like a ship at sea without hands, left to be carried by winds and tides as they happen. It belongs to the rational part of our nature to intend a certain port, as the end of the voyage. . . ."[390] The voyage of the ship of state could not be left undirected by rational principles of action. The Constitution was designed to be a source of rational principles of action strong enough to withstand factions, instability, and a malfunctioning moral sense.

The Constitution, however, is imperfect. In *The Federalist,* Hamilton wrote, "I never expect to see a perfect work from imperfect man. The result of the deliberations of all collective bodies must necessarily be a compound, as well of the errors and prejudices, as of the good sense and wisdom, of the individuals of whom they are composed."[391] Hamilton quoted Hume as follows:

To balance a large state or society . . . is a work of so great difficulty, that no human genius, however, comprehensive, is able, by the mere dint of reason and reflection, to effect it. The judgments of many must unite in the work; experience must guide their labor; time must bring it to perfection, and the feeling of inconveniences must correct the mistakes which they *inevitably* fall into their first trials and experiments.[392]

In order to permit future experience to guide the Republic under the new Constitution, many provisions were left ambiguous.

Reid discussed the problem that occurs "[w]hen men differ about things that are taken to be first principles, or self-evident truths. . . ."[393] His common sense approach took the form of several suggestions. Since *"every man is a competent judge,"*[394] in a controversy "the few must yield to the many, when local and temporary prejudices are removed."[395] Reid wrote that care must be taken to make sure that the many "are not misled by some bias, or taught to renounce their understanding from some mistaken religious principle."[396] His second suggestion is a rationality requirement, although one that gives the benefit of the doubt to the majority. But sometimes the majority may err when the opinions *"are not only false, but absurd*: and, to discountenance absurdity, nature has given us a particular emotion — to wit, that of *ridicule*. . . ."[397] The impartial judge may discountenance absurd opinions that are so plainly wrong "if ever we are to view it . . . stripped of those adventitious circumstances from which it borrowed its importance and authority. . . ."[398]

Reid's third suggestion also described how reasoning can distinguish "vulgar errors and prejudices"[399] from those principles that are truly self-evident. One way is to refer to the consensus of the community for if "we find a general agreement among men in principles that concern human life, this must have great authority. . . ."[400] Similarly, Reid referred to the test of time, noting that the "consent of ages"[401] is persuasive evidence of truth. Another test is the formal justice test of consistency for if one rejects a principle that "stands upon the same footing with others which he admits . . . he [is] guilty of an inconsistency, ..."[402] and any principle that is incompresible is not a true first principle.[403] Reid's suggestions, which include references to the reasonable expectations of society, we shall see, are still among the underpinnings of the modern Supreme Court's dynamic, substantive due process cases.[404]

F. Blending the Elements of Common Sense and Moral Sense into a Valid Constitution

Hutcheson's moral sense doctrine, standing alone, is an inadequate basis for understanding the Constitution or judge-made constitutional law. Hutcheson's doctrine is also too undisciplined for a conventional theory of constitutional adjudication that is concerned with stability and the validity of case rulings. Reid's doctrine needs to be integrated into the humanistic American tradition which recognizes the value, virtue and dignity of man. In brief, Hutcheson was primarily concerned with human desires, while Reid was concerned with the validity of principles. But law without validity is nonsense, while valid law that does not satisfy human desires is useless or worse. Although Hutcheson's moral sense is not unscientific and Reid's common sense is not inhumane, blending elements of both doctrines together provides the ingredients for theories of law and adjudication,[405] which have the power to make good sense of the Constitution.

A fundamental substantive underpinning of the Constitution is the concept of virtue. Eighteenth-century Americans by and large, understood that virtue is indispensable in a self-governing republic. Montesquieu had written that virtue "requires a constant preference of public to private interest."[406] James Madison wrote, "To suppose that any form of government will secure liberty or happiness without any virtue . . . is a chimerical idea."[407] In his First Inaugural Address, George Washington stated, "There is no truth more thoroughly established, than that there exists in the economy and course of nature, *an indissoluble union* between virtue and happiness, between duty and advantage. . . ."[408] But there were disagreements about the optimum relationship between virtue and self-interest.[409]

The Federalists' idea that the central government should be made stronger complicated the problem of defining civic virtue — causing more than one dilemma for those debating the new Constitution. For example, there was grave concern among the Anti-Federalists that a stronger central government would ignore "many significant differences in condition, interest, and habit . . . for the sake of uniform administration."[410] Madison also feared "acts in which the Government is the mere instrument of the major number of its Constituents."[411] Very few believed that the unrestrained will of the majority should always be the law.[412]

Supporters of the proposed Constitution argued that a stronger government could unify the people, preserve peace, promote prosperity, and effectively protect the people from each other. A strong government poses a threat to liberty, but Madison argued that "the people will have virtue and intelligence to select [as representatives] men of virtue and wisdom."[413] The irony is that virtue, rather than force, is the distinguishing hallmark of a Republic, and yet the Founding Fathers augmented the central government's supreme coercive power to protect "we the people"[414] from the people en masse. Hamilton hastened to point out that the strength and stability of the reorganized government would enable it to ameliorate the effects of licentiousness, faction, and turbulence, while it protected liberty and individual rights.[415]

The terms *liberty, individual rights,* and *virtue,* are indistinct and, in 1787, each individual had his own personal view concerning the extent to which *his* happiness should be subordinated to the public interest. His happiness was a concrete reality; the public interest was a glittering generality. While there was profound disagreement over specific issues, at a higher level of abstraction there was a widespread conviction, as Washington had stated, that the union between virtue and happiness was indissoluble.[416] But specification of the precise relationships between liberty and civic virtue was postponed. There was optimism that concrete problems could be solved in the future. Optimism that the government could act as an impartial arbitrator was nourished by Reid's idea that concrete cases will be decided by a recurrence to first principles.[417]

In some respects, this idea of recurrence to first principles begs the ultimate questions since the first principles require clarification. Clarification might favor debtors over creditors, mercantile interests over agrarian interests, and one section of the country over another, but clarification was considered to be an ongoing rational process by the Founding Fathers, who respected common law traditions,[418] constitutionalism, and the symbol of the social contract.[419] Nevertheless, there was and is profound disagreement over the content of the Constitution's first principles.[420]

Does the content of first principles depend upon the subjective desires of the more powerful elements in society?[421] The critics of liberal thought answer this question in the affirmative. In the liberal state, according to the critique, there are not any rules and rights that obtain without reference to individual or group preferences. When a case ruling holds that a law enacted by a majority is oppression that violates constitutional rights, the holding might be perceived as arbitrary. Since individuals do not share the same values in the same way, supposedly someone's purely subjective desires are embodied in the law — either the values of a faction or the majority or the values of the judge who either upholds or invalidates the law. In other words, the indictment is that rules and rights are legal instruments to achieve arbitrary ends that are forcibly imposed on the less powerful. Therefore, liberal "dialogues"[422] are a sham masking the exercise of raw power.

Reid's eighteenth-century doctrine of common sense needs to be supplemented if the ideal of impartial judicial review is to withstand the attack of critical legal scholars. Therefore, it is incumbent upon the Court to develop a methodology that has a legitimate claim on those governed by the Constitution, including the people comparatively disadvantaged by the legal system. The Court has developed such a methodology. In order to describe its complicated nature, it is necessary to introduce the concept of legal hermeneutics,[423] the validity thesis[24] the rationality norm,[425] and the reasonable expectations standard.[426] These steadying factors which engender respect for constitutional law, are discussed in Part III.

Part III   Legitimate and Illegitimate Interpretation
Chapter 5
The Acceptable Meaning of the Constitution

A. Legal Hermeneutics

When a constitutional provision presents a puzzle for solution, judges take into account its line of growth[1] and an almost boundless variety of factors. The Constitution's text, accordingly, provokes a continuing discourse about methods of extracting its meaning. A theory of legal hermeneutics[2] suggests methods that occupy a middle ground between exaggerated descriptions — interpretivism and noninterpretivism — of the interpretive process. It is not the hermeneuticist's "mission to reaffirm the morality of [the] process,"[3] but simply to explain how one arrives at an authentic interpretation of texts.

The Constitution's language is more than "words and phrases,"[4] since the text incomplete, as it stands, has "a generative and creative power."[5] Modern judges know that each application of the Constitution entails a continuous clarification of its meaning. With respect to the framers' intent, the specifics of the original understanding have only limited applicability. The judge who is dealing with the special problems that are presented by a concrete case knows that the relevant period of history neither began nor ended when the framers substituted a new Constitution for the Articles of Confederation. The greater socio-historical context (the conditioning of culture) enters into legal thinking, and determines contemporary textual meaning, which might be quite different from the "supposed opinion of its authors."[6]

It is not always practical to resolve a unique issue solely on the basis of historically distant conceptions. Indeed, there are some contemporary notions of justice that cannot be cabined by eighteenth-century normative perspectives. An informed interpretation of the Constitution's meaning does not disconnect the present from the past, but reflects the essential ties among various previous interpretations of the universal Constitution. The informed interpreter also realizes that each case ruling adding meaning to the text stimulates "its own hermeneutic productivity."[7]

B. The Hermeneutic Insight into Universal Meaning

The Constitution's fluid meaning cannot be reduced to a narrative that recites the burgeoning and development of concepts as if there were an origin or a middle or an anticipated end. The meandering path that a concept takes as it emerges, expands, contracts, deepens, becomes over-shadowed, illuminates, dims, splits, or combines is too dependent on unknown contingencies to be mapped.[8] The interplay between published and unfathomed doctrinal tendencies and countertendencies[9] happens; there are no iron laws of history[10] that determine the basic law's precise content. A judge's theory of constitutional law can have a decisive influence on the case; if his own thesis is inadequate, reflective equilibrium[11] or a new theory[12] must come to mind.

The text yields the general principles that provide an objective justification for a judicial decision. After a series of cases, conscientious habits of interpretation become ingrained as the judge develops a hermeneutic perspective, perhaps without full realization of exactly what that perspective entails. It entails *phronesis,*[13] which reduces the tension between society's basic values and the ruling's articulated objective justification.

The art of judging demands more from the judge than the formal techniques that connect legal norms. The judge, of course, has to evaluate the relevance of normative principles, as well as their weight, equity, and potential consequences. The art of judging also determines which principles are inchoate in the Constitution, and which are not. Despite persistent modes of so-called legal realism in jurisprudential thought, the creative art[14] of disciplined judging is not properly characterized as subjectivism (the theory that holds that the individual conscience is the only valid standard of moral judgment).[15] The very attempt to mediate between the past and the present means the interpreter is not absorbed into mere self-knowledge.

Rainer Maria Rilke symbolically described the importance of understanding the universal meaning of a constitution, which the judge interprets as a participant in its becoming concrete. He wrote:

> Catch only what you've thrown yourself, all is
> mere skill and little gain;
> but when you're suddenly the catcher of a ball
> thrown by an eternal partner
> with accurate and measured swing
> towards you, to your centre, in an arch
> from the great bridgebuilding of God:
> why catching then becomes a power —
> not yours, a world's.[16]

Justice Cardozo apparently understood the reality underlying Rilke's symbolism when he wrote that the standard of justice under the Constitution is "an objective one."[17]

There is tension between the objective and subjective components of a decision, just as there is tension between the universal Constitution and a proposed case ruling. The creative art of disciplined judging dissolves the tension. Unity overcomes tension between the interpreter and the text interpreted when a judicial opinion identifies the authentic mediating principle that justifies a particular case ruling. If the case ruling is compatible with the Constitution and is socially acceptable, a court's decision has an objective dimension which reflects the consent of the governed. The conventional judge is not a prophet[18] but a servant of the governed because society demands decisions, which conform to its reasonable expectations.

C. The Process of Interpreting Texts

Hans-Georg Gadamer's description of the process of understanding texts, which have previously been understood in different ways, brings into view the inadequacies of interpretivism and noninterpretivism. These two schools of juristic thought produce "knockdown arguments"[19] that focus on parts of the hermeneutic problem but not on the relevant whole. Dogmatic scholarly advocacy about the "right" interpretive technique distorts the relationship between the interpreter, the author of a text, and the constitutional language that communicates meaning. Gadamer, although failing to stress the differences between legal hermeneutics and other forms (historical, theological, literary, and artistic hermeneutics), describes "the real experience that thinking is."[20] Something happens to an interpreter of the Constitution "over and above his wanting and doing."[21] What happens?

An interpreter, influenced by his previous experience in a multitude of unexamined ways, has certain preconceived opinions when he approaches a text. He already has an anticipation of its meaning, but he might see that his prejudgment is in error. He may read the text again to determine whether it corresponds to his preconception. If not, it remains a puzzle. By this time, he suspects that none of his prejudgments (prejudices, if you prefer) captures the pertinent meaning of the text as it applies to the pending case, and he protects himself from being victimized by his own hasty or unfocused biases. An experienced interpreter knows that "the tyranny of hidden prejudices"[22] distorts meaning; he realizes that, frequently, he must reformulate his initial impressions and start fresh. He may consult precedent, and then, after reflection, return to the text. Each time he does so, he approaches it with an expectation of its meaning.[23] If he is still doubtful, the decision-making process is prolonged until he is satisfied that he understands the text's applicability to the case. Gadamer writes "that a text does not speak to us in the same way as does another person. We, who are attempting to understand, must ourselves make it speak."[24] To continue Gadamer's metaphor, what *the Constitution is saying* is its affirmed concretization of its meaning. Gadamer expresses the common sense notion that we tend to find in a text what we are inclined to find. We cannot always extricate ourselves from our historicity, nor are all our prejudices incompatible with the text. The careful judge, therefore, will often reexamine his ideas, his values, and the text along with its elaborations.

It is a mistake to think that the hermeneutic perspective of a judge is solipsistic.[25] Solipsism is a "theory that the self is the only thing that can be known and verified."[26] The theory of interpretation that I am describing discloses what happens psychologically to a judge who studies a text over and above that which he consciously realizes.[27] Legal hermeneutics does not suggest that the judge's understanding is whatever he wants it to be. The judge's understanding occurs, as it were, behind his back. Much more than "subjective" preferences is involved when personal experience informs judgment, since personal experience acquaints individuals with the reasonable expectations of others.

The conscientious judge realizes that his private views are subordinate to a socially acceptable standard that requires impartiality. The judge's duty is not to inject peculiar meaning, but rather to extract authentic meaning from the text[28] which is the valid source of law. A judge, having the hermeneutic perspective, is never completely free of the text, since the text suggests the parameters and factors that he must take into account, and place in context. This requires an exercise of will, but it is a mistake to always equate will with improper subjectivism.

The judge cannot dominate the text which is relied upon to channel his discretion. The public expects his judgment to be verifiable as a valid norm by another valid norm contained within the Constitution. Although he is often compelled to look outside the four corners of the Constitution, he is looking outside to determine the acceptable meaning of the language within.

The judge does not interpret the text as if he were a literary critic, a theologian, a critical legal historian, or a moral philosopher. Legal hermeneutics requires a different perspective. For example, the historian uses a text primarily to learn something about the past; the judge uses the past to learn something about the text. The pending case might "have nothing to do with the intended meaning of the text."[29] Hence, the judge's challenging task is to integrate the intended meaning of the Constitution with its perceived applicable and socially acceptable meaning.

The challenging relationship between the interpreter, who has preconceptions, and a puzzling text presents the problem that gives the hermeneutic enterprise its experiential thrust.[30] The Constitution's actual meaning often is extracted from a reluctant text only after the conscientious judge experiments with several plausible alternative interpretations. A similar thinking process occurs when attempts are made to understand, interpret, and apply a case with apparent precedential value. The reader may test the suggestion, presented here, by reading a recent case in order to extract its meaning for a particular legal problem. At some point, the reader will have an anticipation of the case's meaning. He will, however, reread the case until he actually understands the meaning; this understanding occurs at the instant when he is confident that his gradually modified anticipation is finally affirmed. Understanding the import of a case does not necessarily involve reconstruction of its intended meaning at the time it was decided, the object is to understand how it might presently apply to a different — yet perhaps analogous — set of facts.

The process that I have described might again suggest (to those expecting to find it) excessive subjectivity because the interpreter's own reflections are ultimately decisive. The judge's idea of the Constitution's meaning, however, depends, in part, on what others think; indeed the Constitution acquires meaning[31] from evidence that exists independently of the judge's own biases. Thus, judicial discretion is conditioned by the impersonal factors[32] that justify the validity of a case ruling.[33]

D. Legal Hermeneutics and Interpretivism

The framers' intent, a comforting[34] justification for a case ruling, is part of a movement of history that continues. The text is an answer to certain questions the framers asked, and it is an answer to certain questions we have. Our questions are somewhat different from the framers'; so might be the text's answers.

A ruling is not necessarily contraconstitutional nor extraconstitutional when the contemporary interpreter's horizon of thought enables him to influence the previously understood meaning of a constitutional provision. The framers' horizon of thought did not include the present social context, but the present horizon of thought includes important remnants of the past; "together they constitute one great horizon that ... embraces the historical depths of our self-consciousness."[35] Far from being extra or contraconstitutional, the meaning of the Constitution at the moment of decision is properly placed by the judge in a context possibly quite different from anything that was foreseen by the most prescient framers. To put the matter bluntly, the framers' understanding of the Constitution with respect to the pending case is often inadequate.[36] The judge accordingly bases his decision on his "sense of what is feasible, what is possible, what is correct, here and now."[37] Each new decision is the product of accumulated wisdom.

Extremists among interpretivists are wholly concerned with reproducing the original understanding of a text, as if its original meaning could be recaptured or restored.[38] Attempts to recover traces of past meaning that have faded are not always beneficial or useful. It follows that the interpreter with hermeneutic insights restores only the useful remnants of the original core meaning of first principles "in thoughtful mediation with contemporary life."[39]

Now we reach the pith of the controversy that is engendered by an extreme interpretivist point of view. Professor Perry argues that a judge who bans a practice that is not a modern analogue of a particular past practice banned by the framers, is often engaged in illegitimate policymaking.[40] He writes:

> When is a present-day political practice no more than a modern analogue of a past, constitutionally banned practice? The answer, I think, is fairly straightforward: A present-day political practice, *P'*, is simply an analogue of a past constitutionally banned practice, *P*, when a person — one who aspires to logical consistency and moral coherence — who would endorse the political-moral proposition that *P* ought to be banned, could point to no difference between *P* and *P'* that could count as a principled reason for failing to endorse the distinct proposition that *P* ought to be banned.[41]

Is not adequately descriptive of current methods of adjudicating constitutional cases, because the judge charged with the institutionalized duty of interpreting a legal document will not necessarily ignore the whole of a political problem, or a part, simply because the framers were concerned with a different part. Past practices and their analogues are often deemed particular, but not exclusive, applications of the fundamental principles that the framers constitutionalized. The final limit to this endless process cannot be foreseen, for to posit a limit is already to suggest the possibilities beyond it. In short, the framers' intent is a provisionally held guide to the interpreter in search of authentic meaning.

E. Caveat

Legal hermeneutics describes and explains the art of removing textual ambiguity. It is an approach that is misunderstood when some judge's abuse of power is blamed on the hermeneutic process. Blaming legal hermeneutics, a perspective describing the ontology of interpretation, is nonsense. No descriptive theory can guarantee that a rebel, delinquent, or otherwise hyperpolitical judge will not inject unconventional norms into the Constitution to further his political strategy. Obviously, legal hermeneutics, standing alone, can do nothing about judges who refuse to recognize the authority of the universal Constitution.

Legal hermeneutics is a thoroughly conventional explanation of the judicial process. Old wine has been poured in new bottles, but the basic insight merely recognizes the commonplace idea that the judge's power to legislate major changes in legal concepts is limited. The theory of legal hermeneutics presupposes the existence of an orderly legal system that employs traditional methods of adjudication, which facilitate gradual, incremental, and socially acceptable change. Willful judges or visionaries, impatient with this conventional discipline, have no need for legal hermeneutics; indeed, they have no need for a text. The Constitution, for some, has always been expendable.

Chapter 6
The Symbolic Logic of Constitutionalism

A. The Structural Norm and Stability

A conventional theory of constitutional law presupposes the desirability of a responsive, stable government capable of generating reasonable expectations in spite of various unforeseeable contingencies. Conventional theories, however, are being challenged by critics influenced by a new kind of historicism.[42] The type of conventional legal theory under attack has four basic characteristics: (1) It explains how and why the legal system can be "rationally related to some coherent conceptual ordering scheme."[43] (2) It implicitly justifies the existing legal system. (3) It assumes that conventional explanations of the law, which emphasize stability, have practical value for society.[44] (4) It stresses the value of compromise, and is suspicious of the tyrannical tendencies of the cocksure.

The conventional theorist utilizes legal materials (data pertinent to the resolution of legal questions),[45] and a wide variety of other materials[46] disclosing the normative environment[47] (including but not limited to society's political and moral norms). These materials substantially determine the value judgments described by conventional theory. The conventional theorist, however, realizes that society's provisionally held values are part of a fluid historical process which has different characteristics in different times and places.

The genius of the Constitution is its adaptive quality, which enables judges to *affirm* a novel conception of law that appears to change the text's original meaning. There are, however, limits to the Constitution's receptivity to the preferences of its contemporary interpreters. The new historicists ignore these limits when they challenge the authoritative status of the Constitution. If critics who would subordinate the Constitution to their political ideology achieve their objective, the legal system will be radically transformed. Presently, the Constitution is a basic structural norm that is designed to withstand unauthorized actions that create dangerous instability.

The structural analogy, however, is only approximately descriptive of the process of constitutional law development. There are always loose ends, ill-fitting elements, and puzzling discontinuities. Since the very foundation of law is continually shifting, some critics would start from a new rock bottom. The conventional theorist, however, emphasizes the traditional ties that hold the system together. For him, the structural analogy, despite its allegorical character, is a helpful construct that depicts the rationality of constitutional law.

The critical historicists exaggerate the extent of irrationality in legal systems that respect constitutionalism and the idea of law. As an antidote, a conventional theorist writes:

> To the extent that we have in a nation an ordered legal system, and indeed to the extent that any of us has as an individual an ordered system of morality, we owe it to our capacity of reasoning, our gift for imposing an order of universal on a world of particulars.[48]

Our ability to reason, when exercised, imposes order and structure on the world of our experience.[49] Hegel defines reason as the unity of thought and reality.

The structural analogy and the rationality norm enable us to examine and reexamine the eighteenth-century ideas that inspired the Constitution.[50] Indeed, the structural analogy, if not overdrawn, can plausibly describe how our current conception of first principles is but a transitory point in the law's development — a point that becomes meaningful only when other points are traced, linked, and understood by an interpreter with a realistic hermeneutic perspective. The structure of the legal system remains the same (like the fabled ship Thesus in Otto Neurath's figure)[51] when officials keep working with the same set of concepts limiting their quarrels to the means for adapting first principles to unforeseen contingencies. The conventional theorist, however, worries that the law's conceptual structure will disintegrate if the basic concepts are not interlocked and secured by the Constitution, an objective criterion that validates legitimate reforms.

B. The Validity Thesis and the Challenge of the Historicists

The preceding paean to conventional theory will not satisfy the critic who alleges that conventional scholarship underestimates the importance of contingent social and historical factors, which affect the meaning of words, laws, ideas, and actions — indeed, all the manifestations of human life. It is claimed that a theory of constitutional interpretation that is "bound to textual language or the intentions of the drafters"[52] is inadequately attentive to "drastic discontinuities, not only in social conditions and technologies, but in basic assumptions about reality."[53] The critique asserts that conventional theory actually distorts reality, lacks relevance,[54] and can be counterproductive when it fails to explain the harmful contributions of legal texts, like the Constitution, to social context.[55] Conventional theorists, one critic notes, should consider "the possiblilty that their own work, in twenty years, [will] be seen as an apologetic for the current social order."[56]

An apparent justification for this point of view is the uncertain course of history — supposedly the transience of law creates a moral duty to write for social justice. The politically involved writer feels free to criticize the morality of society's reasonable expectations as expressions of arbitrary, human behavior. The Constitution is described by some critical scholars "as a symbolic statement: a legitimating ideology, a utopian aspiration, or a cultural ritual."[57] I will discuss the symbolism of the Constitution[58] after I respond to the message that is being sent by some scholars with radical, political objectives. Their message is clear: "Cite the Constitution as a pretext to achieve political ends, since all political actors, including judges, control the Constitution; it does not control them."

A conventional theorist recognizes "the social contingency of law and legal rationalizations,"[59] without adopting the execration that constitutionalism is not a meaningful, legitimating ideology. Hence, the validity thesis is an indispensable element in a conventional theory. According to the validity thesis, X means that the Constitution governs the judge, and no X means that the judge's political goals govern the Constitution. X, the antithesis of no X, obviously rules out proposed case rulings that are based on the assumption of no X. From the factual statement that X exists, it does not necessarily follow that X exists solely as a fact, for X also means *legally* that X determines validity; this is the suprafactual jurisprudential significance[60] of X. Thus, all case rulings have to be based on X, or they are not valid.

The validity thesis[61] has practical value; for example:

[I]t is good that judicial decisions be predictable and contribute to certainty of law, which they are and do when [judges] apply known rules identified in accordance with commonly shared and understood criteria; . . . it is good that judges stay within their assigned place in the constitutional order, applying established law rather than inventing new law; it is good that lawmaking be entrusted to the elected representatives of the people, not usurped by nonelected and nonremovable judges; the existing and accepted constitutional order is a fair and just system; and accordingly [the Constitution] . . . ought to be observed; and so on.[62]

When critical scholars argue that judges have the legal power to manipulate the Constitution in order to achieve political goals that are unconventional, their advocacy ignores apparent public support of the validity thesis, which is both a social fact and a norm.

If judges were not constrained by the validity thesis, the structure of law, supported by the Constitution, would topple when it stands in the way of a willful judge's political strategy. This is not to say that the judge does not have leeway to introduce into the law inchoate principles, which are ripe for recognition owing to the reasonable expectations of the governed. The inchoate principles, however, have to be demonstrably valid; otherwise no X (which means the judges' objectives are superior to the Constitution) triumphs. The validity thesis narrows judicial discretion, since it stipulates that judges are obligated to justify case rulings on the basis of objectified indicia (that is, criteria derived from the Constitution) which may authoritatively settle disputes about the legitimacy of governmental action.

C. The Symbolism of the Constitution

Whenever the Constitution does not clearly resolve a dispute, which obviously is quite often, an interpreter may rely on the guidance of its inchoate principles. Over time, aspects of these inchoate principles are incorporated into the case law as the Constitution is expounded by judges. Inchoate principles have the power to explain and justify how a proposed case ruling is related to other existing valid case rulings. When the inchoate justifying principle plausibly explains the connections among the proposed case ruling, an existing case ruling, and the Constitution, the inchoate principle itself is demonstrably a valid precedent.

Historicist criticism asserts that the constitutional text is "only . . . a symbolic statement: a legitimating ideology, a utopian aspiration, or a cultural ritual designed to define boundaries between social cleanliness and defilement."[63] Despite the misleading innuendo, the word *symbol* is actually appropriate because the Constitution represents a conscious commitment on the part of judges and citizens, to the reasoned elaboration of first principles. The Constitution is also a symbolic reminder of the people's long-standing distrust for authoritarian ethics imposed by elitist despots. It symbolizes the cultural contributions of a free people who appreciate detailed procedural safeguards that are regularly, and faithfully followed. Having withstood the test of time, the symbol of the Constitution is hardly a utopian aspiration, which is the meaning of a symbol's counter-concept: the fable.[64] In short, the Constitution is a symbol that points the way toward the purity of the political process, and the legitimacy of political outcomes.

The conventional theorist makes no claim that law in the United States is always equitable, perfectly coherent, or logically consistent. However, his reliance upon the reasonable expectations of a free people avoids the perils of a primitive skepticism, although there may be uncertainty about the right moral answer to a difficult question. (Alas, some doubters still question the Supreme Court's answer in *Marbury* v. *Madison*.)[65] Was it morally correct to dismiss a rightholder's case? Maybe it was not. Nevertheless, the conventional theorist, after taking due notice of never-ending controversies, goes about his business of describing the structure and sources of contemporary law, an activity which distinguishes his approach from the theories of the self-righteous who, wittingly or unwittingly, advocate destabilization in the name of abstract justice.

The Constitution does not guarantee perfect social justice; it is solely a source of valid norms which are legally binding. The Constitution is a great matrix of meaning, which admonishes all officials, including judges. It is always saying: "Do not yield to the despotic character of the arbitrary and capricious." In other words, the Constitution is not a utopian document which imposes a judge's authoritarian vision on the public; over time however, the Constitution is capable of affirming the judge's understanding of the public's reasonable expectations, and the community's sense of civic virtue. Conventional theory, in sum, stresses the value of law as an ongoing rational enterprise.

Although rationality is a governing norm for conventional theory, it is recognized that "[r]eason *alone* cannot wholly determine what we ought to do."[66] Conventional theory, however, has nothing to apologize for, because it serves society by acting as a watchdog ever alert for the delinquent judge. It unceasingly insists that a judge who lacks a plausible, ostensible justification for his case ruling has abused his judicial power. Abuse of power is the antithesis and betrayal of constitutionalism.

D. Conventional Historicism

A conventional theory of constitutional law adopts some historicist perspectives, concerning the evolution of law, the particular conditions that affect evolution, and the provisionally held basic values (reasonable expectations) that stimulate ideas of progress. Despite its reliance on a national spirit (*volksgeist*), conventional theory does not reject the possibility of objectified principles of justice. Indeed the validity thesis, the norm of rationality, and the reasonable expectations standard suggest that there are, in fact, adequately objective norms that shape the dimensions of the substantive constitutional law.

For the conventional judge, the reasonable expectations of the public, which have the force of law, have greater constitutional significance than the latest fashionable crusade. Thus, the function of conventional theory is to tame the urgency of those transitory manias that are mistaken for the constitutionalized first principles of civic virtue.

Over time, the integration of the enduring public interest with the Constitution's general principles becomes revealed. The watchful, patient judge with insight into his community's normative environment can avoid rash mistakes causing social chaos. The conventional theorist's reliance on demonstrable social facts about values that evidently are widely shared rescues him from the relativism of those skeptical positivists[67] who deny the jurist's capacity to be objective. In sum, the conventional judge, influenced by historicism, is competent to develop an adequately objective body of case law, which limits the power of the peoples' electorally accountable representatives. We call this case law "constitutional law"; "that special kind of law which establishes a set of preexisting rules within which society works out all its other rules. . . . To deny this idea is . . . to deny the idea of law itself."[68]

Chapter 7 Democratic Despotism and the Inadequacy of a Representation-Reinforcing Point of View

A. Vested Rights Versus the Police Power and Positive Law

Ordinary courts of law, in the early nineteenth century, had the power to mark the limits of legislative sovereignty, and were relied upon to delineate the contours of an individual's constitutionally protected rights. Courts protected rights, not because they were mentioned in the Constitution; they were mentioned because they were fundamental.[69] E. C. Corwin wrote, with reference to the vested rights doctrine: "The written Constitution is . . . but a nucleus or core of a much wider region of private rights, which . . . are as fully entitled to the protection of government as if defined in the minutest detail."[70] The Supreme Court's substantive due process doctrine in many respects is the modern equivalent of the earlier vested rights doctrine. According to the vested rights doctrine, in its strong form, the police power stops short of an enclave of protected rights.

By 1830, the vested rights doctrine was no longer the dominant theory of constitutional law. Its many qualifications and exceptions proved to be its undoing. The case law precedent, which had earlier given the doctrine vitality and legitimacy, was undermined. The idea of unchanging natural rights, which had originally justified the protection of legally vested rights, became less convincing to more people.

The vested rights, most carefully protected by judges, were property rights, but it became increasingly obvious that restrictions on property are necessary to police a variety of nuisances that interfere with the general welfare. When the pertinent judicial question narrows to whether the legislature's goal is legitimate and its means reasonable, the vested rights doctrine becomes a rational basis test, a deferential level of judicial scrutiny. Nevertheless, the police power remains limited in scope, and courts of law properly fix "the outside border of reasonable legislative action, the boundary beyond which the . . . police power, and legislative power in general cannot go."[71] "The ultimate arbitrator of what is rational and permissible is . . . the courts, so far as litigated cases bring the question before them."[72] If it were not so, legislation, incompatible with accepted notions of civic virtue, would be unreviewable.

Chief Justice John Gibson doubting the courts' power of judicial review, wrote "that the people are wise, virtuous, and competent to manage their own affairs."[73] The legal question, however, is the authority of the people's representatives. Chief Justice Gibson disagreed; since "sovereignty and legislative power are . . . convertible terms,"[74] "it is [not] the business of the judiciary, to . . . scan the authority of the lawgiver. . . ."[75]

Although Gibson's views on judicial review were never widely adopted (he later changed his own mind), the vested rights doctrine declined in influence when the police power's domain was expanded by courts. Nevertheless, the great seventeenth and eighteenth-century notions of natural justice and liberty survive. Due process of law is presently a synonym for venerable principles of justice and liberty and as applied, it is also a "synonym for the collective wisdom of civilized mankind. . . ."[76] This gossamer remnant of the ancient ideal of natural law is vague,[77] and presents at least two problems: First, the abstraction does not provide specific guidance when the pending case requires a practical choice between two or more plausible alternatives; a second difficulty is that judges lack special insights into the collective wisdom of civilized mankind. The opinion in the abortion decision, *Roe* v. *Wade,*[78] for example, did not display any unique sagacity, concerning the sanctity of life, on the part of the Supreme Court. After *Roe* v. *Wade,* a controversial case ruling, the stage was set for a theory of judicial review that designated a new limit for judicial activism, one more confining than the "prevailing academic line."[79]

B. The Elysian Challenge to Conventional Theory

The representation-reinforcing point of view propounded by John Ely favors judicial intervention to correct political process defects, yet Ely urges almost total judicial abstinence when political outcomes are challenged by litigants relying upon substantive due process principles.[80] Justice Holmes, an earlier advocate of judicial restraint, once reminded Justice Frankfurter, "A law should be called good if it reflects the will of the dominant forces of the community even if it will take us to hell."[81] Ely's modern process-oriented theory of judicial restraint is less hard-nosed: The road to hell must be paved with good intentions, and it must have no procedural roadblocks.

Ely brings forward certain premises of the framers to justify his thesis. As he describes his position along the spectrum of scholarly thought:

> it is . . . a position . . . capable of keeping faith with the document's promise in a way . . . that a clause-bound interpretivism is not, and capable at the same time of avoiding the objections to a value-laden form of noninterpretivism, objections rooted most importantly in democratic theory . . . and the relative institutional capacities of legislatures and courts. . . ."[82]

Thus, according to Ely, "a representation-reinforcing approach to judicial review, unlike its rival value-protecting approach, is . . . entirely supportive of the underlying premises of the American system of representative democracy."[83] The underlying premises — what Ely calls "*Carolene Prod-*

ucts premises'"[84] — are utilized to minimize the countermajoritarian difficulty of having "justices appointed for life permanently thwarting the will of the people by striking down the work of their elected representatives."[85]

The *Carolene Products* premises[86] are consistent with the modern Court's position that social regulation lies principally in the legislature's domain, and that economic legislation ordinarily enjoys a powerful presumption of constitutionality. Justice Harlan Fiske Stone, after noting that the presumption of constitutionality might not hold with the same force when legislation appears to contravene specific prohibitions of the Constitution, wrote:

> It is unnecessary to consider now whether legislation which restricts those political processes which can ordinarily be expected to bring about repeal of undesirable legislation, is to be subjected to more exacting judicial scrutiny under the general prohibitions of the Fourteenth Amendment than are most other types of legislation . . . . Nor need we enquire whether similar considerations enter into the review of statutes directed at particular religious . . . or national . . . or racial minorities . . .; whether prejudice against discrete and insular minorities may be a special condition, which tends seriously to curtail the operation of those political processes ordinarily to be relied upon to protect minorities, and which may call for a correspondingly more searching judicial inquiry.[87]

This footnote, Professor Ely writes, "can be seen as 'a participation-oriented, reinforcing approach to judicial review,'"[88] since it directs our attention to failures of process rather than to substantive political outcomes that allegedly violate individual rights and liberties.

A supporter of Ely's theory writes:

> The representation-enforcing approach commands judicial intervention where the mechanisms of participatory government have failed to operate, but it also requires deference where no such defect appears. The failure to defer to the legislative product undercuts the democratic process in a multitude of ways. It permits substitution of judicially imposed policies for evenhanded and rationally based state legislative efforts. It encourages politically influential interest groups to seek remedies in judicial rather than legislative tribunals. It induces congressional and agency abrogation of responsibility.[89]

Supporters of Ely's theory try to convey the impression that voters have adequate influence, and that representative government is generally responsive to voters. Ely's critics, however, point out that his process-oriented theory ignores too many social and economic inequalities. His critics also deplore the significant political imbalances that make the very idea of a well-functioning system of representational democracy a delusion.[90]

The difference between Ely's thesis, and the process-oriented theories of previous generations is that Ely rejects a consensus-focused conception of popular consent.[91] For the most part, Ely assumes that a bare majority may take all, and that the Court should not determine whether the political outcome is substantively fair. Since he believes that the elected representatives reliably reflect the relevant consensus, Ely assumes that "our political process works well enough as it is, and is given [only] to rather discrete sorts of malfunction."[92] Not all social and political scientists agree. In terms of resources, skills, and incentives, "citizens by no means exert equal influence over their government."[93] Robert Dahl explains that

political weakness leads to continued political weakness and strength to continued strength. Where a long history of inequality creates a group with a few resources — wealth, income, status, education, official position — the prospects of successful political action are so meager that incentives to act politically are low: As a consequence, political skills are not acquired. So the cycle tends to be perpetuated.[94]

Thinkers who search for ideas to make the legal system more principled will be disappointed in Ely's theory, which encourage courts to enter into the political thicket, but only part of the way. The theory gets bogged down in what American historian Daniel Boorstin call "the thicket of unreality which stands between us and the facts of life."[95] Many conventional specialists in constitutional law, like their intellectual role models, Justices Frankfurter and John Harlan and Professor Bickel, recognize that the need for a disciplined, substantive due process methodology, enabling courts to secure the first principles of liberty and justice. This is not to say that Ely's theisis is not without many supporters. Much support, however, is attributable to, and an overreaction to, the poorly reasoned opinion in the scary abortion decision, *Roe* v. *Wade*.[96] It is therefore necessary to compare the concept of due process of law with the concept of representation in order to discern their common ground: the reasonable expectations of the governed.

C. Comparing the Mischievous Concepts of Due Process of Law and Representation

Due process of law is a legal concept with political ramifications, and representation is a political concept with legal ramifications. Both vague concepts are mischievous since they can be used by zealous advocates to justify worrisome abuses of power. The two concepts are not necessarily in tension with each other, and indeed the two concepts interact harmoniously when a political system, responsive to society's demands, is functioning satisfactorily. Ideally, the concept of due process of law preserves established rights in order to protect reasonable expectations; therefore representatives are obligated to protect their constituents' rights and their reasonable expectations.

Constitutional violations occur when representatives violate their duty by frustrating the people's warranted expectations that they will receive what is their due: what they are owed in the way of a political outcome. Under these circumstances, it would seem that adequate representation is a secondary issue because a violation of due process of law — of constitutionalized principles — is inadequate representation. The situation is somewhat more complicated than a syllogism, however, because the due process clauses are evocative.

The concept of due process, all specialists in constitutional law agree, is constantly in need of clarification. Justice Stanley Matthews stated that law "in furtherance of the general public good, which regards and preserves [principles] of liberty and justice, must be held to be process of law."[97] This conception of the general public good harkens back to John Marshall and Alexander Hamilton "who were responsible for developing a Rousseauan conception of the general will."[98] In *Fletcher* v. *Peck,*[99] for example, Marshall relied upon the "general principles"[100] of society to reinforce his interpretation of the contract clause.[101] Subsequently, the Court occasionally used the *ex post facto* and bill of attainder prohibitions[102] "to do service for the latter-day concept of due process."[103]

Justice Frankfurter ably expounded the latter-day version of the concept of due process in *Joint Anti-Fascist Refugee Comm.* v. *McGrath.*[104] He wrote:

> The requirement of "due process" is not . . . a technical conception with a fixed content unrelated to time, place, and circumstances. Expressing as it does in its ultimate analysis respect enforced by law for that feeling of just treatment which has been evolved through centuries of Anglo-American constitutional history and civilization, "due process" cannot be imprisoned within the treacherous limits of any formula. Representing a profound attitude of fairness between man and man, and more particularly between the individual and government, "due process" is compounded of history, reason, the past course of decisions, and *stout confidence in the democratic faith which we possess.* Due process is not a mechanical instrument. It is not a yardstick. It is a process. It is a delicate process of adjustment inescapably involving the exercise of judgment by those whom the Constitution entrusted with the unfolding of the process.[105]

With those eloquent phrases in mind, one understands why the due process clauses have acquired an independent potency that is neither confined nor comprehended by the more specific provisions in the Constitution. The need for a flexible standard, yet one that provides guidance, was satisfied by Justice Harlan who wrote:

> Due process has not been reduced to any formula; its content cannot be determined by any code. The best that can be said is that through the course of this Court's decisions it has represented the balance which our Nation, built upon the postulates of respect for the liberty of the individual, has struck between that liberty and the demands of organized society. . . . No formula could serve as a substitute . . . for judgment and restraint.[106]

Though lacking a formula, according to Justice Harlan, the Court considers the following factors:

the nature of the individual interest affected, the extent to which it is affected, the rationality of the connection between legislative means and purpose, the existence of alternative means for effectuating the purpose, and the degree of confidence we may have that the statute reflects the legislative concern for the purpose that would legitimately support the means chosen.[107]

Thus, the Supreme Court's flexible due process standard, was given structure by Justice Harlan; his methodology, however, does not give the courts freewheeling authority to circumscribe the choices of representatives.

Justice Harlan's methodology is both too liberating in some areas, and too confining in others for the process-oriented. Elysians claim that the balance our nation has struck between individual liberties and the demands of organized society is a political balance. Judges are not trustworthy or competent enough to strike the obligatory political balance. Why, then, are judges competent enough to use the premises of a representation-reinforcing theory of judicial review to correct the political dysfunctions of our democratic system?

This concept, *representation,* that is being reinforced by the Elysians is no more and no less susceptible to principled elaboration than due process of law. Representation is a concept that initially was not "linked with elections or democracy, nor was [it] considered a matter of right."[108] It is a concept, developed for the most part by politicians and propagandists,[109] and, like the substantive due process concept of liberty, it is a "loose concept, often used in various ways"[110] by different advocates, "each of whom tends to claim that the meaning he attributes to it is the only proper meaning."[111]

Political scientists, after examining several types of normative political theory, have concluded that "none of the traditional formulations of representation are relevant to the solution of the representational problems which the modern day polity faces."[112] Dean Ely, however, insists that judges may actively enforce a somewhat distorted Burkean conception of virtual representation, called "equal concern and respect,"[113] which justifies judicial activism with respect to "the *process* by which the laws that govern the society are made."[114]

Ely, who criticizes the indeterminacy of the due process clauses, advances "a purity of the process" argument that "is indeterminate to the point of virtual uselessness."[115] Ely himself candidly admits that his starting premises "could be elaborated in various ways,"[116] and that they do "not exhaust the set of appropriate constitutional premises for our courts. . . ."[117] I have noted elsewhere that Elysian theory, no less than the Court's substantive due process doctrine, authorize judges to articulate political values that lack support in constitutional text and history.[118] In this chapter, however, I will discuss the unduly deferential component of Ely's representation-reinforcing point of view.

The deferential component is based on a utilitarian/economic model[119] since it is designed to count the preferences of voters according to a one-person, one-vote formula of apportionment. The courts keep their hands off political outcomes, which are compatible, theoretically, with democracy's underlying assumptions. To carry the economic analogy further, representative democracy is "regarded as a sort of economic marketplace in which votes constitute money, and would-be representatives are competitively trying to sell themselves to buyers."[120] Voters, however, do not decide the issues; they choose the representatives who do, and assuming there are no process defects, the only remedy an individual has, when the political check fails, is to use "the ballot" once again in hope of a new and better deal.

Ely's model is unresponsive if not insensitive to some basic values of human dignity, which should command elevated levels of judicial scrutiny in order to protect individual rights. The individual voter in his utilitarian/economic model is represented only in a formal sense and, acting alone, is powerless to undo the irrationality and inefficiency of various voting outcomes that perpetuate inadequate and unresponsive representation.

In contrast, Hanna Pitkin writes that "a representative government is one, . . . responsive to popular wishes"[121] when "there [are] institutional arrangements for responsiveness to those wishes."[122] She recognizes that "institutions develop a momentum of their own...they do not always work as intended. . . ."[123] She concludes that "it is incompatible with the idea of representation for the government to frustrate or resist the people's will without a good reason,"[124] or "to frustrate or resist it systematically over a long period of time."[125] The representation-reinforcing point of view, however, condones the opposite conclusion, absent process defects, and therefore, it is incompatible with Pitkin's vision of substantive representation, which applies to all forms of government whether democratic or not.

The difference between the Elysian approach and Pitkin's is that the latter "has both substantive and formal components."[126] Even Edmund Burke recognized that representation is a concept that "has substantive content."[127] Obviously, if institutions do not respond to the grievances of the represented, virtual representation "becomes an empty formality."[128] It is, therefore, difficult to see the representation-reinforcing nature of a theory that denies the individual meaningful access to courts when the government has violated first principles of justice and liberty.

Some theorists stress the formal aspects of representation, that is, its "outward performance,"[129] and others stress the desired substantive behavior expected of representatives.[130] This is an understandable dichotomy in political science, given the different views of the behavioralists and the normative theorists. Constitutional law, however, deals with behavior, norms, and the grievances of litigants; therefore, a theory of constitutional law is incomplete unless it contains both formal and substantive ingredients. It is not simply how one plays the game, but a matter of protecting losers who are not supposed to lose.

A theory of constitutional law that counsels deference to legislatures should not totally ignore — out of habit, resignation, or the lack of a disciplined but creative imagination — the potential injustice of a system of representation. There are no understandings among the people in the United States, which require courts to accept political outcomes that are demonstrably violative of an individual's reasonable expectations. Although the representation-reinforcing point of view embraces the venerable doctrine of legislative sovereignty, the historic dualism in the United States between individual rights and legislative sovereignty, inevitably in constant tension, was not and could not be eliminated by the Court's *Carolene Products* footnote.[131] The warrant for a surrender of the individual to the political process is hardly implicit in Justice Stone's concise statement[132] about the need for judicial activism in extraordinary situations.

"[P]ermanent reconciliation between the principles of representative government and the opposing principle of judicial authority"[133] is not to be found in Justice Stone's jurisprudence.[134] Elysian theory attempts to resolve the Court's dilemma about double standards[135] but Stone did not measure the stature of American constitutional law "by the number of judicial restraints or by the height of the statutory mortality rate."[136] He recognized that the value of the Constitution will be judged by history on the basis of its strength and responsiveness to the needs of both the society and the individual.[137] *That* ever present political dualism cannot be eliminated by a footnote. When he published his *Carolene Products* opinion, Justice Stone was concerned with the plight of the discrete and insular minorities unable to bring their power to bear because of restrictions that hampered their political freedom. He was also concerned with the unresponsiveness of legislatures to these groups,[138] but he did not attempt in a footnote "to map the entire area of judicial hegemony."[139]

The footnote, at the behest of Chief Justice Charles E. Hughes, indicated that there is a more exacting scrutiny "of the first *ten* amendments, which are deemed equally specific when held to be embraced within the Fourteenth."[140] Clearly, Chief Justice Hughes was concerned with "the nature of the [constitutional] right."[141] He sent a note to that effect to Justice Stone,[142] who replied, "I wish to avoid the possibility of having what I have written in the body of the opinion about the presumption of constitutionality in the ordinary run-of-the-mill due process cases applied as a matter of course to . . . other more exceptional cases."[143] Justice Stone later indicated that he accepted Justice Cardozo's formulation of the due process standard which referred to "those 'fundamental principles of liberty and justice which lie at the base of all our civil and political institutions.' "[144] Justice Cardozo and apparently Stone believed that "neither liberty nor justice would exist [if certain substantive guarantees] were sacrificed."[145]

Further evidence of Stone's acceptance of Justice Cardozo's formulation of the due process of law standard is his concurring opinion in *Skinner v. Oklahoma ex. rel. Williamson.*[146] Stone wrote that the Oklahoma statute, which authorized the sterilization of a thief, had violated "the first principles of due process,"[147] since there was no evidence that a thief's "criminal tendencies are of an inheritable type."[148] Stone, then Chief Justice, added, "There are limts to the extent to which the presumption of constitutionality can be pressed, especially where the liberty of the person is concerned."[149]

Skinner (no run-of-the-mill due process case) was different from the kinds of cases that were identified in the *Carolene Products* footnote. The Court's level of scrutiny, depending on the case, ranges from no scrutiny at all to a completely independent judgment. As J. B. Thayer wrote:

> The laying down of some rule of administration is legitimate, for . . . all courts, in regulating the exercise of their functions, lay down, from time to time, rules of presumption and rules of administration. It is a usual, legitimate, and necessary practice. It is, to be sure, judicial legislation; but it is impossible to exercise the judicial function without such incidental legislation.[150]

The Court, as Stone realized, adjusts its level of scrutiny for special policy reasons in civil liberties cases involving both process values and substantive rights. Although he was very concerned with process, Chief Justice Stone's concurring opinion in *Skinner* demonstrates that his footnote was intended (to use Robert McCloskey's figure) to protect Peter, without abandoning Paul.[151] More specifically, his *Skinner* opinion indicates that he did not approve of legislation which condemns, "all the individuals of a class to so harsh a measure...because some or even many merit condemnation...."[152] Thus, Chief Justice Stone recognized that the concept of due process of law is concerned with individuals — even if the legislature treats many alike — when the nature of the wrong perpetrated by officials puts the government's civilized decency on trial.

Elysian preoccupation with politically powerless *classes* neglects the aspect of the due process clause of the Fourteenth Amendment, which protects privileges and immunities of all "persons,"[153] including the individual "who belongs to no identifiable group at all."[154] The isolated individual can be "about as impotent a minority as can be imagined,"[155] and to think that groups behave like individuals or feel like individuals is to confuse abstractions with life.[156]

A political scientist writes, "If [group] interests are to be given equal representation, the individuals must be denied equal representation. There is no way out of this dilemma,"[157] except by giving each individual access to a responsive court, which has power to accommodate competing interests by giving due respect to each litigant, regardless of his membership or lack of membership in a particular suspect class.[158] Roscoe Pound wrote:

> [T]he liberty guaranteed by our bills of rights is a reservation to the individual of certain fundamental *reasonable expectations* involved in life in civilized society and a freedom from arbitrary and unreasonable exercise of the power and authority of those who are designated or chosen in a politically organized society to adjust relations and order conduct, and so are able to apply the force of that society to individuals.[159]

There will inevitably be disputes about the enclaves of an individual's liberty, its boundaries, its exceptions, its constitutional significance and weight — disputes that will be resolved "by the courts in ordinary proceedings at the suit of the persons aggrieved."[160] Contrary to a theory of process values, however, the individual's constitutional protection is not eliminated simply because he or she had an equal right to participate in the political process.

Not every human desire for gratification can be satisfied by the Constitution, nor should it be. There are, however, some rights that human beings have qua human beings. To put the matter in its crudest terms, there is a distinction between human and animal experience.[161] To be sure, this distinction implies that there are human rights, not all of which are guaranteed explicitly by the Constitution. Some of these basic moral rights, however, can be affirmed by plausible interpretation of the due process concept. The First-Amendment right to read or write about ideas, for example, is a moral right protected by the Fourteenth Amendment's due process clause. It is, however, the substantive dimension of the guarantee that protects "a man's right to read, write, or preach for reasons that go beyond the value of public debate in insuring wise or fair legislation."[162] The point is this: judges do not simply ask how the electorally accountable officials proceed to determine the Constitution's dynamic meaning; they also ask what it means — they ask what is its essence, even as its essence is changing in its endless becoming.

The absorption by the Fourteenth Amendment of substantive First-Amendment values is not a mechanical incorporation of the Bill of Rights. Moreover, the selective incorporation of rights is not based on a theory that focuses solely upon the participational aspects of representation. The Court's focus is upon the enduring basic values, which respect the isolated human being who seeks access to the courts.

A judge does not need any special legal talent to recognize when a person is being treated as a nonperson by the government. This kind of common sense judgment, however, is said to present a problem for the judicial process: "Legal judgment loses its oracular force, and the jurists are robbed of their most visible claim to expertise."[163] But if there is infliction of serious harm, judges have authority to determine whether legislation excessively ignores important and material differences among individuals who have reasonable expectations of more humane treatment.

It is claimed that judicial intervention will "encourage politically influential pressure groups to seek remedies in judicial rather than legislative tribunals."[164] If the reasonable expectations of individuals are demonstrably frustrated by governmental officials, influential groups *should* file class actions seeking Court orders. It is said that judicially imposed policies will be substituted "for evenhanded and rationally based state legislative efforts."[165] When, however, an even-handed and rational legislative effort crudely violates certain basic expectations concerning civic virtue, there *should* be an invalidation of the law.

Judicial review dilutes the apparent importance of a representative's obligation[166] to his constituents. A Court, nevertheless, has a duty to redress legitimate grievances after an official body violates its constitutional obligation to aggrieved constituents. A profoundly cruel law that causes widespread pain and suffering for innocent people is not lightly rubberstamped; it is not a routine case. There are such laws. Finally, it is claimed that judicial review will lead to more governmental abuses requiring more judicial intervention and so on *ad infinitum* and *ad nauseam,* but justified judicial intervention is a saner option than condoning a serious violation of the litigant's reasonable expectation of civilized treatment.

Admittedly judges can often abuse their power. Alexander Hamilton replied to this concern. He wrote in *The Federalist,* "The possibility of particular mischiefs can never be viewed, by a well-informed mind, as a solid objection to a general principle, which is calculated to avoid general mischiefs, and to obtain general advantages."[167] In short, judicial restraint is ordinarily appropriate, but since excessive judicial restraint gives the government an undeserved, unfair and often constitutionally intolerable advantage, undue deference can be a misuse of power.[168]

Representative government can degenerate into an organized form of despotism, contrary to the Constitution's system of checks and balances. The Elysian objection that judicial intervention will interfere with "the democratic process in a multitude of ways"[169] is a telling admission that an institutionalized system of checks and balances substantially influences political behavior in a democracy. The power of judicial review inhibits outrageous behavior by electorally accountable officials who know courts provide effective relief for the system's victims.

Constitutional rules that require due process of law are worthless when, as Madison argued, they are "not buttressed by institutionalized structures of real power, related to social reality. . . ."[170] Madison, although "wrong in detail about the way in which the institutions of the new government would work . . . was right in the long run about the importance of channeling political activity in certain directions."[171] Ely who asserts "that the . . . original Constitution is devoted almost entirely to structure,"[172] finesses Madison's point that the basic skeletal structure was designed to contain the social forces that violate basic values.

Ely notes that the Constitution was not dedicated "to the identification and preservation of specific substantive values."[173] Before its ratification, the absence of a complete list of specific rights concerned many of the Constitution's opponents. Hamilton, however, explained that "a minute detail of particular rights"[174] is applicable only to a constitution that is designed to regulate "every species of personal and private concerns."[175] The United States Constitution, Hamilton pointed out, is not such a document.[176] He also wrote, "It is not . . . to be supposed that the Constitution could intend to enable the representatives of the people to substitute their *will* to that of their constituents."[177] Thus, the need exists for the Court to adopt a methodology that keeps the legislature "within the limits assigned to their authority."[178]

While "it is an awesome thing to strike down an act of the legislature," the power is there to be used "where the occasion is clear beyond fair debate."[179] Constitutional guarantees are not guarantees on paper only so long as courts are empowered to decide what government action constitutes unlawful oppression of innocent individuals. If judicial review were limited to participational rights, an individual's freedom would be a matter of the expediency of group interaction, the casual outcome of whatever pleases the dominant forces in the legislature at a particular time.[180] The Elysians, however, are right about one point: A limit on the people's representatives is countermajoritarian. But there are such limits. This is the essence of constitutionalism. The constraints imposed by constitutionalism "place a limit on supreme political authority without denying its existence."[181] We do not have any maxim that the people's representatives are above the basic law.

The idea that certain individual rights are guaranteed against the majority's will is disconcerting to those who claim democracy is like a monarch above the law. But, however excruciatingly difficult it is to identify society's reasonable expectations of due process of law, "[t]he concept of liberty in the Fourteenth Amendment is hardly adequate if limited to the specific substantive guarantees of the first eight amendments and to procedural guarantees."[182] In short, despite the apparent incongruity of judicial review in a political democracy, the concept of due process of law reinforces a person's rights to the minimum essentials of *substantive* representation.

D. Democratic Despotism

Isaiah Berlin writes, "The desire to be governed by myself, or at any rate to participate in the process by which my life is to be controlled, may be as deep a wish as that of a free area for action, and perhaps historically older. But it is not a desire for the same thing."[183] Indeed, when majorities unduly constrict an individual's free area for action, democracy is "at times, no better than a specious disguise for brutal tyranny."[184] By tyranny, Berlin refers to coerced "service to human masters."[185]

Tyranny in a political democracy, however, is not conceived as such by those whose creed apparently is that the "law cannot be a tyrant."[186] It has been asked, however, by Benjamin Constant (who saw the irony), "why a man should deeply care whether he is crushed by a popular government or by a monarch, or even by a set of oppressive laws."[187] "The triumph of despotism is to force the slaves to declare themselves free."[188] A theory of process values defends participatory self-government as a system that, on the whole, can provide adequate guarantees against tyranny, but it undervalues the connection between representation and oppressive laws. This attitude is difficult to reconcile with the tradition of civic virtue, according to which

> no society is free unless it is governed by . . . two interrelated principles: First, that no power, but only rights, can be regarded as absolute, so that all men, whatever power governs them, have an absolute right to refuse to behave inhumanely; and, second, that there are frontiers, not artificially drawn, within which men should be inviolable, these frontiers being defined in terms of rules so long and widely accepted that their observance has entered into the very conception of what it is to be a normal human being, and therefore, also of what it is to act inhumanely or insanely. . . .[189]

This liberal notion describes a substantive dimension of freedom, but the existence of an area of freedom depends partly on the strength of legally effective barriers that block a representative government's intrusion into the protected enclave.

Democracy can become despotic. The theorists who depend on process values to prevent political malfunctions are depending on the effectiveness of public opinion to protect the enduring values that are usually respected by most American legislatures. Excited public opinion, however, can viciously impinge on traditionally protected substantive liberties. Demagogic representatives can do much damage before the public's sanity is restored. A political outcome, it follows, can be the antithesis of the ideas of fundamental fairness and civic virtue. The point is embarrassingly obvious. Ely's thesis is therefore troubling to the libertarian, the humanist, and the constitutionalist because process values do not cope adequately with the problem of democratic despotism,and democratic despotism, if left unchecked, makes a mockery out of the concept of self-government by and under law.

Chapter 8   Reasonable Expectations and the Supreme Court's Legitimate Political Agenda

A. Overview

In this chapter, I elaborate upon the following conventional justification for the Supreme Court's substantive due process agenda: The social individual's reasonable expectations are a source of basic values and individual rights that give content to the dynamic principles of the Constitution. Part B reveals the roots of the Court's substantive due process doctrine. Part C explains why it is appropriate to confine substantive due process to reasonable expectations.[1] In Part D, the relationship between liberty and reasonable expectations is exposed.[2] Part E further develops the substantive due process agenda under the reasonable expectations standard.[3] In Part F, a methodology for implementing the reasonable expectations standard in due process cases is introduced.[4] Finally, Part G explores the challenging implications of due process methodology.[5]

B. Roots

The decline of the Marshall Court's vested rights doctrine and the rise of positivism did not preclude the courts from taking an active role in government. By virtue of the Court's substantive due process doctrine, certain inchoate principles of the Constitution protect society's reasonable expectations against intolerable and arbitrary government actions. The antecedents of the modern substantive due process doctrine can be traced to *Calder* v. *Bull,* wherein Justice Samuel Chase wrote:

> The people of the United States erected their constitutions or forms of government, to establish justice, to promote the general welfare, to secure the blessings of liberty, and to protect their persons and property from violence. The purposes for which men enter into society will determine the nature and terms of the social compact; and as they are the foundations of the legislative powers, they will decide what are the proper objects of [the legislative power].[6]

Human beings who abide by the social compact expect civilized decency from their government.[7] Justice Chase's views were commonplace when the Republic was young, and *Calder* reflected a basic unwritten tenet of the Constitution: All powers not positively granted to a free government are reserved to the people, who understandably turn to courts of justice when government shatters their reasonable expectations.

Justice Chase upheld the challenged law in *Calder,* a demonstration of judicial restraint on his part. Prudence suggested restraint; the doctrine of judicial review had not been firmly established. The *Calder* Court, however, issued a warning shot that put representative government on notice of the power of judicial review. Earlier decisions also indicated that courts would become guardians of individual rights. For example, Justice William Paterson, three years earlier in *Vanhorne's Lessee* v. *Dorrance,* [8] had charged the jury that a taking of property without compensation "is inconsistent with the principles of reason, justice, and moral rectitude; . . . is contrary both to letter and spirit of the Constitution." [9] On the basis of this charge, an act of the legislature was pronounced void. [10] *Calder* and *Vanhorne's Lessee* are examples of reasoning from the premise that not all legislative acts are valid. These cases relied on a "social alliance" theory as if it were an underpinning of the Constitution. The social alliance notion refers, in part, to the reasonable expectations of the people.

In *Fletcher* v. *Peck,* [11] Chief Justice Marshall noted the nebulous limits separating each branch of government's powers where the Constitution is silent. [12] Marshall thus suggested that an unwritten doctrine of substantive rights can be extracted from the separation of powers principles in the Constitution. Thereafter, the Court in *Murray* v. *Hoboken Land Improvement Co.* [13] stated that the due process clause "cannot be so construed as to leave Congress free to make any process 'due process of law,' by its mere will." [14] While *Murray* dealt with challenged procedures, a landmark state court decision rendered one year later recognized an individual's substantive due process rights. In *Wynehamer* v. *The People,* [15] the state court's reasoning transferred the judiciary's attention further away from the natural justice, social compact, and separation of powers doctrines by emphasizing the limits of legislative power imposed by the due process of law concept.

In 1856, Chief Justice Roger Taney in *Dred Scott* v. *Sandford,* [16] ignored the temper of a large part of the country, which was hostile to his own values. The Chief Justice, referring to an act of Congress, wrote that it "could hardly be dignified with the name of due process of law." [17] In most cases, only a rash Court will nullify legislation when people are sharply divided. History suggests that the unwritten principles of justice, including those guaranteed by the vague due process clauses, cannot be accurately shaped without reference to interests, widely shared, in American society. Expression of these deeply felt needs by judges, attuned to enduring community values, can reduce the tensions between acceptable objective standards and unacceptable judicial subjectivity.

The Court's credible exercise of authority to decide hard cases on the basis of evocative constitutional provisions depends on its ability to provide persuasive reasons for its holdings. When legitimate principles justify a decision, judges are not likely to be regarded as elitists out of touch with reality. Conversely, absent trustworthy evidence of common values held by the diverse segments of society, deference to the political outcome is appropriate in most substantive due process cases.[18]

C. Confining Substantive Due Process Doctrine to Reasonable Expectations

The Constitution approximates a social contract. Historically, the legal concept of a contract has been "a paradigm . . . [of] justice viewed as the satisfaction of reasonable expectations."[19] The reasonable expectation standard is almost as broad as due process itself, and both flexible notions are given content by the Court's interaction with a specific social context.[20] Despite inherent problems with the reasonable expectation standard, it is a guide indicating society's basic values. Accordingly, application of the standard can establish the historic authenticity of a case ruling, which mediates between legal text and social context.

The reasonableness of a litigant's expectation is determined with reference to positive law, custom, and tradition. As precedent builds upon the incomplete meaning of the social contract, the reasonable expectation standard serves as an organizing principle with an empirical basis and objective character which justifies setting aside a political outcome.[21]

The reasonable expectation standard has further merit because it does not grant constitutional significance to all important human rights. The human rights concept is powerful,[22] too powerful to be safely employed without regard to disruptive impacts on society. A judge is not a sage who knows people better than they know themselves. Forcing "human rights" upon people who are unprepared for radical normative change is inconsistent with the reasonable expectation standard. Only a monstrous doctrine equates what a community would choose if it were "morally virtuous" (when it is not), with what it actually seeks and chooses.[23]

There is another reason why the substantive due process doctrine is partly dependent upon the reasonable expectations standard. Substantive due process protects liberties which compete with concepts of equality. Liberty and equality are ultimately imperialistic;[24] as they expand in scope, the tension between them increases. The antimony suggests an inexhaustible source of possibilities. The Court, at best, can effectuate a transient accommodation[25] of competing values by adjusting tensions on a case by case basis.[26] The reasonable expectations standard gives a semblance of continuity, objectivity, and unity to the entire enterprise.

The reasonable expectations of the national community might have little to do with the coherence theories of philosophers. Indeed, the judge who relies solely on sterile logic is likely to be insensitive when legal reasoning is inadequate to resolve a difficult case. The sensitive judge will "enter upon a regressive inquiry into the antecedent postulates of the system of rules which he is applying."[27] The latter judge will often find that a traditional reasonable expectation standard is a legitimate ground for his ruling, even though the pattern of rulings may turn out to be a logician's nightmare. Logic may be deemed less important than tradition, since the latter transmits the meaning of language in a way that logic does not.

Unacceptable social change is not likely to be imposed upon society by a disciplined judge who adheres to the public's shared values. The reasonable expectations limitation on judicial power is thus a practical standard, contemplating the coexistence of individual rights and social justice.[28] The standard does not liberate a judge from the constraints of constitutionalism. As Professor Hart writes, "There still remains a distinction between a constitution which, after setting up a system of courts, provides that the law shall be whatever the supreme court thinks fit, and the actual constitution of the United States. . . ."[29] Kent Greenawalt adds:

> Obviously the law provides the main criteria for judges interpreting the Constitution . . . Although a Court's judgment may be influenced by moral evaluation, rarely, if ever, is the determination a straightforward one about moral acceptability or moral right; the Court will be guided by whatever implicit judgments of acceptability are contained in or underlie the relevant constitutional provision and precedents interpreting it, and often it will grant considerable deference to the judgments made by the political branches.[30]

Any standard of justice that derogates from the authoritative status of the Constitution cannot be justified as a valid interpretation of the due process clauses. To ascertain what is "due," the judge looks outside the document to give it meaning in order to satisfy reasonable expectations. The notion that the judges can discern the authentic consent of the governed (or that of the "real majority") is troublesome. However, it is equally troublesome when, owing to a sudden swing of popular obsession, a transient majority arbitrarily enacts laws offensive to the public's reasonable expectations of fairness. Such deviations from society's prevailing norms offend the fairness component of the due process concept, which protects individuals from democratic despotism.

Judicial despotism is perhaps worse than any other kind. A free people must be protected from despotic judges who arbitrarily invalidate political outcomes under color of law. In outrageous cases, impeachment of judges is an option. Alternatively, Congress should enact legislation to encourage attorneys to challenge controversial decisions when reliable empirical data disclose that the Court's case ruling rests upon a false perception of society's reasonable expectations. An examination of Congress's findings might induce the Court to admit that its precedent is based upon mistaken assumptions of fact.

A conscientious Court will overrule its precedent to correct its mistaken factual assumption about society's reasonable expectations.[31] Inchoate in the separation of powers concept is a system of checks and balances, preventing *each* branch from usurping powers and rights reserved to the people and states by the Ninth and Tenth amendments. The Court, perhaps, has the ultimate power to define and articulate legal standards for the resolution of Article III cases within its jurisdiction. On the other hand, congressional findings of fact about the practices and aspirations of the American people are entitled to respect if based rationally on adequate, trustworthy evidence.[32] If Congress strips the Supreme Court of appellate jurisdiction, the outcome of this political contest is not fore-ordained. You can bet, however, that the reasonable expectations standard will be pertinent.

D. On Liberty

Courts, in modern procedural due process cases, identify innominate liberties protected by the Constitution.[33] This practice, however, should not become a positive law trap[34] requiring a Court to hold that liberties lack constitutional status unless they have first been recognized by a state legislature or by the federal government. The dictionary defines liberty as "[t]he condition of being not subject to restriction or control."[35] This definition "refers to the absence of interference with one's ability to do what one wills."[36] While individuals have desires that lack constitutional significance, the Supreme Court, by a process of inclusion and exclusion, gives content and scope to the liberties that are embraced by the substantive due process concept. Gerald Gunther describes the Court's view of liberty when the policy of politically accountable officials is challenged:

> In the substantive due process cases, the Court adopted a very embracive view of the individual interests encompassed by the term *liberty*. From *Allgeyer*[37] through *Lochner*[38] to *Meyer* v. *Nebraska*,[39] the old Court extended *liberty* far beyond the freedom from physical restraint. And that legacy has not been disavowed by the modern Court: *Griswold*,[40] *Roe*,[41] and their progeny have been increasingly uninhibited in explicitly building upon the *Lochner* era's broad view of liberty. True, justices have differed about what aspects of liberty are sufficiently "fundamental" to warrant special scrutiny by the Court. But those differences . . . have been accompanied by a widespread consensus that *liberty* includes just about every interest of significance to an individual — or, more accurately, that the phrase "life, liberty, or property" in the due process clauses is "a unitary concept embracing all interests valued by sensible men."[42] In the substantive due process area, in short, the typical Court focus has not been on whether a constitutionally protected interest has been impinged upon, but rather on what amount of justification the state must put forth to defend that impingement successfully.[43]

A difficult task is to determine whether the furtherance of legitimate and substantial governmental purposes justifies an impingement on liberty. The

Court cannot make this determination conscientiously unless the government is required to articulate its purposes when its action is challenged in Court.

When the government deprives an individual of liberty without a reasoned justification, it is claiming that it can be as arbitrary as it pleases, notwithstanding the individual's expectations. The government's failure to justify a deprivation of liberty is worse than arbitrary; it treats a human being as "some featureless amalgam, a statistical unit without identifiable, specifically human features and purposes of [its] own."[44] When the Court condones the government's action without any purpose inquiry, the potential is frightening for a free people.

The concept of due process has bite only when the Court does not rubber-stamp an apparently purposeless statute. Whether a means-end instrumental relationship is required, or whether the rationality requirement can be satisfied by a noninstrumental, intuitively plausible explanation,[45] some meaningful rationality requirement ought to obtain.

The rationality standard requires a showing that the official body was aware of what governmental action was taken; that it intended to take that action in the sense of envisaging it; and, that it wanted the action to be taken either for its own sake or for the sake of achieving some stated goal. Without such a showing, the government's legal position is unintelligible and intolerable because the litigant is deprived not only of his liberty but also his position as a respected individual in the community.[46] The notion of a dialogue[47] between the government and the individual defines civilized decency, and a liberal's conception of liberty in a free society.

The Constitution speaks of liberty, but the frontiers of liberty are ever shifting[48] and the minimum essentials of freedom "implicit in the concept of ordered liberty"[49] will thus vary over time. The present meaning of liberty must be drawn out by a constant process of concept formation. It is impractical, if not impossible, to identify the shifting frontier of substantive liberties protected by the due process concept without reference to "quasi-empirical"[50] data providing the basis of a litigant's reasonable expectations.

In the United States, the reasonable expectations of liberty fall short of a dogmatic translation of John Stuart Mill's conception, that liberty means the least restraint of freedom compatible with the liberty of others.[51] Pursuant to the Millian notion, one might argue that he has a right to liberty X, since liberty X does not violate a specific duty to the public or hurt any individual; thus, it is a right that society can "afford to bear for the sake of the greater good of human freedom."[52] Mill's critics "point out that the limits of private and public domain are difficult to demarcate; that anything a man does, could, in principle, frustrate others, that no man is an island; that the social and the individual aspects of human beings often cannot in practice, be disentangled."[53] Rigid formulations of Millian rights often clash with community values, and frequently yield to a more pragmatic quasi-empirical conception of liberty. In other words, judicial review of the government's power to abridge liberty may require the Court to balance competing individual and community interests.[54]

The tension between a liberty and a competing interest cannot be permanently resolved by reasoning from Mill's principles of liberty.[55] For example, an ambivalent individual may simultaneously desire privacy and association, both of which are essential to his development,[56] but certain kinds of required association within the community interfere with someone else's privacy, autonomy, and liberty.[57] If resulting tensions are resolved always by recognizing the priority of social order, individual liberties are sacrificed perhaps arbitrarily.[58] Conversely, if individual liberties always have priority, the societal interests of order, stability, and conventional morality are sacrificed perhaps unnecessarily. Although Mill wanted a maximum of liberty consonant with the just demands of society,[59] he had no conception of what the future would bring, "neither of the political and social consequences of industrialization, nor of the discovery of the strength of irrational and unconscious factors in human behavior. . . ."[60] Thus, the modern Court's mission to protect the liberties of individuals more complicated.

E. The Complicated Nature of the Substantive Due Process Agenda

The following section will survey some of the political complications associated with the Court's controversial substantive due process doctrine. After a brief discussion of the Court's limited role, the focus will shift to criticism of consequentialism in hard cases. The reasonable expectations standard will be suggested as a viable alternative to an excessively teleological approach. Finally, the reasonable expectations standard will be explored with emphasis on its appropiate use in birth control cases and its subsequent abuse in the abortion case, *Roe* v. *Wade*.† – *The objective is to establish a legitimate political agenda for the Court.*

1. A Limited Judicial Role

In our representative democracy, the Supreme Court's legitimate political agenda is limited. The nature of the Court's limited role is not always captured by dicussions about abstract constitutional rights. Legislatures, not federal judges, are answerable directly to the people. As Justice Frankfurter wrote, the "Court's only and very narrow function is to determine whether within the broad grant of authority vested in legislatures they have exercised a judgment for which reasonable justification can be offered."[62] Although the Court's power as the guardian of the Constitution is formidable in a democracy known for its litigious citizens, the legislatures are equally important guardians of liberty.[63]

The Court's consideration of political issues inevitably raises separation of power concerns. As early as 1787 it was asked, "If the judiciary acts as a check on the legeslature, then who is to act as a check on the judiciary?"[64] Even today, one commentator warns, "[g]overnment by judiciary will fail . . . because its present success exalts autocracy over democracy . . . faction over society equality over liberty . . . and even mindlessness over reason."[65] The legal profession keeps its critical eye on the Court. The peer pressure has a salutory impact, tending to restrain judicial autocracy.

The profession should not ask the impossible of the Court. No theory of constitutional law, except one that counsels deference across the board, can completely eliminate discretion. Rigid formulas disable the Court when it attempts to respond to society's deeply felt values. The empirical reasonable expectation standard, however, responds to demands for judicial restraint, yet it protects individuals who are victimized arbitrarily by representatives.

Increased participation by previously powerless segments of the society does not eliminate the problem of "captured"[66] legislatures. When the legislature acts irresponsibly, judicial activity is often justified, but when the judiciary's concerns with substantive justice involve repetitious intervention in routine cases, "the style of legal discourse approaches that of commonplace political or economic argument."[67] Steady doses of instrumental rationality[68] in routine cases involves the Supreme Court in prospective policymaking. It is therefore incumbent upon the Court to exercise self-restraint in what Chief Justice Stone called the "run-of-the-mill" due process case.[69]

Teleologic considerations may be appropriate in hard cases when no rules, principles, or analogies are dispositive, and when counsel's argument persuasively tips the balance of competing consequentialist considerations toward one ruling rather than another.[70] Consequentialist considerations, however, can ultimately undermine and destroy rights.[71] J. Rawls recognizes the subversive tendencies of teleological theories that define the good "independently from the right,"[72] and then define the right as that which maximizes the good.[72] Theories, that allow a determination of goodness without reference to rightness,[73] do not take seriously enough the reasonable expectations of persons, and the "distinction between persons."[74] The implications of consequentialism authorize the judge to sacrifice just claims whenever beneficial social consequences slightly outweigh serious harm to the litigant.[75]

A system of judicial review is not, strictly speaking, rights-oriented or principled when the crucial "legal" issue always is reduced to a determination of the best consequences. Aside from the intractable questions in many cases (best consequences for whom?), evaluating all the possible consequences takes judges beyond their field of competence, which is not forecasting the future. Like representatives, judges are often likely to give undue weight to immediate considerations at the expense of individuals and societal reasonable expectations; such expectations, given an opportunity for more dispassionate judgment, might have superior normative importance.[76] Furthermore, excessive consequentialism subverts the Constitution's distinction between the judiciary and legislature.[77] Finally, excessive judicial consequentialism resembles the "end always justifies the means" rationale fatal to the concept of law.[78]

2. Toward a Theory of Intervention

Although judicial restraint in the routine cases is proper, a judge needs a theory of judicial intervention. How does the judge construct a theory of justified intervention which establishes a legitimate agenda for the Court? If the Court does not rely upon history, tradition, or contemporary consensus for its sources of values, it is dangerously adrift without moorings. If the Court does rely on such sources, cases may be decided on the basis of unreliable evidence.[79] Cognizant of the difficulties in ascertaining society's reasonable expectations, careful judges will rely upon enduring norms and patterns of behavior that, demonstrably, have deep societal roots. The Court can build upon this foundation of trustworthy evidence to justify its decisions.[80]

A competent judge is usually able to recognize when the alleged community consensus is fragmented, shifting, or unknown. Moreover, he can often discern when the traditional values relied upon by a litigant are, in fact, established patterns of social behavior creating reasonable expectations that deserve due process of law. Although history, tradition, and consensus are controversial and elusive value sources, the Court's credibility can be established if the evidence it relies upon is clear and convincing.

Tradition, much maligned these days, is an important ingredient of legitimate authority.[81] Tradition reveals patterns of behavior that are deeply impressed in our social fabric. The nation's continued respect for the judiciary is largely attributable to the judiciary's respect for the tradition that builds upon the excess of meaning that is partially revealed in the Constitution. Without historical perspective or respect for tradition, the Court is more likely to mistake the ripple for the tide, and the fad for essential and enduring societal values.

In a substantive due process case, durable community values have constitutional significance, irrespective of whether any particular judge shares these values. Law and set patterns of morality, however, cannot be kept completely apart for both are concerned with norms of conduct and justice.[82] The typical judge is influenced, at least in part, by the morals and customs of society.

When a judge's pet ideas about the just society are incompatible with the basic values of the nation, he lacks authorization, under the due process clauses, to impose upon an unconsenting public. By contrast, legislation frequently violates due process of law when it denies the humanity of an individual. Under these circumstances, the Court may not conclusively presume the legislation is inoffensive to basic societal values. Of course, in many cases it may be difficult to ascertain whether legislation amounts to the kind of invidious oppression that degrades human dignity.

When there is an evident lack of social agreement on matters of substantive justice, formal justice becomes important. The venerable practice of treating like cases alike is usually sound because it provides an orientation for individuals, representatives, and judges.[83] This practice tends to maintain the status quo, and recognizes that newly emerging rights usually need an incubation period.

Formal justice inhibits judicial activism until a principle of substantive justice is sufficiently ripe to support a novel case ruling. Although the due process concept gradually changes with the ebb and flow of community morality, judges who change the law prematurely in hopes of changing community morality take a dangerous shortcut. In sum, formal justice ensures that the penetration of community morality into the gaps of constitutional law is gradual. In this selective, incremental, and disciplined process of adjudication, only the most appealing inchoate principles of constitutional law, based upon clearly reasonable expectations, are candidates for extraordinary protection from courts.

3. Reasonable Expectations and the Right of Privacy

Judges cannot appear to take partisan sides in political controversies. The judge is expected to be critically aware of most of his prejudices, and to correct them in an effort to understand what the authoritative text says to him in light of the working of tradition. The judge's views of morality may not enter into the law unless his ruling is subsumable by an established or inchoate constitutional principle.

Justice Harlan's approach in the birth control cases[84] is exemplary. By the 1960s, community morality clearly rejected any intrusive governmental experiments with "the mode and manner of the married couple's sexual relations."[85] This reasonable expectation of privacy had not yet been introduced into the case law. Thus when an outmoded Connecticut statute was tested in *Poe* v. *Ullman,*[86] there appeared to be a gap in constitutional law. Since no other state had ever made the *use* of contraceptives illegal,[87] the state's power to regulate the intimacies of married life in the home required clarification. The Court ruled the case nonjusticiable, but Justice Harlan's dissent contended that the statute encroached upon a traditional "private realm of family life"[88] more inviolable than liberties dependent upon the transitory compromises negotiated routinely by politicians.

Justice Harlan noted that an inchoate principle of marital privacy is subsumable under the concept of privacy in the home.[89] He was not suggesting that law and morality are always identical. His *Poe* opinion suggests that the most private intimacies of family life traditionally protected by the government should continue to be so protected, absent some pressing justification for a novel governmental intrusion. Marital sexual privacy is also embraced by the broader principle limiting the extent to which a political body can experiment to the detriment of individuals' personality and dignity.[90] Justice Harlan's views in the birth control cases illustrate how an inchoate right justifying a novel ruling can become established explicitly as a part of constitutional law.[91]

The right of marital privacy was viewed less favorably by Justice Black in his *Griswold* v. *Connecticut*[92] dissent. He wrote, "I like my privacy as well as the next one, but I am nevertheless compelled to admit that government has a right to invade it unless prohibited by some specific constitutional provision."[93] Similarly, Learned Hand believed that

> [j]udges are seldom content merely to annul the particular solution before them; they do not, indeed they may not, say that taking all things into consideration, the legislator's solution is too strong for the judicial stomach. On the contrary they wrap up their veto in a protective veil of adjectives such as *arbitrary, artificial, normal, reasonable, inherently, fundamental,* or *essential,* whose office usually, though quite innocently, is to disguise what they are doing and impute it to a derivation far more impressive than their personal preferences, which are all that in fact lie behind the decision.[94]

Contrary to the beliefs of Justice Black and Learned Hand, nothing in the Constitution prevents a judge from expressing personal preferences consistent with his ruling, as long as the ruling is otherwise *validly* justified on conventional grounds. Justice Harlan, a disciplined judge, recognized that judicial restraint is not accomplished by "hollow"[95] formulas. Rather, judicial restraint is achieved through respect for history and recognition of society's basic values.[96]

Judge Hand also once asked whether judges should be "arbiters of all political authority in the nation with a discretion to act or not, as they please."[97] The question is misleading. Judges do not have discretion to act as they please, but must justify their decisions in accordance with established standards which constrain their discretion. A judge is obligated to employ accepted canons of legal reasoning and to consider the text of the Constitution, its structure, the framers' intent, precedent, notions of formal justice, federalism, rules of justiciability, and the underlying values of a representative democracy, including the majority's demands. Judges, therefore, may not act as they please, since they are expected to persuade the public that their case rulings depend upon legitimate sources of law.

In *Roe* v. *Wade*[98], warnings about abuses of judicial power enunciated by Justice Black and Judge Hand went unheeded. In its rush to judgment, the Court overlooked tradition, consensus, the framers' intent, the constraints of federalism, and the requirements of a principled method of formal justice. The bridge between the politically controversial case ruling and previous precedent did not span the distance. Instead, the newly created right to choose an abortion appeared to depend solely on the will of judges. Because the nation's moral consensus was in a state of flux, such premature judicial intervention was undisciplined.

In pursuit of a new vision of social justice, the *Roe* Court distorted precedent to justify its intensified level of scrutiny. Reliance upon the dictum in *Eisenstadt* v. *Baird*[99] planted to help Justice Harry A. Blackmun write his *Roe* opinion[100] was something of a cheat. Not even the *Griswold* decision supported the holding in *Roe*, since the right of marital privacy in matters concerning the *use* of contraceptives did not clearly encompass the pregnant female's right to choose an abortion. In fact, because the level of scrutiny required in *Roe* was far more exacting than the level of scrutiny in *Griswold* and other analogous precedent,[101] *Roe* appears out of line.[102]

F. Disciplined Due Process Methodology
1. Balancing and Morality

The *United States* v. *Carolene Products Co.*[103] footnote led to two tiers of scrutiny,[104] then apparently three.[105] The more appropriate methodology that often structures the modern Court's discretion in due process cases was described by Justice Harlan.[106] He focused on

> the nature of the individual interest affected, the extent to which it is affected, the rationality of the connection between legislative means and purpose, the existence of alternative means for effectuating the purpose, and the degree of confidence we may have that the statute reflects the legislative concern for the purpose that would legitimately support the means chosen.[107]

Although each substantive due process case involves moral and political issues, the factors identified by Justice Harlan transform the ultimate moral questions into technical legal questions. For example, "the nature of the individual interest affected" refers only to interests of demonstrable constitutional significance. An empirical examination of "the extent to which [the interest] is affected"[108] does not focus upon abstract ideals of morality. Similarly, "the rationality of the connection between legislative means and purpose"[109] provokes technical questions about the required quantity and quality of evidence supporting official findings of fact. Clearly, when the government's policy is challenged, "the existence of alternative means for effectuating the purpose,"[110] is a factor that helps the Court compare the incremental benefits of the policy with its incremental interference with individual liberties. This evaluation does not focus solely upon moralistic considerations. Instead, the Court decides whether there is a reasoned explanation for the resection of a less burdensome policy. The final factor in Justice Harlan's analysis considers the genuineness of the government's articulated purpose.[111] Again, technical rules of statutory construction and a rule bound inquiry into the legislature's intent are specialized techniques.

A Court applying this technical methodology examines problems that result from a decision adverse to the government. Some of the technical questions presented include the following: whether federalism or separation of powers concerns are adversely affected; whether the law's continuity will be interrupted; whether the Court will be entering into a delicate area of controversy where it lacks information, expertise, self-confidence, and the public's confidence; whether judicial intervention causes undue disruption to governmental operations will occur; and, whether the Court is interfering with the political process and the often necessary compromises reached by political actors. These are not questions usually entertained by the moral philosopher. His methodology is different.

When moral questions have only secondary importance, and political questions are reserved for officials accountable to the public, the danger that a decision imposes socially unacceptable ethics upon society diminishes. Thus, the Court's methodology, not its ideology, becomes paramount. For example, assume that it is immoral to force an involuntarily committed patient to ingest antipsychotic drugs with dangerous side effects.[112] Nevertheless, if the patient's state-employed physicians determine that the drugs reduce the patient's propensity for violence, and that the risks of side effects are slight, the Court might reduce its level of scrutiny, especially if the government's management of such patients has built-in procedural safeguards. Otherwise, the Court becomes involved in the day-by-day management of mental patients, taxing its resources in areas where it lacks expertise. It is thus possible that a variation of a deferential rational basis test will be applied by the Court, even though basic liberties are burdened. This is not to say that professional judgment is immune from judicial review. Rather, it is to recognize that the Court is not usually in a position to second guess medical judgment.

Each factor in a multifactor balancing test affects the significance of other factors. The interaction is complex. Obviously, the Court's scrutiny tends to become more exacting as the burden on constitutionally protected interests increases.[113] On the other hand, the greater the dislocation likely to be caused by a ruling adverse to government, the more circumspect the Court. Circumspection was evident in *Youngberg* v. *Romeo*.[114] The state's medical care, although interfering with an institutionalized person's core liberties of movement and bodily security, survived the Court's deferential test. The Court was understandably unwilling to allow a jury to second-guess professional judgment, an intrusion which would disrupt a specialized institution's ongoing internal operations. Thus the remedy requested by a challenger of governmental policy, here a damages award, may also affect the Court's balancing process.[115] The nature of the remedy requested is often relevant.

The piecemeal development of a substantive due process agenda includes case rulings that specify proper levels of judicial review.[116] A level of judicial scrutiny created by a series of cases "grows slowly by gradual accretion from the resolution of specific problems."[117] It becomes a working hypothesis requiring continuous testing in the laboratory of the law.[118] Eventually principles will clarify the developing law,[119] but the quest has been described as "a sort of connect-the-dots exercise."[120] Nevertheless, the painstaking process of groping for justice is preferable to rigid levels of scrutiny which do not reflect society's reasonable expectations. Moreover, a multi-factor, but structured approach is judicially manageable, and preferable to a purely *ad hoc* approach.

2. Balancing Versus Fixed Levels of Scrutiny

A multifactor, flexible balancing test is sensitive to the dynamics of the reasonable expectations standard. The test, when properly structured, avoids excessive reliance upon ambiguous "buzzwords,"[121] such as *compelling* and *substantial* (government interests) which can mean all things to all people[122] and different things to each judge. A tractable yet disciplined methodology compares well to a rigidly dichotomous test that is either "strict in theory and fatal in fact"[123] or excessively deferential.

As *Romeo*[124] indicates, substantial burdens on core liberties do not necessarily trigger intrusive judicial review. The circumstances of each case affect the Court's level of scrutiny.[125] Moreover, all types of rights and governmental restrictions are not alike. There are countless possibilities. Therefore, references to a two or three tiered due process concept can be misleading. For example, the abstract right of privacy subsumes countless concrete rights, not all of which are equally constitutionally significant. Thus, in the abortion cases, a parental notification requirement triggers a slightly different level of scrutiny than a parental consent requirement.[126] A spousal notification requirement may require yet another level of scrutiny.[127] Obviously, not every case involving disputes about fundamental rights necessarily triggers the same fatal scrutiny applied in *Roe*.[128]

Personal autonomy issues are not resolvable solely by mechanistic concepts of judicial review,[129] especially during the throes of a sexual revolution. For example, in abortion funding debates, some argue that a pregnant female has a duty to protect prenatal life, but would not extend this duty to victims of rape. When ambivalent human feelings are involved, cliches about privacy have limited usefulness, and do not necessarily indicate the Constitution's answer to controversies involving basic human instincts. The legislature is often insensitive to the plight of the pregnant female. On the other hand, the legislature might be concerned that many indigent females worried about lack of money, are unable to evaluate impartially society's interest in the sanctity of prenatal life. The government's use of economic pressure through denial of abortion funding reflects an official belief that a pregnant female is not responsible enough to make the right moral decision on her own.[130] Is such a case to be decided always by a level of scrutiny fatal in fact?

The Court was "uncertain and adrift"[131] when burdens on fundamental interests always triggered strict scrutiny. It is less likely that a person's reasonable expectations will be characterized as a fundamental right if the result is the demise of a network of state laws.[132] Conversely, more fundamental rights will be recognized when the ascription does not interfere with the task of balancing competing interests.

A court required to balance competing interests after the legislature has canvassed the subject is always faced with a delicate task.[133] A sober second evaluation by an impartial tribunal, however, is desirable when evidence suggests that a serious political malfunction has occurred. Often, the Court's balancing of competing interests is different than the legislatures'. A legislative compromise appeasing special interest groups might fail to assign the requisite weight to constitutionally significant interests. Long after the legislation is enacted, changed conditions may generate reasonable expectations. Moreover, the legislature's judgment may have been a response to public hysteria, panic, or obsession. True, a balancing test might require the Court to substitute its view for that of the legislature when laws that appear despotic are enacted with little or no deliberation. Under these circumstances, the Supreme Court has a duty to discern the constitutional balance "which our nation, built upon postulates of respect for the liberty of the individual, has struck between that liberty and the demands of organized society."[134] The constitutional balance is the source and product of the discernible reasonable expectations of fair-minded people.

Many a question about a reasonable expectation standard dependent in part on empirical is without a permanently settled answer. For example, who are the fair-minded people? How long must a value endure before it is recognized as a constitutionally significant reasonable expectation? What percentage of the nation's population must cherish a particular value before it becomes a reasonable expectation? On what side does the Court throw its weight when the country is polarized as in 1954 when *Brown* v. *Board of*

Education[135] was decided? Further, to what extent can the Court uphold reasonable expectations which are, in its view, becoming morally regressive? The difficulty of these and other questions[136] suggests that the Court must eschew rigid formulas and platitudinous generalizations when it decides hard cases. The Supreme Court, although not infallible, is often capable of identifying some of society's reasonable expectations. It must be sensitive and responsive to views, which are not shortsighted. Even Learned Hand wrote, "[J]udges are perhaps more apt than legislators to take a long view" although he did add that this "varies so much with the individual that generalization is hazardous."[137] The value of a credible application of the reasonable expectation standard is this: it elevates the Court's judgment to a universality higher than the judgment of a demonstrably despotic legislature. Moreover, the standard is compatible with the "consent of the governed" precept.

G. The Challenge of Due Process Methodology

In a rapidly changing, dispute-ridden society, a Court of nine independent justices will not always produce a consistent body of case law. When logical coherence is the Court-watcher's sole criterion, the Supreme Court's cases appear to be a doctrinal mess.[138] The critical observer, however, cannot fairly accuse the Court of abusing judicial power when its members conscientiously exercise their detached judgment and provide a valid justification for each ruling. Conventional theory attempts to explain that the apparently incoherent and contradictory case law has an organizing methodology.

A flexible but structured methodology for weighing competing interests provides the basis for a descriptive and modestly prescriptive theory of law enabling the legal profession to understand the due process concept. There are of course, several problems associated with balancing. All balancing tends to focus on the particular factors relevant in a given case.[139] Even excessively particularized opinions, which seem *ad hoc*, can congeal over time into broad rules of general application that lead to predictable results. Toward that end, when judges engage in balancing, they should articulate the valid criteria that guide resolution of value conflicts.[140] A judge's opinion, when practicable, should conjoin the case ruling with more general principles and standards. Since the scope, content, and weight of rights frequently expand and contract, continuous clarification of the law is essential. Otherwise, the judicial system will produce a bevy of disconnected case rulings inadequate to meet the needs of lawyers and their clients.

Depending on the nature of the right, overinclusive prophylactic rules might be necessary to prevent any chilling effect produced by the unpredictability of balancing.[141] On the other hand, depending on the interest of the individual, it may be appropriate to presume that the government's action is constitutional.[142] Unfortunately, constitutional rules and presumptions provide either too much or too little protection;[143] in such circumstances, gradual reformulation of the rules and presumptions pursuant to a disciplined methodology is often warranted.[144]

A key question is always whether an equal protection[145] or substantive due process case requires the risks associated with judicial discretion. In due process cases, Justice Harlan recognized that judicial discretion is "more conducive to judicial restraint than an approach couched in slogans. . . ."[146] While stressing restraint,[147] Justice Harlan also realized that due regard for an individual's reasonable expectations occasionally requires the risk-laden flexible balancing approach. Risks are taken in order to protect the individual from democracy run riot. Democracy is not the ultimate end of our government, but a means for working out, under law, a reasonable socially acceptable relationship between the legal liberties of individuals and the community's welfare. Thus, the need for a constitutional requirement of due process of law, which limits the power of elected representatives.

The Court's critics claim that the due process concept is too "evocative,"[148] and that "a principled approach to judicial enforcement of the Constitution's open-ended provisions cannot be developed. . . ."[149] In the hardest kind of a constitutional case, the applicable principle and its weight is not obvious. This is a problem. Article III imperatives, however, obligate the Court to develop a credible theory of legitimate judicial intervention. We do not have a government where "anything goes." Although the reasonable expectation standard provides a guide, judicial efforts to apply the reasonable expectations standard occasionally appear as creative groping for a plausible justification in due process cases.[150] Chief Justice Marshall, mindful of similar challenges, wrote:

> The judiciary cannot, as the legislature may, avoid a measure because it approaches the confines of the constitution. We cannot pass it by because it is doubtful. With whatever difficulties, a case may be attended, we must decide it, if it be brought before us. We have no more right to decline the exercise of jurisdiction which is given, than to usurp that which is not given. The one or the other would be treason to the Constitution. Questions may occur which we would glady avoid, but we cannot avoid them. *All we can do is, to exercise our best judgment, and conscientiously to perform our duty.*[151]

The litigant has a reasonable expectation that the Supreme Court will perform its duty conscientiously. When it does not, the Court itself violates due process of law.

Chapter 9 Concluding Note on Skepticism, Radicalism, and Constitutionalism

A. Excessive Skepticism

We cannot govern ourselves under law without adherence to principles, but we hold to our principles provisionally and with some healthy skepticsm[152] to avoid being cocksure. Skepticism while healthy in moderation can become excessive. The skeptic claims that "the conclusion of a valid deduction can contain no reference to sense impressions which do not already figure in its premises."[153] The skeptic also claims that inductive argument "cannot justify a passage from the occurrence of sense impressions to the existence of anything which is not an object of experience. . . ."[154] The neurotic skeptics who take their claims too seriously are paralyzed by doubt. Some specialists in constitutional law are excessively skeptical. As noted earlier, however, the common sense doctrines of Thomas Reid counsel against neurotic skepticism,[155] and the American concept of constitutionalism is grounded on a common sense view of the judicial role.

A common sense theory of constitutional law is not excessively skeptical about adequate judicial objectivity, and denies that values with constitutional significance are always arbitrarily generated "out of the [judicial] stomach."[156] A human being's inclinations, of course, inevitably influence his choice of starting premises. However, the steadying factors of formal justice, the validity thesis, the rationality norm, and society's reasonable expectations, which control judicial discretion, are safeguards against unacceptable arbitrariness. Consequently the conscientious judge attempts to acquire disciplined habits of self-control, by adhering to the steadying factors in the law.

Some skeptics, nevertheless, argue that their notions of legal realism explain the nature of the judicial process, but their explanations mislead. The judge, of course, cannot help being intellectually involved in a case. However, his involvement is not necessarily some inherently dangerous form of judicial subjectivity; but rather the mere act of thinking. Judges who think naturally have discretion to clarify law in many different ways. The task of hermeneutical reflection is to bring to the language of the law the plausible possibilities that words suggest, but which have remained unexpressed — until the hard case is decided. It is neurotic, however, to claim that a plausible justification for a case ruling is inevitably dictated by arbitrary personal preferences.

Berlin points out "the major fallacy"[157] of the skeptic's critique of objective judgments when he writes:

We are told that we are creatures of our environment, or of history, and that this colors our temperament, our judgments, our principles. Every judgment is relative, every evaluation subjective, made what . . . it is by the interplay of the [contingent] factors of its own time and place, individual or collective. But relative to what? Subjective in contrast to what? Made to conform as it does to some ephemeral pattern as opposed to what conceivable timeless independence of such distorting factors? Relative terms (especially perjoratives) need correlatives, or else they turn out to be without meaning themselves, mere gibes, propagandist phrases designed to throw discredit, and not to describe or analyze.[158]

Contrary to the skeptics' discrediting gibes, the judge's case ruling is hardly arbitrary when he weighs evidence, determines the credibility of the evidence, reasons, and applies traditional canons of constitutional interpretation consistently from case to case. He is expected to employ time-tested methods to verify facts, to control his bias, and to attain that personal detachment which is expected of judges. "The [judicial] function is canalized by the adversary process, which . . . tends to structure issues and narrow their scope to manageable proportions."[159] Thus, the disciplined judge, although at times moved by irrational forces, is not "mysteriously doomed to [an unacceptable] degree of relativism and subjectivism."[160]

In constitutional law, the word *objective* refers primarily to "standards of analytical candor, rigor, and clarity."[161] The legal profession and society imposes these standards of impartiality on its judges, and requires faithful adherence. Concerning the word *subjective,* Berlin writes:

If words like *subjective* and *relative, prejudice* and *biased,* are terms not of comparison and contrast — do not imply the possibility of their own opposites, of *objective* (or at least *less subjective*) of *unbiased* (or at least *less biased*), what meaning have they for us? To use them to refer to everything whatever, to use them as absolute terms, and not as correlatives, is a rhetorical perversion of their normal sense . . . but not a serious doctrine concerned with the question of attribution of responsibility in history, relevant to any particular group of . . . statesmen or human beings.[162]

Since judges are often fairly criticized as being unduly subjective, some correlative concept of adequate objectivity has to be the critics' standard. Contrary to some critics, however, adherence to a standard of adequate objectivity is attainable by conscientious judges who believe in fidelity to law.

Fidelity to law is determined by a judge's willingness to maintain the requisite degree of personal detachment. This kind of impartial mediation was stressed in the eighteenth century by those Founding Fathers influenced by Hutcheson and Reid. The transmittal over time of these enduring assumptions about the desirability and possibility of objectivity enables us to identify with preceding generations.[163] "It is only a very vulgar historical materialism that . . . says that ideals [of impartiality] are mere material interests in disguise."[164] The neurotic skeptic cannot support the concept of fidelity to law; he doubts his own judgments and the judgments of others. Hence, he has no capacity to be objective, impartial, or faithful to an authoritative but indeterminate Constitution. On the other hand, conventional theory attempts to transcend the dualism of subjectivity and objectivity.

Adequate objectivity, I contend, is an indispensable ingredient in any political agenda for the Supreme Court. Without it, the very idea of the judicial process is perverted. Paul Freund's interesting statement is not at odds with the preceding argument. He wrote:

> Much of law is designed to avoid the necessity for the judge to reach what Holmes called his can't helps, his ultimate convictions or values. The force of precedent, the close applicability of statute law, the separation of powers, legal presumptions, statutes of limitations, rules of pleading and evidence, and above all the pragmatic assessments of fact that point to one result whichever ultimate values be assumed, all enable the judge in most cases to stop short of a resort to his personal standards. When these prove unavailing, as is more likely in the case of courts of last resort at the frontiers of the law, and most likely in a supreme constitutional court, the judge necessarily resorts to his own scheme of values. It may therefore be said that the most important thing about a judge is his philosophy; and if it be dangerous for him to have one, it is at all events less dangerous than the self-deception of having none.[165]

Surely Freund is right; there are occasions when the judge has discretion to resort to his own scheme of ultimate values. However, some values are ruled out by virtue of his position. When a lawyer becomes a judge, he can no longer actively pursue the values that always favor his former clients. Indeed, he may not misuse the law by favoring any of the litigants in a case. After he rules out various options because of their incompatibility with his institutional role, and after he realizes that his case ruling has to be based on convictions that will have general application in all like cases, it still, in a sense, comes down to a judge's scheme of values. However, they are expected to be the fair-minded values of a person who has an obligation to subordinate his lawless inclinations to the institutional standards that channel judicial discretion.

Even the judge's personal standards of justice under law are less subjective in nature than Professor Freund's phrase "his own scheme of values" indicates. Freund recalls Holmes who immortalized the "can't helps" criterion, but Justice Holmes also wrote: "The very considerations which judges most rarely mention, and always with apology, are the secret root from which the law draws all the juices of life. I mean, of course, considerations of what is expedient for the community concerned. . . ."[166] I regard Holmes's "can't helps" to be dictates of conscience that express what Francis Hutcheson called the impartial moral sense; a deeply felt sense of civic virtue.

The impartial judge with moral sense, if he is blessed with the minimum essentials of common sense, will act to prevent unauthorized acts by officials. The skeptic, all the while, counsels restraint because his neurotic doubts disable him from identifying and resisting tyranny. Even the will to be impartial is considered subjectivism by the skeptic. If excessive skepticism prevents the judge from following the dictates of his moral and common sense, officials could, with impunity, disobey the Constitution. A judge paralyzed by doubt is incapable of satisfying society's requirements and its reasonable expectations. Society, however, expects an independent judiciary to resist the tyranny of representatives who abuse their trust.

B. Unacceptable Radicalism

Radical extremists are not skeptical concerning the values which courts should impose upon the public. Some radicals, so confident about their own views of social justice, would have courts impose their ideas of progress. Even the Constitution's authoritative status is challenged by some radical legal thinkers. Why? The impartiality of judges is deemed a fable, and the system of law is regarded as a mask that hides the real concentrations of power that are inimical to a more just social order.

Advocates of radical social transformation, insist that the superstructure of "rational" liberal thought is an illusion, and refer to it as

> that system of political, social economic, and religious institutions, those "myths," dogmas, ideals, categories of thought and language, modes of feeling, scales of values, "socially approved" attitudes and habits (called by Marx superstructure) that represent "rationalizations," "sublimations," and symbolic representations, which cause men to function in an organized way, prevent chaos, [and] fulfill the function of the Hobbesian state.[167]

Admittedly, powerful groups in a representative democracy erroneously equate their selfish interests with the public interest. Since the government cannot equitably reconcile all the competing interests in a pluralistic society, the critics of conventional theory stress the contradictions of liberal thought, and, accordingly, ridicule the eighteenth-century dream of harmony. Radicals actively pursue their political objectives unhampered by what they perceive as the intellectual baggage of mainsteam liberals and conservatives.

Radicals deny that individuals seeking private gain in a democracy can be voluntarily persuaded to work for the common good. The political compromises accomodated by a Constitution receptive to negotiated outcomes are deemed intolerable. It follows that the radicals downgrade the Constitution's status as an authoritative text. Judges are perceived as political actors who presently are acting in behalf of certain vested interests. The moral imperfection of the Constitution is, therefore, used as a justification for the radical's advocacy of contraconstitutional judicial activism. Moreover, critics of constitutionalism contend that any deferential judge who claims he is relying on neutral principles, when he condones inequality, is either fooling the public or himself. The question is whether this verbal assault is realistic. The critique unrealistically claims that the judge lacks incentive and the ability to secure lawful justice impartially. Though the judge's views are naturally colored by his subjective assessments, I submit that he tends to conform to the standards of impartiality imposed upon him by society. The judge, unless he is a zealot, realizes that the Constitution, properly interpreted, is not incompatible with the reasonable expectations that animate society.

Although conventional theories of law are pliable and tolerant of judicial discretion in hard cases, the judge's legal duty to be impartial is not one that he is free to ignore. He knows that not all theories of social justice can be derived from valid existential premises of constitutional law. A judge, with integrity, is constrained by the norms of constitutionalism that he might unofficially desire to subvert. This subversion he cannot accomplish as an official of the United States, lacking power to redefine his official role. When judges radically redefine their office, without a legal warrant in the Constitution, as it is commonly understood and interpreted, their abuse of power is an impeachable offense. Moreover, it is within Congress's power to prohibit repeated abuses of power by regulating the jurisdiction of any federal court, which regularly defies the limits placed on the judiciary by the Constitution — the supreme norm that holds the legal system together. Without some strong political support, any holding that a statute, which strips the Court of jurisdiction, is unconstitutional will be hortatory.

The need for Congress to let this "Sword of Damocles" drop has not yet arisen, and the need will never arise, so long as the Court rejects proposed case rulings that are socially unacceptable in a political democracy. If necessary, a free people will have to decide whether the destabilization likely to occur as a result of legislation that strips federal courts of jurisdiction poses less risks than the judiciary's unacceptable redefinition of their duty.

The point, in other words, is that the judicial power falls far short of the power needed by a dictatorship of the self-righteous.[168] In sum, "[t]here are those who think we need a new Constitution, and their views may someday prevail."[169] But under the Constitution we have, courts lack authority to impose upon the governed an intolerably radical ideology simply because it is, in the court's opinion, profoundly wise, morally right, or good for the masses or an elite.

C. Constitutionalism and the Judge's Conventional Role

Our deep down feelings (values) are conditioned by the world around us.

We express these personal feelings very imperfectly. Judges share this inadequacy. The law articulated by a Court, which might be a product of the judge's socially conditioned feelings, has to be articulated *and justified*. The justifications of a case ruling are part of the law, and sources of the law in gestation. Justifications are sometimes implausible when they do not conform to the reasonable expectations of the public. Thus, the people's fairminded expectations, their perceptions of civic virtue, and their constitutive rules for recognizing valid legal principles influence the judge, channel his discretion, rule out certain interpretations of the Constitution, and produce the law. In this respect the people are both ruled and rulers, and courts are not immune from their power.

The judge occasionally fails to read accurately the reasonable expectations of the public. However, when he makes a flagrant mistake, he feels the pressures of public opinion — down deep with his other feelings. His court's prestige,perhaps its legitimacy and survival, is at stake. As a result, or as a prophylactic, the cautious court develops techniques of judicial circumspection. These techniques of constitutional adjudication are captured by a theory of conventional law that focuses, in part, upon methodology — the disciplined methodology for *not* misreading the nation's reasonable expectations. In this way, the law in the Constitution *becomes* constitutional law.

The judge, attentive to the community consensus of feelings, judgments, and norms which generate a litigant's reasonable expectations, can explain why politically accountable officials have failed to give the public its due. There is a healthy balance between the law's continuity and the public's perceptions of fairness when the literal or intended meaning of the Constitution is synthesized with commonly held perceptions of its contemporary legal significance. In sum, there is a warrant for judicial activism on a litigant's behalf when rights based on values deemed basic by society, are subsumed by the legal system's basic norm.

Public perceptions of fairness enter into the law and are affirmed by the Constitution, but judicial opinions do not always successfully separate the factual and normative components of applicable fundamental fairness and reasonable expectations standards. Moreover, there is an unclear overlap between these standards, and their relationship to the Constitution's more evocative provisions. In some respects the reasonable expectation standard is countermajoritarian; in other respects, it is not. The resultant uncertainty about constitutional law is not a ground for despair. Uncertainty increases the judges' awareness that their understanding of the law in motion is imperfect. Uncertainty encourages the prudent interpretive approach that carefully adjusts the case law to society's gradually changing perceptions of the Constitution's present and future meaning. Its meaning is immanently formative, which is to say it continues to form itself out of itself. Judges who assist in this process, if they are impartial mediators, bolster the public's faith in a transcendent legal order.

Citation of the Constitution is linguistic legerdemain when its ambiguity is exploited as a pretext for imposing socially unacceptable political doctrines upon an unreceptive majority. The Constitution, when properly cited, is not a pretext, but a metaphor that likens the real meaning of the text (that is, the meaning existing at the present moment) with the dominant social perception of its meaning. Our basic *grundnorm* symbolically combines the principles of self-government with the warranted expectations of the social alliance. To determine which expectations are truly warranted, the social context cannot be ignored. When the authoritative text is considered in its normative setting, a responsive Court can impartially determine the socially acceptable meaning of the Constitution: its actual meaning.

Footnotes for Introduction

1. *See, e.g., Gordon, Historicism in Legal Scholarship,* 90 **Yale L. J.** 1017, 1024 (1981).
2. Freund, "Social Justice and the Law," in **Social Justice** 110 (Brandt, ed. 1962).
3. *See also,* Cox, Book Review, 94 *Harv. L. Rev.* 700, 706 (1981). ("One way or another . . . the Court is always deciding whether in its judgment the harm done to the disadvantaged class by the legislative classification is disproportionate to the public purpose the measure is likely to achieve.")
4. MacCormick, **Legal Reasoning and Legal Theory** 242 (1978).
5. *See, e.g.,* Bolling v. Sharpe, 347 U.S. 497 (1954). (The Court held that *de jure* segregation in Washington, D.C., violated the Constitution.)

Footnotes for Part I, Chapter 1

6. Francis, **Formal Models of American Politics: An Introduction** 16 (1972).
7. Dworkin "condemns the practice of making decisions that seem right in isolation, but cannot be brought within some comprehensive theory of general principles and policies that is consistent with other decisions also thought right." **Dworkin, Taking Rights Seriously 87 (1978).** In his chapter, "Hard Cases" (*id.* at 81-130), Dworkin refers to a remarkable number of discrete theories that he would like to embrace under a comprehensive theory. He refers, *inter alia,* to a general theory of precedent (*id.* at 111), a "theory of mistakes" (*id.* at 121-22), "constitutional theory" (*id.* at 117), "political theory" (*id.* at 92-93, 95, 109), "full political theory" (*id.* at 94 n. 1), a "theory of hard cases" (*id.* at 81), a "theory of dignity" (*id.* at 128), a "theory of adjudication" (*id.* at 82, 126), a "theory of law" (*id.* at 118), a "theory of statutory interpretation" (*id.* at 109), "moral theory" (*id.* at 147), a "theory of moral rights against the state" (*id.* at 147, 149), a "theory of political skepticism" (*id.* at 138), a "theory of judicial deference (*id.* at 138), and a theory of institutional history (*id.* at 89). Nozick also refers wistfully to the dream of "one general and unified theory of value." **Nozick, Philosophical Explanations** 417-18 (1981).
8. Raz, **The Concept of a Legal System** 212 (2d rev. ed. 1980).
   Id. at 211.
10. *Id.* at 212.
11. *Id.* at 211.
12. **Ely, Democracy and Distrust: A Theory of Judicial Review** (1980).
13. United States v. Carolene Products Co., 304 U.S. 144, 152-53, n. 4 (1938).
14. **Kelsen, General Theory of Law and State** (1961).
15. **Hart, The Concept of Law** (1961)
16. **Ely,** *supra* note 12.
17. **Perry, The Constitution, The Courts, and Human Rights** (1982).
18. MacCormick, *supra* note 4.
19. For descriptions of political science theories dealing with groups, elites, and power, see **Meehan, Contemporary Political Thought: A Critical Study** 100-05 (1967).
20. *Id.* at 111-89.
21. *Id.* at 287-349.
22. *Id.* at 190-286.
23. **Pennock, Democratic Political Theory** (1979).
24. **Meehan,** *supra* note 19, at 144 [quoting **Parsons, The Social System** 486 (1951)].
25. *Id.* at 55; *see also,* Kuhn, **The Structure of Scientific Revolutions** 206 (2d ed. enlarged 1970).
26. Durant's list of the ultimate questions include the following:
    What is the nature of the world? What are its matters and form, its constituents and structure, its ultimate substances and laws? What is matter in its innermost quality, in the secret essence of its being? What is mind? — and is it forever distinct from matter

and master of it, or a derivative of matter, and its slave? Are both the external world which we see in perception, and the internal world which we feel in consciousness, subject to mechanical or deterministic laws. . . . **Durant, The Pleasures of Philosophy** 33 (1953).

27. **Gadamer, Truth and Method,** xxv (2d rev. ed. 1975).
28. **The American Heritage Dictionary of the English Language** 1335 (1969).
29. **Meehan,** *supra* note 19, at 24.
30. **Meehan,** *Id.* "The variables are linked by their common focus on the phenomenon — *x*."
31. *See* **Wechsler, Principles, Politics, & Fundamental Law** 3-28 (1961).
32. **Meehan,** *supra* note 19, at 24.
33. *Id.*
34. *See generally* **Bickel, The Supreme Court and the Idea of Progress** (1970) (a critical discussion of the Warren Court).
35. **Meehan,** *supra* note 19, at 111-89.
36. *Id.* at 113.
37. *Id.*
38. *Id.* at 190-286.
39. *See, eg.,* **Perry,** *supra* note 17, at 111.
40. *See* Kim, "Explanations in Science," in 3 **The Encyclopedia of Philosophy** 159-60 (reprint ed. 1972); **Meehan,** *supra* note 19, at 19-22.
41. **Meehan,** *supra* note 19, at 20.
42. *Id.* at 19-20.
43. For an excellent study of systems which distinguish between axioms and postulates, <u>see</u> **Maki and Thompson, Mathematical Models and Applications** 9-12 (1973). The term *first principles* is used to signify a starting premise, and I discuss how the framers used this term in my discussion of Reid on pp. 61-66 *infra*. Jefferson, of course, used the term *self-evident truths* in the Declaration of Independence. *See* **Wills, Inventing America: Jefferson's Declaration of Independence** 181-92 (1979).
44. Meehan writes, "For the present, political science deals almost entirely with probabilistic generalizations and tendency statements. Universal generalizations are rare and perhaps nonexistent." **Meehan,** *supra* note 19, at 20. He adds, "The social sciences may have very few 'genuine' theories. . . ." *Id.* at 23.
45. *But, see* Professor Dworkin's instructive attempts. Dworkin, "No Right Answer?" in **Law, Morality, and Society Essays in Honor of H.L.A. Hart** 58-84 (Hacker and Raz, eds. 1977).
46. *See generally* **Copi, Introduction to Logic** 510-30 (5th rev. ed. 1978) (a discussion of probability from the logician's point of view).
47. The different kinds of models are too numerous to mention in this project. The most basic kind of classification distinguishes between mathematical models, logical models, and real models. *See* **Maki and Thompson,** *supra* note 43, at 16.
48. **Meehan,** *supra* note 19, at 294.
49. *Id.* at 292.
50. *See* **Dworkin,** *supra* note 7, at 17.
51. **Meehan,** *supra* note 19, at 31-32.
52. *Id.* at 32.
53. More generally, Meehan writes, "Unfortunately, there are no formal rules for evaluating the usefulness of models in political inquiry. The judgment and experience of the individual must come into play, obviously, but the rules of evaluation have thus far defied formalization." I do not believe that the structuralist approach of Claude Levi-Strauss, and his disciples does the job. *See* **Kurzweil. The Age of Structuralism: Levi-Strauss to Foucalt** (1980).
54. *See* **Dworkin,** *supra* note 7, at 14-80.
55. *See* **Francis,** *supra* note 6, at 21-38.
56. **Meehan,** *supra* note 19, at 33.

57. Ely, *supra* note 12.
58. Parker, *The Past of Constitutional Theory — And its Future,* 42 **Ohio St. L. J.** 223, 229 (1981).
59. *Id.*
60. Ely, *supra* note 12, at 151.
61. Meehan, *supra* note 19, at 295.
62. Ely, *supra* note 12, at 183.
63. Gordon, *Introduction: J. Willard Hurst and the Common Law Tradition in American Legal Historiography,* 10 **Law & Soc'y Rev.** 9, 29-33 (1975).
64. Meehan, *supra* note 19, at 28-29.
65. Kuhn, *supra* note 25, at 9 (2d ed. enlarged 1970).
66. Meehan, *supra* note 19, at 71.
67. Ely, *supra* note 12, at 72.
68. Meehan, *supra* note 19, at 161.
69. *Id.* at 164.
70. *Id.*
71. Parker, *supra* note 58, at 240.
72. Meehan, *supra* note 19, at 165.
73. Parker, *supra* note 58, at 240.
74. Meehan, *supra* note 19, at 108.
75. U.S. Const. amend. IX; *see* Berger, *The Ninth Amendment,* 66 **Corn. L. Rev.** 1 (1980)
76. 77. example, the privileges and immunities clause of the Fourteenth Amendment U.S. **Const. Amend. XIV, § 1.** *See* **Ely, Democracy and Distrust: ATheory of Judicial Review** (1980).
77. U.S. Const. amend. XIV, § 1.
78. Interpretation is an intellectual activity which accompanies the process of law application in its progression from a higher to a lower level norm. During this process, the more general norm becomes more concrete in its meaning. It acquires, in other words, a more particular meaning. *See* **Kelsen, Pure Theory of Law** 348 (1967).
79. Hart, *supra* note 15, at 123. Professor Hart writes:

   . . . there still remains a distinction between a constitution which, after setting up a system of courts, provides that the law shall be whatever the supreme court thinks fit, and the actual Constitution of the United States. . . . '[T]he Constitution . . . is whatever the judges say it is,' if interpreted as denying this distinction is false. At any given moment, judges, even those on a supreme court, are parts of a system the rules of which are determinate enough at the center to supply standards of correct judicial decision.

80. Professor Brest makes the helpful distinction between literalism or strict textualism and strict intentionalism:

   Strict intentionalism requires the interpreter to determine how the adopters would have applied a provision to a given situation, and to apply it accordingly. The enterprise rests on the questionable assumption that the adopters of constitutional provisions intended them to be applied in this manner. Brest, *The Misconceived Quest for the Original Understanding,* 60 **B.U.L.** Rev. 240, 222 (1980).

81. "A thorough-going literalist understands a text to encompass all those and only those instances that come within its words read without regard to its social or perhaps even its linguistic context." *Id.*
82. Hamilton, Introduction, in **The Constitution Reconsidered,** xiii (Read, ed. 1938).
83. **Kammen, The People of Paradox** 1 (1973).
84. U.S. Const. art. III,§ 2.
85. For a discussion of how the doctrine of judicial sovereignty developed during the tenure of Chief Justice Marshall, <u>see</u> **McCloskey, The American Supreme Court** 53-80 (1960). The Court has added further gloss by stating that "the federal judiciary is supreme in the

exposition of the law of the Constitution, and that principle has . . . been respected by this Court and the country as a permanent and indispensable feature of our constitutional system." Cooper v. Aaron, 358 U.S. 1, 18 (1958).

86. *See, e.g., Constitutional Adjudication and Democratic Theory,* 56 N.Y.U. L. Rev. 259-582 (1981).

87. *See* Ely, *supra* note 76.

88. *See, e.g., Judicial Review versus Democracy,* 42 **Ohio St. L. J.** 1 (1981).

89. *See, e.g.,* **Berger, Government by Judiciary** (1977); Bork, *Neutral Principles and Some First Amendment Problems,* 47 **Ind. L. J.** 1 (1971), Bork, *The Impossibility of Finding Welfare Rights in the Constitution,* 1979 **Wash. U. L. Q.** 695; Rehnquist, *The Notion of a Living Constitution,* 54 **Tex. L. Rev.** 693 (1976).

90. *See, e.g.,* Brest, *supra* note 80, at 204.

91. **Perry, The Constitution, the Courts, and Human Rights** (1982).

92. **Hand, The Bill of Rights** (1958).

93. *See* **Ely,** *supra* note 76.

94. *See generally* **Miller, The Supreme Court: Myth and Reality** (1978).

95. *See* **Dworkin, Taking Rights Seriously** 166, 283-90, 362 (1977).

96. Easterbrook, *Ways of Criticizing the Court,* 95 **Harv. L. Rev.** 802, 832 (1982).

97. **Bickel, The Least Dangerous Branch** 32 (1962).

98. **Buchanan, Understanding Political Variables** 316 (1969).

99. *See* **Perry** *supra* note 91, at 61-69, 103-7.

100. Perry writes, "[Noninterpretivism] can explain and justify a policymaking institution whose morality is 'open,' not 'closed' — an institution that resolves moral problems not simply by looking backward to the sediment of old moralities, but ahead to emergent principles in terms of which fragments of a new moral order can be forged." *Id.* at 111 (footnote omitted). He adds that "constitutional theory must not be propounded in a historical vacuum; it must be sensitive to context — the context of our own time." *Id.* at 119. In an even stronger statement, Perry writes, "I prefer to let the framers sleep. Just as the framers, in their day, judged by their lights, so must we, in our day, judge by ours." *Id.* at 75.

101. *See* **Dworkin,** *supra* note 95, at 180.

102. *See* **Ely** *supra* note 76, at 135.

103. *See infra* note 146 and accompanying text.

104. *See* **Ely** *supra* note 76, at 88.

105. **Kuhn, The Structure of Scientific Revolutions** 182 (2d. rev. ed. 1970).

106. *Id.*

107. *Id.* at 146.

108. *See* Dworkin, "No Right Answer?" in **Law, Morality, and Society: Essays in Honor of H.L.A. Hart** 58 (Hacker and Raz, eds. 1977).

109. **Allen, Law in the Making** 1-8 (7th rev. ed. 1964).

110. *Id.*

111. Dworkin, *The Forum of Principle,* 56 **N.Y.U. L. Rev.** 469 (1981).

112. **Ely,** *supra* note 76, at 1.n.*

113. **U.S. Const. amend. X.**

114. **U.S. Const. art. I, § 8, cl. 18.**

115. National League of Cities v. Usery, 426 U.S. 833 (1976).

116. *See, e.g.,* Roe v. Wade, 410 U.S. 113 (1973).

117. Snead v. Stringer, 454 U.S. 988, 989 (1981) (Rehnquist, J., dissenting from denial of cert.).

118. **Nozick, Philosophical Explanations** 3 (1981).

119. Note, *'Round and 'Round the Bramble Bush: From Legal Realism to Critical Legal Scholarship,* 95 **Harv. L. Rev.** 1669, 1673 (1982).

120. **MacCormick, Legal Reasoning and Legal Theory** 238 (1978).

121. If I understand Dworkin correctly we differ on this point to the extent that he conveys the impression that the theory, which explains the Constitution, is the basic norm, and not the

other way around. *See* Dworkin, *supra* note 111. However, my position is not inconsistent with the following statement by Dworkin: "[S]cholars who say they simply start from the premise that the Constitution is law underestimate the complexity of their own theories." *Id.* at 475 (footnote omitted). Obviously, a description of the Constitution as the basic norm is, itself, a theory of sorts.

122. **Neely, How Courts Govern America** 18 (1981).
123. Dworkin writes, "There is no such thing as the intention of the framers waiting to be discovered, even in principle. There is only some such thing waiting to be invented." Dworkin, *supra* note 111, at 477. This is an overstated position, although I cannot deny that a faulty reconstruction of the framers' intent is perceived correctly as an invention.
124. Sandalow, *Constitutional Interpretation,* 79 **Mich. L. Rev.** 1033, 1038 (1981).
125. **MacCormick,** *supra* note 120, at 16.
126. *Id.* at 17.
127. Sandalow, *supra* note 124.
128. **Neely,** *supra* note 122, at 18.
129. **MacCormick,** *supra* note 120, at 16.
130. Judge Frank wrote:

> But talks with candid judges have begun to disclose that, whatever is said in opinions, the judge often arrives at his decision before he tries to explain it. With little or no preliminary attention to legal rules or a definite statement of facts, he often makes up his mind that Jones should win the lawsuit not Smith. . . . Frank, *What Courts Do in Fact,* 26 **Ill. L. Rev** 645, 653 (1932).
>
> The law, however, was not made when the judge made up his mind because of his breakfast or other reasons that are not mentioned in the opinion that justifies his decision. Certain reasons are not mentionable because technically they are not legally relevant. The are not law.

131. **MacCormick,** *supra* note 120, at 15.
132. Bork, *Neutral Principles and Some First Amendment Problems,* 47 **Ind. L. J.** 1, 4 (1971).
133. For critiques of the practice of bringing forward the framers' intentions, <u>see</u> Munzer and Nickel, *Does the Constitution Mean What it Always Meant?* 77 **Colum. L. Rev.** 1029 (1977); Bridwell, Book Review, **Duke L. J.** 907 (1978); Nathanson, Book Review, 56 **Tex. L. Rev.** 579 (1978).
134. Frankfurter, *Some Reflections on the Reading of Statutes,* in Bobbs-Merrill Reprint PS-86, at 216 (1947) [reprint of Justice Frankfurter's Address before the Association of the Bar of the City of New York (Mar. 18, 1979)].
135. 198 U.S. 45 (1905).
136. *See* Hamilton, *The Path of Due Process of Law,* 48 **Ethics** 269, 293–94 (1938).
137. Black, *The Bill of Rights,* 35 **N.Y.U. L. Rev.** 865, 881 (1960). (Justice Black argues that the framers did not intend to balance away First Amendment rights.)
138. **White, Social Thought in America: The Revolt Against Formalism,** xvi–xvii (1976).
139. **Schauer,** *An Essay on Constitutional Language,* 29 **UCLA L. Rev.** 797, 809 (1982) (footnote omitted).
140. 377 U.S. 533 (1964).
141. Santa Clara County v. Southern Pac. R.R., 118 U.S. 394, 396 (1886).
142. Graham, *The "Conspiracy Theory" of the Fourteenth Amendment,* 47 **Yale L. J.** 371 (1938).
143. In 1930 Radin wrote, "[T]hat the intention of the legislature is undiscoverable in any real sense is almost an immediate inference from a statement of the proposition." Radin, *Statutory Interpretation,* 43 **Harv. L. Rev.** 863, 870 (1930).
144. **Perry,** *supra* note 91, at 70.
145. *Id.*
146. **The Federalist No. 37,** at 224–32 (Madison) (Mod. Libr. ed. 1937).
147. *Id.* at 229.
148. *Id.*
149. *Id.*

150. *See* **The Federalist No. 51,** at 335–41 (Madison) (Mod. Libr. ed. 1937). Some believe Hamilton wrote this essay.
151. **The Federalist No. 37,** at 229 (Madison) (Mod. Libr. ed. 1937).
152. *Id.*
153. *Id.* at 230.
154. *Id.*
155. *Id.*
156. *Id.*
157. *Id.* at 229.
158. *Id.*
159. *Id.* at 231.
160. *Id.*
161. **The Federalist No. 82,** at 534 (Hamilton) (Mod. Libr. ed. 1937). Hamilton also wrote that "a minute detail of particular rights is certainly far less applicable to a Constitution like that under consideration, which is merely intended to regulate the general political interests of the nation, than to a constitution which has the regulation of every species of personal and private concerns."
    The Federalist No. 84, at 559 (Hamilton)(Mod. Libr. ed. 1937). Hamilton was writing to allay the fears that the government was empowered to nullify the reserved rights of the people. *Id.*
162. See *infra* notes 370–85 and accompanying text in Chapter 4 *infra.*
163. Perry, *supra* note 91, at 140.
164. Proceedings of a Special Session of the United States Court of Appeals for the Second Circuit to Commemorate Fifty Years of Federal Judicial Service by the Honorable Learned Hand 37 (Apr. 10, 1959). (W.N. Seymour, Esquire quoting Hand).
165. *Id.*
166. **Kuhn, The Structure of Scientific Revolutions** 76 (2d rev. ed. 1970).
167. *Id.* at 196.
168. *Id.* at 183.
169. *Id.* at 179.
170. Perry, *supra* note 91, at 143–44.* Perry acknowledges and maintains that Dworkin is mistaken in his belief that judges "make substantive decisions of political morality . . . in place of judgments made by the [framers] . . . rather [than] in service of those judgments." *Id.* at 113–14.*
171. *Id.* at 147.
172. *Id.* at 50–51. His primary justification is the ability of the courts to "function in part by interacting, in a dialectic way, with *other* agencies of moral reevaluation and growth." *Id.* at 163. This is called, at times, its prophetic function. *Id.* at 162.
173. Neely, *supra* note 122, at 11.
174. 377 U.S. 533 (1964).
175. *Id.* at 558.
176. For a discussion of reapportionment cases, see Ely, *supra* note 76, at 119–24.
177. Perry, *supra* note 91, at 146–62.
178. *See* Monaghan, *Our Perfect Constitution,* 56 **N.Y.U. L. Rev.** 353 (1981).
179. *Id.* at 375.
180. *Id.* (footnotes omitted).
181. *Id.* at 376–77.
182. *Id.* at 378.
183. *Id.* at 379 [citing **Dworkin, Taking Rights Seriously** 132–37 (1978)]. Monaghan, however, does not join this fashion parade; the courts do.
184. *Id.* at 396.
185. 377 U.S. 533 (1964).
186. **Friedrich, Tradition and Authority** 49 (1972).
187. *Id.* at 57.
188. Dworkin, *supra* note 111, at 469.
189. **Holmes, The Common Law** 36 (1881).

190. Gadamer, **Truth and Method** 292 (1975).
191. Dworkin, *supra* note 111, at 488–91.
192. *See* Perry, *supra* note 91, at 70.
193. Neely, *supra* note 122, at 19.
194. *Id.*
195. Horwitz, **The Transformation of American Law:** 1780–1860, at 5 (1977).
196. *Id.* at 18. While it appears that a great danger was perceived to be the *judicial* construction of statutes (even as the judges claimed that they were not making law) my effort is to show that the interpreter of the Constitution, in whatever branch, has some leeway to fill in general concepts with unforeseen particularized applications, and that this possibility was apprehended by the framers.
197. For a discussion of Reid's influence on Madison, see **Wills, Explaining America** 15–17 (1981).
198. *See generally* **Reid, Essays on the Intellectual Powers of Man** (1971).
199. **Friedrich, The Philosophy of Law in Historical Perspective** 217 (2d rev. ed. 1963).
200. Ely, after noting that the Court has not backed away from its narrow interpretation of the Fourteenth Amendment's "privileges and immunities" clause in the Slaughter-House cases, 83 U.S. (16 Wall.) 36 (1873), writes: "The reason has to be that the invitation extended by the language of the clause is frightening. . . ." **Ely,** *supra* note 76, at 23 (footnote omitted).
201. 6. F. Cas. 546 (C.C.E.D. Pa. 1823) (No. 3230).
202. Berger, *supra* note 89, at 138. *See id.* at 22, 29, 38–45.
203. Civil Rights Act of 1866, ch. 31, 14 Stat. 27. Neither the Civil Rights Act of 1866 nor the Fourteenth Amendment conferred or guaranteed political rights. *See* **Berger,** *supra* note 89, at 30.
204. U.S. Const. amend. XIV, § 5. *See Berger, supra* note 89, at 221-29.
205. Boutwell, a member of the Joint Committee that drafted the Fourteenth Amendment, recalled that the phrase *privileges or immunities* came from Representative Bingham. 6 **Fairman, History of the Supreme Court of the United States** pt. 1, at 1270 (1971). Representative Kelley, a radical, supported the Fourteenth Amendment, and stated that it would " 'more explicitly empower Congress to enforce and maintain' the rights of the people." *Id.* at 1277.
206. Woodbridge, a member of the Judiciary Committee, stated that the object of the amendment was to "enable Congress to give to all citizens the inalienable rights of life and liberty. . . ." *Id.* at 1270. Most radicals construed the term *privileges or immunities* in a far-reaching way. *Id.* at 1287-96. Reverdy Johnson, a leading constitutional lawyer, who took a moderate pro-Southern line most of the time, complained that he did not "understand what will be the effect of the [the priveleges and immunities clause]." *Id.* at 1297. Fairman notes, "[C]oming from him, that amounted to a certificate that, for purposes of litigation, the privileges and immunities clause did not have a definite meaning." *Id.*
207. The moderates in Congress who were trying to achieve a consensus were walking a tightrope. Brock writes: "Caught between the dogmatism of [President] Johnson and the extremism of Stevens they tried to reach a solution which would satisfy everyone . . . and the result was an impossible situation. **Brock, An American Crisis: Congress and Reconstruction** 1865–1867, at 151 (1966).
208. The Civil Rights Cases, 109 U.S. 3, 25 (1883) ("special favorite of the laws"). Tannenbaum wrote, "One must always remember that the Negro started after the Civil War with nothing at all; he had neither education, nor property, nor position, nor the psychological readiness for achievement and personal growth." **Tannenbaum, Slave and Citizen** 113 (1946). The free blacks in the United States before emancipation were relatively few in number and too weak in influence to provide adequate leadership for the vast numbers of new freedmen. *Id.* at 104. Regarded as a chattel for many years, the emancipated blacks were thrust into a new and undefined status, a halfway level between slave and equal — a freedman. *Philadelphia Inquirer,* Oct. 12, 1865 (report of a speech by Beecher).
209. **Fairman,** *supra* note 205, pt. 1 at 110–11.

210. *Id*. at 115, 330–33. Steps were taken to provide a system of public schools in the South, open to all, without distinction of race or color. *Id*. at 330.
211. **Woodward, The Strange Career of Jim Crow,** 67–102 (2d rev. ed. 1966).
212. *See generally* **Fairman,** *supra* note 205, at pt. 1.
213. *Id*. at 315.
214. Fairman noted that Justice Nelson, in the case of *In re* Egan, wrote that the moment a rebel state's government became reorganized, "the ancient laws resumed their accustomed sway" since the state is "entitled to the full enjoyment, of her constitutional rights and privileges." *Id*. at 148. This "Portentous dictum" was announced in1866. *Id*.
215. *Ex parte* Garland, 71 U.S. (4 Wall.) 333 (1867); Cummings v. Missouri, 71 U.S. (4 Wall.) 277 (1867); *Ex parte* Milligan, 71 U.S. (4 Wall.) 2 (1866).
216. **Fairman,** *supra* note 205, pt. 1 at 1300.
217. *See* Hamilton, *supra* note 82, at 167–90.
218. *See, e.g.,* United States v. Cruikshank, 92 U.S. 542 (1875). (The Court drastically curtailed the privileges and immunities recognized as being under Congress's protection.)
219. *See, e.g.,* The Civil Rights Cases, 109 U.S. 3 (1993), United States v. Reese, 92 U.S. 214 (1875).
220. *Ex parte* Yarbrough, 110 U.S. 651, 658 (1884). Other decisions which disclose judicial creativity in the late nineteenth century before the era of substantive due process include the following: Motes v. United States, 178 U.S. 458 (1900); Logan v. United States, 144 U.S. 263 (1892); *In re* Neagle, 135 U.S. 1 (1890); United States v. Waddell, 112 U.S. 76 (1884).
221. Slaughter-House cases, 83 U.S. (16 Wall.) 36, 123 (1873) (Bradley, J., dissenting). Justice Bradley also wrote:

> It is possible that those who framed the article were not themselves aware of the far-reaching character of its terms. They may have had in mind but one particular phase of social and political wrong which they desired to redress. Yet, if the amendment as framed and expressed, does in fact bear broader meaning and does extend its protecting shield over those who were never thought of when it was conceived and put in form, and does reach social evils which were never before prohibited by constitutional enactment, it is to be presumed that the American people in giving it their imprimatur, understood what they were doing and meant to decree what has in fact been decreed. Livestock Dealers' and Butchers' Ass'n v. Crescent City Livestock Landing & Slaughter-House Co. 15 F. Cas. 649, 652 (C.C.D. La. 1870) (No. 8408).

222. 83 U.S. (16 Wall.) at 123.
223. **Fairman,** *supra* note 205, pt. 1 at 1363.
224. Dartmouth College v. Woodward, 17 U.S. (4 Wheat.) 518 (1819).
225. *Id*. at 644. *See also* **Fairman,** *supra* note 205, pt. 1 at 1301.
226. *See* The Civil Rights Cases, 109 U.S. 3, 22 (1883).
227. 83 U.S. (16 Wall.) 36 (1873).
228. *Id*. at 69–70.
229. *See generally* **Kluger, Simple Justice** (1976) (an elaborate description of the development of the relevant legal precedent in school segregation cases).
230. 347 U.S. 483 (1954).
231. **Perry,** *supra* note 91, at 72.
232. **Woodward,** *supra* note 211, at 97–102, 108.
233. *Id*. at 99–100.
234. 217 N.Y. 382, 111 N.E. 1050 (1916).
235. **Levi, An Introduction to Legal Reasoning** 1–19 (1948).
236. *See generally* **Cross, Precedent in English Law** (1961) (a discussion of Anglo-American doctrine of precedent).
237. **Gadamer,** *supra* note 190, at 292.
238. *Id*.
239. **The Federalist No. 78,** at 510 (Hamilton) (Mod. Libr. ed. 1937). *Id*. at 510–11.
240. *Id*. at 510–11.

241. **Cross,** *supra* note 236, at 251 (1961).
242. **Perry,** *supra* note 91, at 102.
243. *Id*. at ix.
244. **The Federalist No. 78,** at 506 (Hamilton) (Mod. Libr. ed. 1937).
245. *Id*. at 507.
246. Kelsen writes:

> Legal norms are not valid because they themselves . . . have a content the binding force of which is self-evident. They are not valid because of their inherent appeal. Legal norms may have any kind of content. There is no kind of human behavior [from the standpoint of legal science] that, because of its nature, could not be made into a legal duty corresponding to a legal right. The validity of a legal norm cannot be questioned on the ground that its contents are incompatible with some moral or political value. **Kelsen, General Theory of Law and State** 113 (Wedberg, trans. 1961).

247. Hill makes a distinction between being legally obliged and a legal obligation. He admits "that it is possible to give an adequate, clear, hardheaded account of legal validity, free of any appeal to the principles of justice and morality. . . ." Hill, *Legal Validity and Legal Obligations,* 80 **Yale L. J.** 47, 75 (1970). Hill, however, is of the view "that an adequate analysis of legal *obligation* must appeal to the principles of justice and morality." *Id*.
248. **Perry,** *supra* note 91, at 141.
249. *Id*. at 139.
250. *Id*. at 138.
251. *Id*. at 139.
252. *Id*. at 138.
253. *Id*.
254. Kelsen tries to capture the dynamic quality of authorizing norms in the following passage:

> The judge authorized by a statute (that is, a general norm) to decide concrete cases, applies the statute to a concrete case by a decision which constitutes an *individual* norm. Again, authorized by a judicial decision to execute a certain punishment, the enforcement officer "applies" the individual norm of a judicial decision. **Kelsen,** *supra* note 78, at 16. *See id*. at 39–45.

255. The Federal Administrative Procedure Act provides in part: General Notice of proposed rule making shall be published in the Federal Register, unless persons subject thereto are named and either personally served or otherwise have actual notice thereof in accordance with law. The notice shall include —

> (1) a statement of the time, place, and nature of the public rule-making proceedings;
>
> (2) *reference to the legal authority under which the rule is proposed;* and
>
> (3) either the terms or substance of the proposed rule or a description of the subjects and issues involved. 5 U.S.C. § 533(b) (1976) (emphasis added). The act further provides: "After notice . . . the agency shall give interested persons an opportunity to participate in the rule making through submission or written data, views, or arguments with or without opportunity for oral presentation." *Id*. § 533(c).

256. **Perry,** *supra* note 91, at 112.
257. *Id*. at 111 (emphasis added).
258. *Id*. at 118.
259. *Id*. at 143. n.*
260. *Id*. (emphasis added).
261. **Rawls, A Theory of Justice** 235 (1971). Rawls maintains that the rule of law is compatible with injustice. *Id*. at 236. The wide realm of judicial discretion provided by Perry's theory is likewise compatible with injustice. Indeed, some theories of justice articulated by judges are, according to other theories, injustice.
262. *Id*. at 236.
263. *Id*. at 238.
264. **Perry,** *supra* note 91, at 93.

265. *Id.* at 105.
266. *See id.* at 140.
267. Wolff, **The Rule of Law** 8 (1971).
268. Perry, *supra* note 91, at 134.
269. *Id.*
270. *Id.* at 135.
271. **The Federalist No. 51,** at 337 (Madison) (Mod. Libr. ed. 1937) (hereinafter cited as Earle, ed. 1937).
272. The point in the text concerning Madison is not free from doubt. Perhaps Madison's theory, derived from Hume and spelled out at length in *The Federalist,* was this: at a local level, one "faction" might well have sufficient clout to be able to tyrannize others. In the national government, however, no faction or interest group would constitute a majority capable of exercising control. *See* **Ely,** *supra* note 76, at 80.
273. Perry, *supra* note 91, at 118.
274. *Id.* at 111 [citing **Cardozo, The Nature of the Judicial Process** 113 (1921)].
275. Snyder v. Massachusetts, 291 U.S. 97, 105 (1934).

Footnotes for Part II, Chapter 3

1. **Berlin, Four Essays on Liberty** 17 (1970).
2. *Id.* at 63.
3. *Id.* at 33–34.
4. *Id.* at 101.
5. **Perry, The Constitution, The Courts, and Human Rights** 111 (1982).
6. *Id.* at 113.
7. *Id.* at 118.
8. **Berlin,** *supra* note 1, at 8.
9. **Kennedy, Notes on History of American Legal Thought** 874 (Jan. 1979) (emphasis added) (instructional materials used at Harvard Law School) [hereinafter cited as Kennedy materials].
10. *Id.*
11. **Copleston, A History of Philosophy, Modern Philosophy, The French Enlightenment to Kant,** vol. 6, pt. I, 26 (1964); *See also,* **Stein, Legal Evolution: The Story of an Idea** 15–19 (1980).
12. **Gay, The Enlightenment: An Interpretation — The Science of Freedom** 327 (1969) [quoting **Neumann, Introduction to Montesquieu, The Spirit of Laws,** xxxii (1949).
13. *Id.* at 189.
14. **The Federalist No. 37,** at 228–29 (Madison) (Earle, ed. 1937).
15. **The Federalist** app. IV, at 585–86 (Earle, ed. 1937) (reprinting Washington's Letter of Transmittal of the Constitution to Congress) (Sept. 17, 1787).
16. *Id.* at 586.
17. *See* notes 97–101 *infra,* and accompanying text.
18. *See* notes 83–85 *infra,* and accompanying text.
19. Proceedings of a Special Session of the United States Court of Appeals for the Second Circuit in Commemoration of Fifty Years of Federal Judicial Service by the Honorable Learned Hand 33 (Apr. 10, 1959) (reprinting Seymour, *Tribute to the "Old Chief" of the Bench: Learned Hand Has Set a Record of Fifty Years as a Federal Judge, but the Breadth of His Career Is Even More Noteworthy than its Length).*
20. **Hart, The Concept of Law** 97–107 (1961).
21. Robinson, "In the Basement of History" (Book Review), *N.Y. Times,* May 16, 1982, sec. 7 (Book Review), at 9 (reviewing and quoting **Braudel, The Structures of Everyday Life: The Limits of the Possible — Civilization and Capitalism, 15th–18th Century** vol. I).
22. *See* notes 271–78 *infra,* and accompanying text.
23. *See* notes 339–41 *infra,* and accompanying text.

24. *See* note 350 *infra,* and accompanying text.
25. *See* note 361 *infra,* and accompanying text.
26. *Selections from the Scottish Philosophy of Common Sense* 172 (Johnston, ed. 1915) [quoting 2 **Reid,** "Essays on the Active Powers of Man," in **Works 580**-81 (Hamilton, 6th rev. ed. 1863)].
27. **Reid, Essays on the Intellectual Powers of Man** 435 (Walker, 2d rev. ed. 1851).
28. *Id*. at 435-36.
29. *See* note 73 *infra,* and accompanying text.
30. *See* note 74 *infra,* and accompanying text.
31. *See* note 73 *infra,* and accompanying text.
32. *See* notes 121-22 *infra,* and accompanying text.
33. *See* note 206 *infra,* and accompanying text.
34. *See* note 188 *infra,* and accompanying text.
35. **Stein,** *supra* note 11, at 9-12.
36. Madison wrote:

    Would it be wonderful if . . . the convention should have been forced into some deviations from that artificial structure and regular symmetry which an abstract view of the subject might lead an ingenious theorist to bestow on a Constitution planned in his closet or in his imagination? The real wonder is that so many difficulties should have been surmounted. . . . **The Federalist No. 37,** at 231 (Madison) (Earle, ed. 1937).

37. See Gompers v. United States, 233 U.S. 604, 610 (1914) (Holmes, J.).
38. **Scott, Francis Hutcheson: His Life, Teaching and Position in the History of Philosophy** 1 (1900 & reprint 1966).
39. **Pole, The Pursuit of Equality in American History** 8(1978) [citing **Davis, The Problem of Slavery in Western Culture** 348-64 (1966)].
40. **Bailyn, The Ideological Origins of the American Revolution** 40 (1967).
41. **Smith, The Constitution: A Documentary and Narrative History** (1978).
42. **Hayek, The Constitution of Liberty** (1960).
43. **Ely, Democracy and Distrust: A Theory of Judicial Review** (1980).
44. **The Constitution Reconsidered** (Read, ed. 1938).
45. MacIver, "European Doctrines and the Constitution," in **The Constitution Reconsidered** 52 (Read, ed. 1938) (emphasis added).
46. *Id*. at 55.
47. **Wood, The Creation of the American Republic** 403-29 (1969).
48. MacIver, *supra* note 45, at 53.
49. Schneider, "Philosophical Differences Between the Constitution and the Bill of Rights," in **The Constitution Reconsidered** 155 (Read, ed. 1938).
50. *Id*.
51. *Id*.
52. *See* notes 171-75 *infra,* and accompanying text.
53. MacIver, *supra* note 45, at 57 (quoting 4 **Madison, Writings** 186).
54. *Id*.
55. **Scott,** *supra* note 38, at 228 (emphasis added) [quoting 1 **Hutcheson, A System of Moral Philosophy** 281 (1755)].
56. *Id*. [quoting 1 **Hutcheson, A System of Moral Philosophy** 253 (1755)].
57. **U.S. Const.** Preamble.
58. **Unger, Knowledge & Politics** 106 (1975).
59. *Id*. at 6.
60. *See* notes 116-20 *infra,* and accompanying text.
61. **Scott,** *supra* note 38, at 274.
62. *See* notes 83-89 *infra,* and accompanying text.
63. *See* notes 90-109 *infra,* and accompanying text.
64. *See* notes 110-22 *infra,* and accompanying text.
65. *See* notes 123-215 *infra,* and accompanying text.
66. *See* notes 216-40 *infra,* and accompanying text.

67. Wills reports that eighteenth-century Americans concentrated on Scottish Enlightenment figures and writes, "There should be nothing surprising in this concentration on Scottish thinkers. By the middle of the eighteenth century, Scotland's five universities had far outdistanced somnolent Oxford and Cambridge in the study of science, philosophy,and law." **Wills, Inventing America: Jefferson's Declaration of Independence** 175-76 (1979).
68. Sprague, "Francis Hutcheson," in 4 **The Encyclopedia of Philosophy** 99 (1967).
69. *Id.* Sprague writes:

> The Presbytery of Glasgow tried him for teaching, in contravention to the Westminster Confession, the following "false and dangerous" doctrines: (a) that the standard of moral goodness is the promotion of the happiness of others; and (b) that it is possible to have a knowledge of good and evil without, and prior to, a knowledge of God.

70. Hume was in basic agreement. *See* note 98 *infra,* and accompanying text.
71. **Blackstone, Francis Hutcheson and Contemporary Ethical Theory** 6 (University of Georgia monograph No. 12, 1965).
72. **Halevy, The Growth of Philosophic Radicalism** 13 (1972).
73. **Scott,** *supra* note 38, at 273.
74. *Id.* at 230-243.
75. **Wills,** *supra* note 67. *See also* **Wills, Explaining America** 16-18 (1981).
76. **White, The Philosophy of the American Revolution** (1981).
77. *See* notes 269-405 *infra,* and accompanying text for a discussion of Reid.
78. Frankena, *Hutcheson's Moral Sense Theory,* 16 **J.** Hist. **Ideas** *356, 375 (1955).*
79. **Blackstone,** *supra* note 71, at 1.
80. **Wills,** *supra* note 67, at 279 (quoting Jefferson's "Head and Heart" letter to Cosway).
81. Peach, Introduction, **Hutcheson, Illustrations on the Moral Sense** 9 (1971) [citing **Edwards, The Nature of True Virtue** (1765 & reprint 1960)].
82. Peach, *supra* note 81, at 9. Edwards "until recently . . . has been thought of as a fiery Puritan preacher who merely made an apology for Calvinism, but he is now coming to be recognized as a theologian and philosopher of importance." *Id.*
83. **Wills,** *supra* note 67, at 176-77.
84. Peach, *supra* note 81, at 15.
85. *Id.* at 3.
86. **Scott,** *supra* note 38, at 287.
87. *Id.*
88. *Id.*
89. *Id.* at 285.
90. *See* Peach, *supra* note 81, at 49.
91. Sprague, *supra* note 68, at 99.
92. *Id.* at 100; **Wills,** *supra* note 67, at 195-96; **Scott,** *supra* note 38, at 187-90.
93. *See* Sprague, *supra* note 68, at 99-100.
94. **Blackstone,** *supra* note 71, at 25.
95. *Id.* at 15.
96. Peach, *supra* note 81, at 19.
97. *See id.* at 19, 82-90; **Blackstone,** *supra* note 71, at 17-19.
98. **Blackstone,** *supra* note 71, at 17.
99. *Id.* at 13 [quoting **Hutcheson, An Essay on the Nature and Conduct of the Passions and Affections with Illustrations upon the Moral Sense** 206 (3d rev. ed. Glasgow 1769) (1st rev. ed. Glasgow 1728)].
100. Peach, *supra* note 81, at 32.
101. **Blackstone,** *supra* note 71, at 17 [quoting **Bentham, An Introduction to the Principles of Morals and Legislation** 6 [sic] (London 1823) (1st rev. ed. London 1789)].
102. Peach, *supra* note 81, at 92.
103. *See id.* at 88.
104. *Id.* at 96-97.
105. Peach, *supra* note 81, at 93.
106. *Id.*

107. Hutcheson "held that moral philosophy is something more than ethical geometry. . . ." Scott, *supra* note 38, at 197.
108. *Id*. at 287-88.
109. *Id*. at 286.
110. Blackstone, *supra* note 71, at 72.
111. **Mackie, Ethics: Inventing Right and Wrong** 31 (1977 & reprint 1979).
112. *Id*.
113. Peach, *supra* note 81, at 26-27.
114. *See generally* Blackstone, *supra* note 71, at 72-75.
   Id. at 77.
116. Peach, *supra* note 81, at 20.
117. *Id*.
118. *Id*. at 97.
119. *Id*. at 20-21.
120. *Id*. at 22.
121. *Id*. at 40.
122. Blackstone refers to the moral sense as the "impartial judge" and the "impartial spectator." **Blackstone**, *supra* note 71, at 70. Elsewhere he refers to it as the "ideal observer." *Id*. at 71. The idea is that the moral sense will "act in the interest of mankind, not oneself." *Id*. at 70.
123. Kennedy, *Form and Substance in Private Law Adjudication,* 89 **Harv. L. Rev.** 1685, 1768 (1976).
124. **Pennock, Democratic Political Theory** 371 (1979).
125. *Id*. at 125.
126. **MacPherson, The Political Theory of Possessive Individualism: Hobbes to Locke** 3 (1962 & reprint 1972).
127. *Id*. at 231 [citing **Locke, Two Treatises of Government** (Second Treatise) sec. 27 Laslett, ed. 1960)].
128. *See* MacIver, *supra* note 45, at 51-61. MacIver also notes that Harrington who "combined a republican philosophy with an aristocratic respect for landed property . . . ranks next to Locke among the English writers who had vogue in America." *Id*. at 54.
129. "The individualist holds that all social behavior can be reduced to individual behavior in the sense that it can be explained in terms of the motivations or 'dispositions' of individuals." **Pennock**, *supra* note 124, at 66.
130. **Gay, The Enlightenment: An Interpretation, The Science of Freedom,** vol. II, 200 (1969).
131. **Wills,** *supra* note 67, at 251-52 [quoting **Hutcheson, An Essay on the Nature and Conduct of the Passions and Affections** 208 (1728) and citing 1 **Hutcheson, A System of Moral Philosophy** 10 (1755)].
132. Scott, *supra* note 38, at 235 [quoting 1 **Hutcheson, A System of Moral Philosophy** 287-90 (1755)].
133. *Id*. at 237 [quoting 1 **Hutcheson, A System of Moral Philosophy** 287-90 (1755)].
134. Ely, *supra* note 43 at 79 (footnotes omitted) (citing Rossum, *Representation and Republican Government: Contemporary Court Variations on the Founders' Theme,* 23 **Am. J. Juris.** 88, 91 (1978) and **The Federalist No. 39,** at 280-81 (Madison) (Wright, ed. 1961) among other works).
135. **Pennock,** *supra* note 124, at 28.
136. **White,** *supra* note 76, at 128.
137. *Id*. at 130.
138. *Id*. at 128.
139. *Id*. at 131. Hutcheson, however, did believe that those "manifestly superior in wisdom" should be in charge of "matters relating to the safety and advantage either of individuals or the whole body." **Wills,** *supra* note 67, at 236 [quoting **Hutcheson, A Short Introduction to Moral Philosophy** 281-82 (1747)].
140. Hutcheson writes "There can be no government so absolute as to have even an *external right* to do or command everything. For wherever any invasion is made upon *inalienable rights,* there must arise either a *perfect,* or *external right* to *resistance.*" White, *supra* note

76, at 242 [quoting **Hutcheson, Inquiry Concerning Moral Good and Evil,** sec. VII, pt. VII, at 294 (2d rev. ed. London 1726)]. An external right of government is its power and authority to enforce its will contrary to the individual's imperfect rights which are rights that the individual cannot protect by using force. See **White,** *supra* note 76, at 241; **Blackstone,** *supra* note 71, at 32.

141. Hutcheson defines perfect rights as those "of such a nature that the interest of society requires that they should ever be maintained and fulfilled to all who have them," even through the use of force if necessary. **Blackstone,** *supra* note 71, at 32 [quoting 1 **Hutcheson, A System of Moral Philosophy** 257 (1755)]. White writes, "The difference between a perfect moral right and a perfect legal right involves the distinction between what can be done in a state of nature and what can be done in civil society." **White,** *supra* note 76, at 241 n. 13.

142. **White,** *supra* note 76, at 241; **Wills,** *supra* note 67, at 216.

143. *See* **Blackstone,** *supra* note 71, at 32–33. Stein states that Hutcheson makes much of the difference between "perfect rights, enforceable in a law court, and imperfect rights, which are recognized by morality but not by law." **Stein,** *supra* note 11, at 10.

144. **Wills,** *supra* note 67, at 216.

145. *Id.* at 231; *see* **White,** *supra* note 76, at 196–210.

146. **White,** *supra* note 76, at 197–202.

147. *Id.* at 197.

148. *Id.*

149. Hutcheson wrote, "Whenever it appears to us that a faculty of doing, demanding, or possessing anything, universally allowed in certain circumstances, would in the whole tend to the general good, we say that any person in such circumstances has a right to do, possess, or demand that thing. And according as this tendency to the public good is greater or less, the right in question is greater or less." **Wills,** *supra* note 67, at 216 [quoting **Hutcheson, An Inquiry into the Origin of our Ideas of Beauty and Virtue** 256 (1725)].

150. **White,** *supra* note 76, at 209 [quoting **Hutcheson, Inquiry Concerning Moral Good and Evil** 283 (2d rev. ed. London 1726)].

151. **Wills,** *supra* note 67, at 217 [quoting 1 **Hutcheson, A System of Moral Philosophy** 294 (1755)].

152. Wills writes that Hutcheson believed that "[d]uty is simply one's right considered from another aspect." *Id.* Actually, Hutcheson preferred to speak of rights and justifications for actions rather than to speak of an *obligation,* which he believed was a confusing term. *See* **Blackstone,** *supra* note 71, at 80. Wills, however, is probably correct in writing that Hutcheson thought that the coin has two sides — rights and duties — and that one is the concomitant of the other; but the matter is not free of difficulty. *See* **White,** *supra* note 76, at 199–202.

 The idea that natural rights are derived from natural laws of duty is an ancient idea, and it is found in Hamilton's papers *Id.* at 147 n. 7. Witherspoon, a signer of the Declaration, also wrote that "whatever men are in *duty* obliged to do . . . they have a *claim* to." Jefferson often spoke of rights as duties and duties as rights; but White, contrary to Wills, thinks Jefferson followed Burlamaqui rather than Hutcheson. *Id.* at 162–63. Burlamaqui believed that the content of duties comes from the essence of man and "that God *gave* man that essence." *Id.* at 169. Hutcheson believed that God endowed man with a moral sense, but he did not stress the point because he preferred not to refer to the nature of virtue as merely an immutable aspect of God. **Blackstone,** *supra* note 71, at 51.

153. **Wills,** *supra* note 67, at 236.

154. *Id.* at 231 [quoting from both **Hutcheson, A Short Introduction to Moral Philosophy** 147 (1747) and 1 **Hutcheson, A System of Moral Philosophy** 309 (1755)].

155. **Blackstone,** *supra* note 71, at 33.

156. **Wills,** *supra* note 67, at 233 [quoting **Hutcheson, A Short Introduction to Moral Philosophy** 246–47 (1747)].

157. **Blackstone,** *supra* note 71, at 32.

158. *Id,* at 34 [quoting 1 **Hutcheson, A System of Moral Philosophy** 329 (1755)]

159. *Id.* [quoting 1 **Hutcheson, A System of Moral Philosophy** 327 (1755)].
160. **Wills,** *supra* note 67, at 231.
161. *See* **Becker, The Declaration of Independence** 4 (1942) for a list identifying committee members.
162. **White,** *supra* note 76, at 214 [quoting 1 **Parrington, Main Currents in American Thought: The Colonial Mind, 1620-1800** at 344 (1930)].
163. A natural right from the secondary natural law is a right that is acquired, and not one derived from the essence of man. This is Burlamaqui's explanation. Burlamaqui, a disciple of Hutcheson, **Wills,** *supra* note 67, at 250, who also influenced Jefferson, believed that one essential natural right is the right to pursue happiness. *See* **White,** *supra* note 76, at 219–20.
164. As White notes, Blackstone, in his **Commentaries on the Laws of England,** "finds it necessary to make the qualified statement that 'the origin of private property is *probably* [White's emphasis] founded in nature.' " **White,** *supra* note 76, at 223 [quoting 2 **Blackstone, Commentaries on the Laws of England** 138 (Philadelphia 1803 & reprint 1969)]. Blackstone went on to explain that there is a right in the community to God-given property, but this was "the right of common ownership." *Id.* at 224. The individual has "a transient right . . . to possess a given thing only so long as he use[s] it." *Id.* White's explanation notwithstanding, there is little doubt that most Americans (as he himself concedes) read Blackstone to say that property is one of the absolute rights that "every man is entitled to enjoy, whether out of society or in it." *Id.* at 223.

But what this meant to Americans in the eighteenth century is hard to say. In a fascinating essay, Whelan undertakes to document the reasons that Blackstone gives for the importance of property: "Blackstone's theory of property rests on a premise similar to Hume's: that the rules establishing and regulating it constitute an elaborate social artifice that is to be evaluated in the final analysis by its consequences for the happiness of society. There is no question, moreover, with Blackstone, that these rules constitute a legal artifice and that property rights are conferred by positive, or as he often calls it, municipal law." Whelan, "Property as Artifice: Hume and Blackstone," in **Property, Nomos XXII,** 115 Pennock and Chapman, eds. 1980).

Whelan goes on to show that "the common law is subordinate to statutory law," and that the statutes may regulate property "according as the municipal legislator sees proper, for promoting the welfare of the society, and more effectually carrying on the purposes of civil life." *Id.* at 116 [quoting 1 **Blackstone, Commentaries on the Laws of England** 55 (1879)].

Whelan explains that the term *absolute right* when used in connection with property is misleading. "The alleged 'absoluteness' or inviolability of property rights under the law of England is in reality a tautology, since property consists of rights defined and qualified by law." *Id.* at 120 [citing **Boorstin, The Mysterious Science of the Law** 176–78 (1973)].

In the United States as late as 1800, "there still existed a perhaps dominant body of opinion maintaining that individuals held their property at the sufferance of the state." **Horwitz, The Transformation of American Law, 1790–1860,** 64 (1977).

165. Whelan, *supra* note 164, at 101.
166. *Id.* at 108.
167. **Blackstone,** *supra* note 71, at 35 [quoting 2 **Hutcheson, A System of Moral Philosophy** 4 (1755)].
168. *Id.* [quoting 2 **Hutcheson, A System of Moral Philosophy** 4 (1755)].
169. *Id.* at 36.
170. *Id.* at 37.
171. *See* **White,** *supra* note 76, at 133–34.
172. **Wills,** *supra* note 67, at 248 (quoting Wilson).
173. *Id.* at 251.
174. *Id.* at 255.
175. Scott, referring to Hutcheson's conception of natural rights, writes, "To further reinforce society against the individual, Hutcheson introduces an extended scheme of rights du from the individual to the general body of his fellows, which are obviously intended t

outweigh the claims of any single member." **Scott,** *supra* note 38, at 229 (footnote omitted). Scott also notes that Hutcheson insisted "upon the duties of persons in easy circumstances, in a civilized community, to devote themselves gratuitously in aiding in movements of public utility." *Id*. Scott opines that Hutcheson subordinated both property and natural rights to the overall objective of "Universal Happiness *and* Perfection." *Id*. at 228.

176. White, *supra* note 76, at 198, 203-4.
177. These rights were, in part, linked with rights that were morally unalienable. *Id*. at 203-5.
178. Adams had written, "[T]he logos of Plato . . . plausible and specious . . . will be three thousand years longer more delusive than useful." Adams, "Debate with Condorcet," in **The Portable Age of Reason Reader** 622 (Brinton, ed. 1956). Jefferson, in a letter to Adams dated July 5, 1814, wrote of Plato's *Republic:* "While wading through the whimsies, puerilities, and unintelligible jargon of this work, I laid it down often to ask myself how it could have been, that the world should have so long consented to give reputation to such nonsense as this?" Jefferson, "Plato Be Damned," in **The Portable Age of Reason Reader** 615 (Brinton, ed. 1956).
179. Hamilton, "1937 to 1787, Dr.," in **The Constitution Reconsidered**, xiv (Read, ed. 1938).
180. Hayek, *supra* note 42, at 54.
181. **Davis, The Problem of Slavery in Western Culture** (1966).
182. Hayek, *supra* note 42, at 55-56.
183. *Id*.
184. *Id*. at 55.
185. *Id*. at 431 n. 2 (quoting Groethuysen, "Rationalism," in 13 **Encyclopedia of Social Sciences 113**).
186. *Id*. at 54.
187. *Id*. at 56 [quoting **Talmon, The Origins of Totalitarian Democracy** 2 (1952)] [Talmon's work is hereinafter cited as *Talmon's Origins.*]
188. *Id*. (quoting *Talmon's Origins, supra* note 187, at 71).
189. *Id*.
190. *Id*. (quoting *Talmon's Origins, supra* note 187, at 2).
191. *Id*. at 57.
192. Sprague, *supra* note 68, at 99.
193. Kennedy materials, *supra* note 9, at 145.
194. *Id*. at 195.
195. *See generally* **Pound, The Development of Constitutional Guarantees of Liberty** (1946).
196. Hayek, *supra* note 42, at 60.
197. Kennedy materials, *supra* note 9, at 196.
198. Hayek, *supra* note 42, at 63. Hayek adds, "The evolutionary view is based on the insight that the result of the experimentation of many generations may embody more experience than any one man possesses." *Id*. at 62.
199. *Id*. at 6.
200. **Davis,** *supra* note 181, at 433-36. Hutcheson did recommend slavery for idle vagrants who would not support themselves and their families. *Id*. at 376 [quoting 2 **Hutcheson, A System of Moral Philosophy** 202 (1755)]. Davis discusses Hutcheson's moral sense. *Id*. at 374-78.
201. Hayek, *supra* note 42, at 63.
202. **Davis,** *supra* note 181, at 442.
203. *Id*. at 433.
204. *See generally* **Gay,** *supra* note 130, at 328-31 (a discussion of Montesquieu's influence on the eighteenth-century Enlightenment). Montesquieu believed that slavery is "useless and uneconomical — then he adds a little parenthetically, 'I do not know if this chapter was dictated to me by my mind or my heart.'" *Id*. at 330-31 [quoting **Montesquieu, De L'esprit Des Lois,** bk. xv, ch. viii, in 1 **Oeuvres Completes,** pt. 1, 334 (Masson, ed. 1950-55)].

205. Kennedy materials, *supra* note 9, at 77. Kennedy's passionate liberalism "is committed not to ratifying the results of social struggle, but to setting ground rules for it, even if those rules should lead to constant revolutions in the actual distribution of power and welfare." *Id.*

206. *See* Scott, *supra* note 38, at 244–56.

207. Kennedy writes, "But, at least for rights, there were . . . substantive aspects to the pre-Classical concepts that allowed legal thinkers to fit them together with a degree of harmony long since passed beyond our powers." Kennedy materials, *supra* note 9, at 604. He adds, "Within this tradition, it was possible to order the concepts of right and power in such a way as to sharply reduce what we regard as inherent incompatibilities." *Id.*

208. Kennedy writes, "The pre-Classical notion was that men created the sovereign, namely the people gathered in their constitution-making capacity, in order to secure their natural rights against lawless neighbors. This the sovereign did by creating legal powers, legislative, and judicial, which in turn operated to protect the citizen against his neighbors' encroachments." *Id.* at 607.

209. **Blackstone,** *supra* note 71, at 39.

210. *See* notes 121–22 *supra,* and accompanying text.

211. *Id.*

212. Kennedy materials, *supra* note 9, at 47.

213. *Id.*

214. *Cf. id.* at 50.

215. *Id.* at 63.

216. **Stein,** *supra* note 11, at 9.

217. **Cassirer, The Philosophy of the Enlightenment** 55 (1951). Cassirer described the Cartesian system as follows:

> For Descartes the certainty and stability of all knowledge was founded in its first principles, while everything factual as such remained uncertain and problematical. We cannot trust the appearances of things to the senses, for sense perception always involves the possibility of sense deception. We can escape such deception only by penetrating beyond mere appearance, by relating the empirically given to concepts and expressing it in concepts which carry their proof within themselves. There is then an immediate and intuitive certainty regarding principles: regarding facts knowledge is mediate and derivative. *Id.* at 54–55.

218. **Burns, The American Experiment: The Vineyard of Liberty** 33 (1982).

219. *Id.*

220. *Id.*

221. *Id.* Many questions were left open after the Constitution was ratified. The framers defined liberty in varying ways; and their expectations, as well as their answers to the following questions, varied:

> What *kind* of liberty? Liberty for *whom*? Liberty *from* whom? Liberty expressed through what kinds of channels or vehicles (press, church, assembly, or other)? Liberty in what kind of context (war or peace, a crowded street, or a philosopher's study)? Liberty expressed through — or protected from — what level of government (state or national) and what branch of government (executive or legislative or judicial)? And the toughest question of all — to what degree, and in what way, should public authority be used to protect individual liberty against private power, such as that of a corporation or a tavernkeeper? Or a slaveowner? *Id.* at 130–31.

Equality was a concept no less amorphous in meaning. Burns writes:

> As in the case of liberty, few Americans asked the tough explicit questions about the meaning of equality. What kind of equality — legal, political, economic, social? Equality to be achieved how — by the natural workings of the social and economic order, by religious teachings, by the deliberate intervention of the community, perhaps even through government? And above all, equality for whom? All men, rich and

poor? Between men and women? Between adults and children? Equality for Indians, immigrants, aliens? Equality for black people? *Id*. at 142.

Indeed, was the purpose of the wider union simply for prosperity, safety, and national defense; or was it also formed to satisfy "higher needs — for individual liberty and self-expression, for a sense of sharing and fraternity, for the equal rights and liberties proclaimed in the Declaration of Independence [and if so] [h]ow would such aspirations and expectations be fulfilled?" *Id*. at 21.

222. How did Americans conceive of virtue? By virtue, the framers "meant at the least good character and civic concern; at the most . . . a heroic love for the public good, a devotion to justice, a willingness to sacrifice comfort and riches for the public weal." *Id*. at 62. Washington, in his Inaugural Address, referred to the "indissoluble union between virtue and happiness, between duty and advantage." *Id*. at 67.

223. **Stein,** *supra* note 11, at x.

224. It cannot be denied that "union and order and national strength were far more important to most of the framers than were the rights or liberties of black men and women." **Burns,** *supra* note 218, at 40.

225. **Stein,** *supra* note 11, at 12.

226. **Scott,** *supra* note 38, at 275 [quoting **Hutcheson, A Short Introduction to Moral Philosophy** 117 (1747)].

227. *Id*. at 276 [quoting 1 **Hutcheson, A System of Moral Philosophy** 69 (1755)].

228. *Id*. [quoting **Hutcheson, A Short Introduction to Moral Philosophy** 56, 64, 76 (1747)].

229. **Stein,** *supra* note 11, at 12.

230. *Id*. at 10.

231. *Id*.

232. *Id*. at 9.

233. *Id*.

234. *Id*.

235. *Id*. at 10.

236. Hutcheson's writing on contractual obligations was sensitive to the modern point that the binding force of a contract is derived from the contracting parties' reasonable expectations. *Id*. at 39 n. 14; *see also, id*. at 11.

237. *Id*. at 12.

238. *Id*. at 11.

239. Stein, speaking generally, writes, "In an age when religious freedom was being asserted, it was important to separate man's civil and political duties from his religious obligations." *Id*. at 1.

240. *Id*. at 12 [quoting **Hutcheson, A System of Moral Philosophy** 328 (1755)].

Footnotes for Part II, Chapter 4

241. **The Federalist No. 10,** at 55 (Madison) (Earle, ed. 1937)

242. *Id*. at 54.

243. *Id*. at 59.

244. **The Federalist No. 53,** at 347 (Hamilton or Madison) (Earle, ed. 1937).

245. **The Federalist No. 10,** at 57 (Madison) (Earle, ed. 1937).

246. *Id*. at 54.

247. *Id*. at 53.

248. *Id*.

249. *Id*. at 62.

250. **Wills, Explaining America** 268 (1981).

251. **Gay, The Enlightenment: An Interpretation, The Science of Freedom,** vol. II, 397 (1969).

252. **Wills,** *supra* note 250, at 270.

253. **The Federalist No. 37,** at 230 (Madison) (Earle, ed. 1937).

254. *Id*. at 229–30.

255. *Id*. at 229.
256. *Id*.
257. **The Federalist No. 82,** at 534 (Hamilton) (Earle, ed. 1937).
258. **The Federalist No. 84,** at 559 (Hamilton) (Earle, ed. 1937).
259. *Id*.
260. *Id*. at 563.
261. *Id*.
262. Hamilton, when referring to the power of the Court to act as an impartial judge, wrote: "The courts must declare the sense of the law; and if they should be disposed to exercise WILL instead of JUDGMENT, the consequences would equally be the substitution of their pleasure to that of the legislative body." **The Federalist No. 78,** at 507–8 (Hamilton) (Earle, ed. 1937). He added, "It is far more rational to suppose, that the courts were designed to be an intermediate body between the people and the legislature, in order, among other things, to keep the latter within the limits assigned to their authority." *Id*. at 506.
263. *See* **The Federalist Nos. 78–83,** at 502–55 (Hamilton) (Earle, ed. 1937).
264. Hamilton wrote:

> The complete independence of the courts of justice is peculiarly essential in a limited Constitution. . . . Limitations . . . can be preserved in practice no other way than through the medium of courts of justice, whose duty it must be to declare all acts contrary to the manifest tenor of the Constitution void. Without this, all the reservations of particular rights or privileges would amount to nothing. **The Federalist No. 78,** at 505 (Hamilton) (Earle, ed. 1937).

265. After noting that the Court's function is to accord priority to the Constitution over repugnant legislation, Hamilton wrote, "Nor does this conclusion by any means suppose a superiority of the judicial to the legislative power. It only supposes that the power of the people is superior to both." *Id*. at 506.
266. *Id*. at 507.
267. *Id*. at 510.
268. **The Federalist No. 84,** at 563 (Hamilton) (Earle, ed. 1937).
269. **White,** *supra* note 76, at 114.
270. *See generally id.* According to White, most Americans believed that moral sense and intuitive reasoning were basic components of morality.
271. Feinberg, "Introduction to Mind and its Place in Nature," in **Reason and Responsibility: Readings in Some Basic Problems of Philosophy** 244 (Feinberg, 5th rev. ed. 1981).
272. Johnston writes:

> The analogies between Reid's work and Kant's are many and striking. Reid began, as Kant did, by comparing the slow progress made by philosophy with the rapid advance of physical science. And, like Kant, Reid determined that, if philosophy were to advance, the attitude of physical science must be adopted. Like Kant, Reid was a competent mathematician and physicist, with a great respect for Newton, but his general philosophical method differs from that of Kant. While Kant's work is written, in the main, from the epistemological standpoint, Reid remains true to the traditional British psychological method. Johnston, Introduction, **Selections from the Scottish Philosophy of Common Sense** 12–13 (Johnston, ed. 1915).

273. Gadamer writes that Kant "totally excluded the idea of *sensus communis* from moral philosophy." **Gadamer, Truth and Method** 31 (1975). Kant was attempting to exclude totally any trace of *moral sense,* as Hutcheson used the term, from his idealism. *Id*.
274. *See* note 377 *infra,* and accompanying text.
275. Johnston, *supra* note 272, at 3 [quoting 1 **Reid, Works** 95 (Hamilton, 6th rev. ed. 1863)].
276. Duggan, Introduction, **Reid, An Inquiry into the Human Mind,** at x (Duggan, ed. 1970) [quoting **Fraser, Thomas Reid** 41 (1898)].
277. **Reid, An Inquiry into the Human Mind** 87 (Duggan, ed. 1970).
278. *Id*. at 36.

279. Seth, Scottish Philosophy: A Comparison of the Scottish and German Answers to Hume 7 (1895) (quoting **Reid, Works** 283). Seth consistently cites Reid's *Works* as edited by Hamilton without identifying the volume, edition, or date of publication. Hereinafter, Seth's citations of Reid's *Works* will utilize his incomplete form.

280. Reid wrote that "skepticism is inlaid" in "Descartes's system of the human understanding." *Id.* at 6 (quoting **Reid, Works** 103).

281. Descartes, "Meditations on First Philosophy," in **Reason and Responsibility: Readings in Some Basic Problems of Philosophy** 120 (Feinberg, 5th rev. ed. 1981). Descartes added, "I am nevertheless assured that these modes of thought that I call perceptions and imaginations, inasmuch only as they as modes of thought, certainly reside [and are met with] in me." *Id.*

282. **Seth,** *supra* note 279, at 15.

283. **Locke,** "An Essay Concerning Human Understanding," in **The English Philosophers from Bacon to Mill** 248 (Burtt, ed. 1939).

284. *Id.* at 344.

285. Locke considered innate ideas to be "the root of dogmatism and the chief obstacle to the progress of knowledge." *Id.* at 247, n. 2 (note inserted by editor Burtt).

286. Feinberg, "Introduction to Human Knowldge: Its Ground and Limits," in **Reason and Responsibility: Readings in Some Basic Problems of Philosophy** 108 (Feinberg, 5th rev. ed. 1981).

287. **Locke,** *supra* note 283, at 265.

288. *Id.* at 265–66.

289. *Id.* at 267.

290. *Id.* at 248.

291. *Id.* at 249.

292. *Id.*

293. *Id.*

294. *Id.*

295. *Id.*

296. *Id.*

297. *Id.*

298. *Id.*

299. *Id.* at 372.

300. *Id.*

301. **Seth,** *supra* note 279, at 19.

302. **Locke,** *supra* note 283, at 317.

303. **Russell, The Problems of Philosophy** 12–13 (1912 & reprint 1971).

304. Feinberg, *supra* note 286, at 109.

305. **Russell,** *supra* note 303, at 13.

306. **Ayer, The Central Questions of Philosophy** 61 (1975).

307. *Id.*

308. **Seth,** *supra* note 279, at 45 [quoting **Hume, A Treatise of Human Nature,** i. 559 (Green, ed.)].

309. **Hume, A Treatise of Human Nature, Abstract** 658 (Selby-Bigge and Nidditch, 2d rev. ed. 1978).

310. *Id.* app. at 634.

311. *Id.* app. at 636.

312. Foot, Introduction, **Theories of Ethics** 1 (Foot, ed. 1967 & reprint 1977).

313. *Id.*

314. *Id.*

315. **MacCormick, Legal Reasoning and Legal Theory** 3–4 (1978).

316. *Id.* at 4.

317. *Id.* at 5.

318. **Reid,** *supra* note 277, at 18.

319. Duggan, *supra* note 276, at xxvi.

320. *See id.* at xxvii–xxix.
321. **Reid,** *supra* note 277, at 44–45.
322. **Seth,** *supra* note 279, at 99. Seth writes, "Reid himself binds us to no such order; and we ought to guard ourselves, above all things, against importing the idea of chronological succession into an analysis of knowledge. For in a real sense, it may be said that one such judgment involves and contains all." *Id.* at 100–101.
323. **Reid, Essays on the Intellectual Powers of Man** 175 (Walker, 2d rev. ed. Cambridge 1851).
324. **Seth,** *supra* note 279, at 112.
325. *Id.*
326. *Id.* at 110.
327. Berlin, Interpretive Commentary, **The Age of Enlightenment: The 18th Century Philosophers** 261 (Berlin, ed. 1956).
328. *Id.* at 261–62.
329. Putnam, Foreword, **Daniels, Thomas Reid's Inquiry: The Geometry of Visibles and the Case for Realism,** v (1974).
330. *Id.*
331. *Id.*
332. *Id.* at iv.
333. **Seth,** *supra* note 279, at 113.
334. *Id.* at 112.
335. *Id.*
336. **Reid,** *supra* note 277, at 272.
337. *Id.* at 268–69.
338. **Selections from the Scottish Philosophy of Common Sense** 181–82 (Johnston, ed. 1915) [reprinting 2 **Reid, "Essays on the Active Powers of Man,** in **Works** 586–90) (Hamilton, 6th rev. ed. Edinburgh 1863)].
339. **Wills, Inventing America** 183 (1979).
340. Concerning the relationship between a self-evident truth and common sense, Reid wrote:

 We ascribe to reason two offices, or two degrees. The first is to judge of things self-evident; the second to draw conclusions that are not self-evident from those that are. The first of these is the province, and the sole province, of common sense; and, therefore, it coincides with reason in its whole extent, and is only another name for one branch or one degree of reason. **Selections from the Scottish Philosophy of Common Sense,** *supra* note 338, at 149–5] [reprinting 1 **Reid,** "Essays on the Intellectual Powers of Man," in **Works** 425–26 (Hamilton, 6th rev. ed. Edinburgh 1863)].

341. Reid distinguished between necessary and contingent self-evident truths. An example of a necessary or immutable truth is the axiom of geometry "that a cone is the third part of a cylinder of the same base and the same altitude." *Id.* at 153 (reprinting 1 **Reid,** "Essays on the Intellectual Powers of Man," ,in **Works** 441–52 (Hamilton, 6th rev. ed. Edinburgh 1863) [hereinafter all references to Reid's "Essays on the Intellectual Powers of Man," will be material reprinted in Johnston's *Selections* from Hamilton's sixth edition of Reid's **Works,** *Id.*, and will be cited as *Intellectual Powers*].

 Reid notes that "the minds of men are occupied much more about truths that are contingent than about those that are necessary. . . ." *Id. (Intellectual Powers, supra* at 441–52). For example, Reid took for granted the principles that what will be is probably like what has previously been in similar circumstances. *Id.* at 156 (*Intellectual Powers, supra,* at 441–52). Thus, weight will fall to the ground, and this is a contingent truth that we can rely upon, although "[i]t depends upon the power and will of that Being who made the sun and all the planets. . . ." *Id.* at 153 (*Intellectual Powers, supra,* at 441–52). Reid was not overly concerned about the cause-and-effect relationships that troubled Hume.

342. *Id.* at 161–62 (reprinting 2 **Reid,** "Essays on the Active Powers of Man," in **Works** 558–60 (Hamilton, 6th rev. ed. Edinburgh 1863) [hereinafter all references to Reid's "Essays on the Active Powers of Man" will be material reprinted in Johnston's *Selections* from Hamilton's sixth edition of Reid's **Works,** *Id.*, and cited as *Active Powers*].

343. *Id.* at 164 (*Active Powers, supra* note 342, at 558-60).
344. *Id.* at 172 (*Active Powers, supra* note 342, at 580-81).
345. *Id.* at 165 (*Active Powers, supra* note 342, at 558-60).
346. *Id.*
347. *Id.* at 164 (*Active Powers, supra* note 342, at 558-60).
348. *Id.*
349. *Id.* at 165 (*Active Powers, supra* note 342, at 579-80).
350. *Id.*
351. *Id.* at 170 (*Active Powers, supra* note 342, at 580-81).
352. *Id.* at 171-72 (*Active Powers, supra* note 342, at 580-81).
353. *Id.* at 172 (*Active Powers, supra* note 342, at 580-81).
354. *Id.*
355. *Id.*
356. "Smith's expression of the 'invisible hand' . . . described how man is led 'to promote an end which was no part of his intentions.' " **Hayek, Law, Legislation and Liberty: A New Statement of the Liberal Principles of Justice and Political Economy, Rules and Order,** vol. I, 37 (1973) [quoting 1 **Smith, Wealth of Nations** 421 (Cannan, ed.)].
357. **Selections from the Scottish Philosophy of Common Sense,** *supra* note 338, at 174 (*Active Powers, supra* note 342, at 586-90).
358. *Id.* at 173 (*Active Powers, supra* note 342, at 586-90).
359. *Id.*
360. *Id.*
361. *Id.* at 179 (*Active Powers, supra* note 342, at 586-90).
362. Reid wrote:

    Moral obligation is a relation of its own kind, which every man understands, but is, perhaps, too simple to admit of logical definition. Like all other relations, it may be changed or annihilated by a change in any of the two related things — I mean the agent or the action. *Id.* at 178 (*Active Powers, supra* note 342, at 586-90). Hume, unlike Reid, wrote that morality is not susceptible of demonstration because it is not a matter of fact and is not applicable to relations. **Hume, A Treatise of Human Nature** 463-64 (Selby-Bigge and Nidditch, 2d rev. ed. 1978).
363. **Selections from the Scottish Philosophy of Common Sense,** *supra* note 338, at 167 (*Active Powers, supra* note 342, at 579-80).
364. *Id.* at 193 (*Active Powers, supra* note 342, at 670-73).
365. *Id.* at 192 (*Active Powers, supra* note 342, at 670-73).
366. *Id.* at 194 (*Active Powers, supra* note 342, at 670-73).
367. *Id.*
368. Putnam, *supra* note 329, at iv.
369. Reid rejected Hutcheson's and Hume's position that morality was purely a matter of taste or feeling because he insisted that morality was primarily a matter of judgment. He stated:

    [I]f it be true that there is judgment in our determinations of taste and of morals, it must be granted that what is true or false in morals or in matters of taste, is necessarily so. For this reason, I have ranked the first principles of taste under the class of necessary truths. **Selections from the Scottish Philosophy of Common Sense,** *supra* note 338, at 160-61 (*Intellectual Powers, supra* note 341, at 452-57).

    The first principle of morals is to do "[t]hat which, taken with all its discoverable connections and consequences, brings more good than ill." *Id.* at 170 (*Active Powers, supra* note 342, at 580-81). If the rational principle of action is true, it will bring more good than ill.
370. **Reid,** *supra* note 323, at 255-97.
371. *See* notes 322-24 *supra,* and accompanying text.
372. **Reid,** *supra* note 323, at 331-32.
373. *Id.* at 256.
374. *Id.*
375. *Id.* at 257.

376. *Id.* at 261.
377. *Id.* at 261-62.
378. *Id.* at 262.
379. *Id.* at 267.
380. *Id.*
381. *Id.* at 287.
382. *Id.* at 289.
383. *Id.* at 292-93.
384. *Id.* at 290.
385. *Id.* at 291.
386. **Hayek,** *supra* note 356, at 11.
387. *Id.*
388. *Id.* at 147-48 [quoting **Peters, The Concept of Motivation** 5 (1959)].
389. *Id.* at 11.
390. **Selections from the Scottish Philosophy of Common Sense,** *supra* note·338, at 173 (*Active Powers,* *supra* note 342, at 586-90).
391. **The Federalist No. 85,** at 570-71 (Hamilton) (Earle, ed. 1937).
392. *Id.* at 574 (quoting 1 **Hume,** "The Rise of Arts and Sciences," in **Essays** 128).
393. **Reid,** *supra* note 323, at 370.
394. *Id.* at 371.
395. *Id.* at 372.
396. *Id.*
397. *Id.*
398. *Id.* at 373.
399. *Id.* at 378.
400. *Id.* at 375.
401. *Id.*
402. *Id.* at 374.
403. *See supra* text accompanying notes 333-38. Walker, editor of Reid's *Essays on the Intellectual Powers of Man,* wrote:

> On the means of discriminating and determining first principles which is one of the most difficult points in the philosophy of common sense, Sir W. Hamilton in Note A, § 4, expresses himself thus: — "Those characters, I think, may be reduced to four: — 1°, their *incomprehensibility;* 2°, their *simplicity;* 3°, their *necessity* and *absolute universality;* 4°, their *comparative evidence* and *certainty.*" **Reid,** *supra* note 323, at 378 (editor's footnote).

404. For a discussion of the Supreme Court's substantive due process doctrine, see chapter 8 *infra.*
405. A theory of adjudication provides methods which judges use to gauge the validity of a proposed case law ruling. Theories of adjudication are primarily concerned with technical matters, such as the need for principled decisionmaking. As such, they are controversial, but less controversial than theories of law. No theory of law can totally ignore the norms of morality and the ends that should be furthered by the legal system. Theories of law and adjudication require each other, since neither alone can wholly determine what judges ought to do. *Cf.* **MacCormick, Legal Reasoning and Legal Theory** 265 (1978) ("[T]heories of legal reasoning and law require and are required by each other; both in turn have to be based in some general theory of practical reason and its limits." *Id.*).
406. 1 Montesquieu, **The Spirit of the Laws** 34 (Nugent, trans., 1949).
407.· **Storing, What the Anti-Federalists Were For** 72 (1981) (citing 3 **The Debates of the State Conventions on the Adoption of the Federal Constitution, as Recommended by the General Convention at Philadelphia in 1787,** 536-37 (Elliot, 2d rev. ed. Philadelphia 1866) [hereinafter cited as Elliot, **Debates**].
408. **Burns, The American Experiment: The Vineyard of Liberty** 67 (1982). (emphasis added).
409. Kenyon, "Constitutionalism in Revolutionary America," in **Constitutionalism: Nomos XX,** 117 (Pennock and Chapman, eds. 1979).

410. **Storing,** *supra* note 407, at 15.
411. *Id.* at 39 [citing letter from Madison to Jefferson (Oct. 17, 1788) in 5 **Madison, Writings** 272 (Hunt, ed.)].
412. "There were very few 'democrats' among the Anti-Federalist writers (or probably among Americans of any kind) . . . who believe[d] that the will of the majority of the people is law and that that will ought to be exercised as directly and with as little restraint as possible." *Id.* at 40 (footnote omitted).
413. *Id.* at 72 (quoting Madison).
414. **U.S. Const. Preamble.**
415. **Storing,** *supra* note 407, at 71 (citing 2 Elliot, **Debates,** *supra* note 407, at 301.
416. **Burns,** *supra* note 408, at 67.
417. Kenyon, *supra* note 409, at 116, 120.
418. *Id.* at 114.
419. *Id.*
420. *See* text accompanying notes 338-42, 368-403 *supra.*
421. The text is but a brief allusion to Unger's critique of liberal thought. **Unger, Knowledge & Politics** (1975), which does not do justice to Unger's careful development of the antinomies between reason and desire, rules and values, and theory (ideas) and facts (events). Unger also outlines the antinomies of liberal thought in a helpful chart. *Id.* at 138.
422. Ackerman relies on a continuing neutral dialogue among the individuals in the liberal state to justify rational outcomes. *See generally* **Ackerman, Social Justice in the Liberal State** (1980). After each citizen recognizes each other's claim to self-respect, *id.* at 75, each citizen must "be prepared to offer a reason in defense of every aspect of his power position when challenged to do so by anyone disadvantaged by his claim of dominion." *Id.* at 372. Ackerman argues that "[n]eutral dialogue [is] the most sensible way of regulating our power struggle." *Id.* at 357.
423. There is a distinction between the United States Constitution and the Supreme Court's interpretation of the Constitution. *See* **Hart, The Concept of Law** 141 (1961). The power of a Court to say what the Constitution means is a power conferred by a system of rules derived from the Constitution, which the judges are not free to disregard. *Id.* at 141-42.
424. Professor MacCormick refers to inchoate principles as "an intermediate terra incognita of principles struggling for legal recognition." **MacCormick,** *supra* note 405, at 238.
425. *See e.g.,* **Dworkin, Taking Rights Seriously** 14-149, 294-359 (1978).
426. **MacCormick,** *supra* note 405, at 235.
427. *Cf.* Radin, "Case Law and Stare Decisis," in **Essays on Jurisprudence from the Columbia Law Review** 15 (1963 & reprint 1977).
428. *Cf.* Douglas, "Stare Decisis," in **Essays on Jurisprudence from the Columbia Law Review** 18 (1963 & reprint 1977).
429. *See* discussion of Griswold v. Connecticut (Chapter 8 in text accompanying notes 84-91 *infra*) for a more concrete example illustrating how inchoate principles introduce into the law those basic values of society which have constitutional significance, and are ripe for recognition by courts.

    MacCormick writes, "The rules which are rules *of law* are so in virtue of their pedigree; the principles which are principles *of law* are so because of their function in relation to those rules, that is, the function which those who use them as rationalizations of the rules thus ascribe to them." **MacCormick,** *supra* note 405, at 233.
430. MacCormick writes, "It is . . . a shared thesis as between positivistic and natural law thinking that legal systems have criteria, sustained by 'acceptance' in the society whose system it is, satisfaction of which is at least presumptively sufficient for the existence of a rule as a 'valid rule' of the system." *Id.* at 62 (emphasis added).

Footnotes for Part III, Chapter 5

1. Gompers v. United States, 233 U.S. 604, 610 (1914) (Holmes, J.).

2. The theory that is presented in the essay is a revision of the theory of interpreting texts propounded by Gadamer. *See generally* **Gadamer, Truth and Method** (1975) (a discussion of the problem of "[t]he phenomenon of understanding and of the correct interpretation of what has been understood" from a hermeneutic perspective. *Id* at x). Since Gadamer is not primarily interested in methodology, I have adapted Gadamer's theory, with some substantial modifications. I have, however, tried to preserve the essence of Gadamer's epistemology.

3. *See* Brest, *Interpretation and Interest,* 34 **Stan. L. Rev.** 765, 765 (1982).

4. **Gadamer,** *supra* note 2, at 475.

5. *Id.*

6. *Id.* at 473.

7. *Id.* at 472.

8. *See generally* Parker, *The Past of Constitutional Theory — And its Future,* 42 **Ohio State L. J.** 223 (1981) (an appeal by Parker to his generation — "the generation of the 1960s" — to free themselves from "self-imposed orthodoxy." *Id.* Parker looks forward to **"The Future of Constitutional Theory: Without Maps."** *Id.* at 257.

9. *See* **Cardozo, The Nature of the Judicial Process** 28 (1921).

10. *See* Gordon, *Historicism in Legal Scholarship,* 90 **Yale L. J.** 1017 (1981). Gordon uses the term *historicism* to refer loosely "to the perspective that the meanings of words and actions are *to some degree* dependent on the particular social and historical conditions in which they occur. . . ." *Id.* at 1017 n. 1 (emphasis added).

11. Rawls discusses a version of reflective equilibrium. See **Rawls, A Theory of Justice** 48–51 (1971).

12. *See* **Dworkin, Taking Rights Seriously** 81–149 (1978) (a description of the enterprise of theory-building by judges).

13. Gadamer distinguishes the art of wise and prudent judging, *phronesis,* from the artisan's craft, *techne.* Following Aristotle's distinction, his point is that the interpreter with a hermeneutic perspective brings to bear on his project a greater degree of creative imagination. He is no mere mechanic. **Gadamer,** *supra* note 2, at 280–89.

14. Hand stressed the fact that the great judges are better at the art of judging because of their creative imagination in interpreting texts, Proceedings of a Special Session to Commemorate Learned Hand held at United States Courthouse, New York, N.Y., Apr. 10, 1959 (remarks by Hand).

15. **The American Heritage Dictionary of the English Language** 1282. (1969).

16. Rilke (quoted in **Gadamer,** *supra* note 2 at v.

17. Cardozo, *supra* note 9, at 88–9.

18. Perry suggests that the courts may make policy in human rights cases since "judicial review represents the institutionalization of prophecy." **Perry, The Constitution, The Courts, and Human Rights** 98 (1982). Perry explains that Americans have a "religious understanding of themselves . . . the notion of prophecy." *Id.* This involves "a commitment — though not necessarily a fully conscious commitment — to the notion of moral evolution. . . ." *Id.* at 99.

19. The literature on the difference between interpretivism and noninterpretivism is growing at an accelerated rate. *See, e.g., Constitutional Adjudication and Democracy Theory,* 56 **N.Y.U. L. Rev.** 259–582 (1981), *Judicial Review versus Democracy,* 41 **Ohio St. L. J.** 1–434 (1981), Grey, *Origins of the Unwritten Constitution: Fundamental Law in American Revolutionary Thought,* 30 *Stan L. Rev.* 843 (1978); Grey, *Do We Have an Unwritten Constitution?* 27 **Stan. L. Rev.** 703 (1975) Brest, *The Misconceived Quest for the Original Understanding,* 60 **B.U. L. Rev.** 204 (1980); **Ely, Democracy and Distrust: A Theory of Judicial Review** (1980). Perry, *supra* note 18. Wellington, book review, 97 **Harv. L. Rev.** 326 (1983).

For a discussion of the coercive use of the "knockdown argument," see **Nozick, Philosophical Explanations** (1981).

20. **Gadamer,** *supra* note 2, at xxiv.

21. *Id.* at xvi.

22. *Id*. at 239.
23. *Id*. at 237-50, 273.
24. *Id*. at 340.
25. Professor Brest writes that Gadamer holds an "essentially solipsistic view of historical knowledge." Brest's statement at best is misleading. Brest, *The Misconceived Quest for the Original Understanding*, 60 **B.U. L. Rev.** 204, 222, (1980).
26. **The American Heritage Dictionary of the English Language** 1229 (1969).
27. **Gadamer,** *supra* note 2, at xvi.
28. *Id*. at 297.
29. *Id*. at 301.
30. *Id*. at 239, *see also, Id*. at 310-25.
31. Fiss writes, "Adjudication is interpretation: Adjudication is the process by which a judge comes to understand and express the meaning of an authoritative legal text and the values embodied in that text." Fiss, *Objectivity and Interpretation*, 34 **Stan L. Rev.** 739, 739 (1982). He adds, "Viewing adjudication as interpretation helps to stop the slide toward nihilism. It makes law possible." *Id*. at 750.
32. Fiss writes,

> Objectivity in the law connotes standards. It implies that an interpretation can be measured against a set of norms that transcend the particular vantage point of the person offering the interpretation. Objectivity implies that the interpretation can be judged by something other than one's own notion of correctness. It imparts a notion of impersonality. The idea of an objective interpretation does not require that the interpretation be wholly determined by some source external to the judge, but only that it be constrained. *Id*. at 744.

> *But see* Brest, *supra* note 3, at 765. Brest writes that the notion of "constitutional adjudication as hermeneutics. . ." is "sophisticated" but "by making constitutional law inaccessible to laypersons" it tends to augment a coercive power relationship. *Id*. at 771-72. Gadamer, however, simply recognizes that the immanent meaning of words is that which is filtered through the mind set of the existing dominant cultural forces in society. He is a sophisticated messenger bringing the news.

33. See generally **MacCormick, Legal Reasoning and Legal Theory** (1978).

> MacCormick relies on the conventional theory of formal justice which "requires that the justification of decisions in individual cases be always decided on the basis of universal propositions to which the judge is prepared to adhere as a basis for determining other like cases and deciding them in the like manner to the present one." *Id*. at 99. The judge is certainly expected to conform to this elementary notion of the rule of law when he can.

> Fiss writes that the judge can preserve objectivity that is compromised by "a number of disparate and conflicting roles" and "the pressures of instrumentalism" by a proper response: "increased effort, clarity of vision and determination, not surrender." Fiss *supra* note 31, at 762.

34. *See* Sandalow, *Constitutional Interpretation*, 79 **Mich. L. Rev.** 1033, 1038-39, (1981).
35. **Gadamer,** *supra* note 2, at 271.
36. Sandalow writes that "[b]y wrenching" ourselves from the framers' particular judgments, "we are not serving larger ends determined by the framers but making room for the introduction of contemporary values." Sandalow *supra* note 34, at 1046. He adds, quoting Llewellyn, "The 'quest does not run primarily in terms of historical intent. It runs in terms of what the words can be made to bear, in making sense in the new light of what was originally unforeseen.' " *Id*. at 1060.
37. **Gadamer,** *supra* note 2, at xxv.
38. Gadamer refers to this undertaking as "the recovery of a dead meaning." *Id*. at 149. He also refers to it as "this romantic reflective enjoyment of history." *Id*. at 172.
39. *Id*. at 150. Gadamer noted that Hegel went far beyond romantic hermeneutics but Gadamer, in part, rejects the ultra-metaphysical Hegelian approach for understanding history. Gadamer is however influenced by Heidegger's development of "the fore-

structure of understanding." *Id*. at 235. Heidegger warned that the approach described in somewhat modified form in the text (see text above note 22 *supra* "is not to be reduced to the level of a vicious circle. . . ." *Id*. at 235. While "[a] person who is trying to understand a text is always performing an act of projecting" it is always necessary for him to keep his gaze on the text "as he penetrates into the meaning. . . ." *Id*. at 236. Although this projective process will result in a large variety of readings depending on the reader, "it is not the case that within this variety . . . everything is possible." *Id*. at 238. "The important thing is to be aware of one's own bias, so that the text may present itself in all its newness and thus be able to assert its own truth against one's own fore-meanings." *Id*.

40. **Perry,** *supra* note 18, at x, 4–8.
   Perry himself is not an interpretivist. He wears an interpretivist strawman's hat which he knocks off and replaces with a wrong-headed emphasis on a "functional justification of non-interpretive review with respect to human rights issues. . . ." *Id*. at 7. The functional justification involves the judiciary "as an agency of ongoing, insistent moral reevaluation, and ultimately of moral growth." *Id*. at 163. The approach attempts to reconcile judicial review with the demands of representative democracy since Perry envisions a congressional supervisory role, in the form "of a broad jurisdiction-limiting power." *Id*. at 138.

41. **Perry,** *supra* note 18, at 74. Perry writes that evidence is "wholly lacking" to support the proposition that the framers "intended to constitutionalize broad 'concepts' rather than particular 'conceptions.' " *Id*. at 70. *But see* **The Federalist Nos. 37, 84, Fairman, History of the Supreme Court of the United States: Reconstruction and Reunion** 1864–88 [vol. VI of the Holmes Devise] 1207–1388 (1971).

Footnotes for Part III, Chapter 6

42. The word *historicism* is used by Professor Gordon as a reference "to the perspective that the meanings of words and actions are to some degree dependent on the particular social and historical conditions in which they occur, and to interpretations and criticisms that are suggested by that perspective." Gordon, *Historicism in Legal Scholarship, supra* note 10, at 1017 n. 1. He adds, "It is not intended to describe the view that meanings may be derived *exclusively* by reference to the unique conditions of a specific time and place." *Id*.
   This definition does not conform to Popper's definition of historicism. The historicism which Popper rejected was the claim that the future depends on historical necessity. **Popper, The Open Society and Its Enemies, The Spell of Plato** vol. 1, 3 (5th rev. ed. 1966). Popper wrote, "[Historicists] also believe that they have discovered laws of history which enable them to prophesy the course of historical events." *Id*. This essay does not undertake to discuss all the varieties of historicism, Marxist, Hegelian, or otherwise.

43. Gordon, *supra* note 10, at 1018.

44. *Id*. at 1018–19.

45. Gordon refers to the "legal texts," which include "the basic data of the field, the work-product of the legal agencies, and of lawyers doing or anticipating business before them, including cases, statutes, regulations, briefs, pleadings, indentures, deeds, settlement offers, negotiation . . . advice to clients, and so forth." *Id*. at 1019.

46. Gordon refers to the "data from the social field in which the legal text is embedded. This could be the 'facts' of a dispute, the 'social problem' inspiring statutory action, the 'difficulties of enforcement' of a tax levy. . . ." *Id*.

47. Gordon refers to the "normative context." This context, he writes, "is the apparatus of normative conceptions to which the legal scholar tries to relate the legal texts." *Id*. at 1019–20. These conceptions can be drawn from "perceptions of customary morality, historical tradition, political economy, ordinary language, moral philosophy, and so forth." *Id*. at 1020. He adds, "I trust that no one will suppose that normative and social contexts are meant to represent categories easily defined to be mutually exclusive." *Id*.

48. **MacCormick,** *supra* note 33, at 267.

49. *Id.*
50. *See* Gordon, *supra* note 10, at 1050.
51. *See* **Quine, Word and Object** 124 (1960).
52. Gordon, *supra* note 10, at 1020.
53. *Id.* (citing **Ely,** *supra* note 19, at 11–41, 45; Brest, *supra* note 19, at 204, 220–21.
54. Gordon *supra* note 10, at 1021.
55. *Id.* at 1023–24.
56. *Summary of Discussion of Historicism in Legal Scholarship,* 90 **Yale L. J.** 1060, 1061 (1981) (summary of symposium participants' discussion).
57. Gordon, *supra* note 10, at 1024. This reference to symbolism seems to denigrate the importance of symbolic statements. The process of symbolization, however, is so fundamental to human history that the whole history of ideas should be reviewed in the light of the power of social structures to generate symbols, which have a meaningful impact beyond that which can be conveyed by mere discursive language. The symbolization process is profoundly social in nature. A symbolic statement suggests mysticism, which in a rational society is not necessarily a compliment, but as Popper citing McTaggert, writes

   > [T]he fundamental ideas of mysticism are two: (a) the doctrine of the *mystic union,* i.e., the assertion that there is a greater unity in the world of realities than that which we recognize in the world of ordinary experience, and (b) the doctrine of the *mystic intuition,* i.e., the assertion there is a way of knowing which 'brings the known into closer and more direct relation with what is known' than is the relation between the knowing subject and the known object in ordinary experience. **Popper,** *supra* note 42, at 314 (citing **McTaggert, Philosophical Studies** 47 (Keeling, ed. 1934)).

   Popper himself adds a third characteristic which possibly describes the American people's affection for the United States Constitution: "the *mystic love,* which is an example of mystic unity *and* mystic intuition." *Id.* For the Constitution to remain symbolically viable, it must connect credibly with experience, and be a medium of expression, which provides patterns of continuity, orientation, and a sense of group identity.
58. *See infra* text accompanying notes 63–64.
59. Gordon, *supra* note 10, at 1045.
60. See **Kelsen, What Is Justice** 179–180 (1957).
61. A synthesis between the validity thesis and its antithesis can be accomplished by a disciplined judge attentive to reasonable expectations. MacCormick also discusses the validity thesis. *See* **MacCormick,** *supra* note 33, at 62, 65, 71, 107, 139, 155, 194, 242, 244–45.
62. *Id.* at 63–64.
63. Gordon, *supra* note 10, at 1024.
64. A symbol represents the unity between an ideal (moral, political or religious) and the world of the senses. *See generally* **Gadamer,** *supra* note 2, at 65–73 (discussion of symbolism in Kantian and classical liberal thought), **Langer, Philosophy in a new key: A study in the Symbolism of Rite and Act** (1970)
65. 5 U.S. (1 Cranch) 137 (1803).
66. **MacCormick,** *supra* note 33, at 265.
67. For a helpful discussion of historicism, positivism, and the tension between universal and particular norms of justice, see **Brecht, Political Theory** 185–86 (1959).
68. **Bickel, The Morality of Consent** 30 (1975).

Footnotes for Part III, Chapter 7

69. Corwin, *The Basic Doctrine of American Constitutional Law,* 12 **Mich. L. Rev.** 247–48 (1914).
70. *Id.* at 248.
71. **Thayer, Legal Essays** 27 (1927).
72. *Id.* at 32.
73. Eakin v. Raub, 12 Serg & Rawle 330, 335 (Pa. 1825).

74. *Id*. at 347.
75. *Id*.
76. Corwin, *The Higher Law Background of American Constitutional Law, 42* **Harv. L. Rev.** 149, 408-09 (1938) quoting **Pollock, Expansion Of The Common Law** 128 (1904).
77. **Ely, Democracy and Distrust: A Theory of Judicial Review** 51 (1980).
78. 410 U.S. 113 (1973).
79. **Ely**, *supra* note 77, at 43.
80. There should be strict judicial scrutiny when the courts determine that "representative government cannot be trusted." **Ely**, *supra* note 19, at 180. Ely favors judicial intervention, not prudence, in the area of voting rights, freedom of speech, and areas where the Court can ensure a "broadened access," *id*. at 74, to representative government. He favors a higher level of judicial scrutiny to protect the politically powerless minorities who are not benefiting from adequately responsive representative government. *Id*. at 135-72.
81. **Parrish, Felix Frankfurter and His Times: The Reform Years** 65 (1982).
82. **Ely, Democracy and Distrust: A Theory of Judicial Review** 88-89 (1980).
83. *Id*. at 88.
84. Ely, *Democracy and the Right to be Different, 56* **N.Y.U. L. Rev.** 397 (1981) (a reference to United States v. Carolene Products Co., 314 U.S. 144, 152 n. 4 1938).
85. The phrase is borrowed from Professor Wellington and others. *See* Wellington, *The Nature of Judicial Review,* 91 **Yale L. J.** 487 (1982).
86. United States v. Carolene Products Co., 304 U.S. 144, 152 n. 4 (1938).
87. *Id*.
88. **Ely**, *supra* note 82, at 87.
89. Eule, *Laying the Dormant Commerce Clause to Rest, 91* **Yale L. J.** 425, 422 (1982).
90. Parker, *The Past of Constitutional Theory — And its Future,* 42 **Ohio St. L. J.** 223, 242-46 (1981).
91. *Id*. at 231.
92. *Id*. at 240.
93. **Dahl, Democracy in the United States** 448* (3d rev. ed. 1976).
94. *Id*. at 488.
95. Boorstin is quoted in **The American Heritage Dictionary of the English Language** 1337 (1969)
96. 410 U.S. 113 (1973).
97. Hurtado v. California, 110 U.S. 516, 535 (1884) (California statute which permitted criminal proceedings to be instituted by information was upheld on the basis of its conformity with the principles of liberty and justice).
98. **Wright, The Growth of American Constitutional Law** 244 (1967).
99. 6 Cranch 87 (1810).
100. *See* **Wright**, *supra* note 98, at 42.
101. U.S. Const. art. I § 10.
102. U.S. Const. art. I §§ 9, 10.
103. **Wright**, *supra* note 98, at 84. Wright explains that in Cummings v. Missouri, 4 Wall. 277 (1867) and *Ex parte* Garland, 4 Wall. 33 (1867) the Court set aside "state and federal statutes requiring a highly inclusive oath of nonsupport of the late wicked Rebellion as a prerequisite to the practice of certain professions. . . ." *Id*. at 83. The holdings were based upon the *ex post facto* and bill of attainder provisions of the Constitution. **U.S. Constitution**, Art. I, §§ 9, 10.
104. 341 U.S. 173 (1950) (Frankfurther, J., concurring).
105. *Id*. at 162-63 (emphasis added.)
106. Poe v. Ullman, 367 U.S. 497, 542 (Harlan, J.,dissenting).
107. Williams v. Illinois, 399 U.S. 235, 260 (1970) (Harlan, J., concurring in result).
108. **Pitkin, The Concept of Representation** 3 (1972).
109. **Birch, Representation** 124 (1971).
110. *Id*.
111. *Id*.
112. *Id*. at 101.

113. Ely, *supra* note 82, at 98.
114. *Id.* at 74.
115. Ely, *supra* note 84, at 397.
116. *Id.* at 398.
117. *Id.*
118. Leedes, Book Review, "Democracy and Distrust: A Theory of Judicial Review," 59 N.C. L. **Rev.** 628 (1981), Leedes, *The Supreme Court Mess,* 57 **Tex. L. Rev.** 1361, 1421-37 (1979).
119. **Ely,** *supra* note 82, at 187 n. 14.
120. **Pitkin,** *supra* note 108, at 291. (Pitkin refers to Schumpeter's economic model of democracy.)
121. *Id.* at 233.
122. *Id.*
123. *Id.* at 235.
124. *Id.* at 233.
125. *Id.*
126. *Id.* at 235.
127. *Id.* at 175.
128. *Id.* at 175-76.
129. *Id.* at 238.
130. *Id.*
131. United States v. Carolene Products Co. 304 U.S. 144, 152 n. 4 (1938).
132. *Id.*
133. **Jackson, The Struggle for Judicial Supremacy** vi (1941).
134. **Mason, Harlan Fiske Stone: Pillar of the Law** (1965) (passim).
135. **Lusky, By What Right?** 80-112 (1975) (a discussion of the footnote's genesis and double standards). See also, Hand, *Chief Justice Stone's Conception of the Judicial Function, 46* **Col. L. Rev.** 696,698 (1946). Judge Hand mistakenly presumed that Stone shared his views, just as Mason assumed Stone shared his views on civil liberties. Stone was somewhere in between, but less process-oriented than Ely.
136. The phrase is borrowed. *See* **Wright,** *supra* note 98, at 259.
137. *Id.* Wright is referring to Madison's conception of the Constitution, namely that the Constitution is flexible and adaptable but not flabby.
138. Other indications of Justice, then Chief Justice, Stone's interest in the political check of adequate representation are found in Helvering v. Gerhardt, 304 U.S. 405 (1938), South Carolina State Highway Dep't v. Barnwell Bros., 303 U.S. 177, 184 n. 2 (1938).
139. **Lusky,** *supra* note 135, at 109.
140. United States v. Carolene Products Co., 304 U.S. 144, 152 n. 4 (1938). (emphasis added).
141. **Mason, Harlan Fiske Stone: Pillar of the Law** 513 (1956) (quoting letter, Hughes to Stone, Apr. 19, 1938).
142. *Id.* at 514 (quoting letter, Stone to Hughes, Apr. 19, 1938).
143. *Id.*
144. Palko v. Connecticut, 302 U.S. 319, (1937). For quotations from Stone's letters indicating his approval, see **Mason,** *supra* note 141, at 516.

Justice Cardozo actually phrased the determinative question in due process cases in a number of ways:

whether the procedure in issue was "of the very essence of a scheme of ordered liberty"; whether to employ it violated a "principle of justice so rooted in the traditions and conscience of our people as to be branded as fundamental"; whether a "fair and enlightened system of justice would be impossible without it"; whether "liberty and justice" would exist if it were sacrificed; whether its use subjects a person to "a hardship so acute and shocking that our polity would not endure it"; whether it is among "those immutable principles of justice, acknowledged *semper ubique et ab ominibus* . . . wherever the good life is a subject of concern. *See* Kadish, "Methodology and Criteria in Due Process Adjudication: A Survey and Criticism."

Professor Kadish was quoting from Palko v. Connecticut, 302 U.S. 319 (1937) and Snyder v. Massachusetts, 291 U.S. 97 (1934). Kadish refers to these formulations as examples "of flexible-natural law due process." *Id.*

145. Palko v. Connecticut, 302 U.S. 319, (1937).
146. 316 U.S. 535 (1942).
147. *Id.* at 545.
148. *Id.* at 544.
149. *Id.*
150. Thayer, *supra* note 71, at 150.
151. *See* McCloskey, "Economic Due Process and the Supreme Court: An Exhumation and Reburial" in **The Supreme Court and the Constitution: Essays in Constitutional Law from the Supreme Court Review,** 172 (Kurland, ed. 1965). (hereinafter McCloskey).
152. Skinner v. Oklahoma *ex rel* Williamson, 316 U.S. 535, 544 (1942) (Stone, Ch. J., concurring). Stone's opinion illustrate that the concepts of substantive and procedural due process are sometimes inextricable related.
153. **U.S. Const. amend. XIV, § 1.**
154. McCloskey *supra* note 151, at 174.
155. *Id.*
156. For the same thought, see **Curtis, Lions Under the Throne** 253 (1947).
157. **Dahl,** *supra* note 93, at 184.
158. Regents of the University of California v. Bakke, 438 U.S. 265, 289, 297–99, 305, 318 n. 52, 320 (1978) (Powell, J., opinion of the Court).
159. **Pound, The Development of Constitutional Guarantees of Liberty** 1 (1956) (emphasis added).
160. *Id.* at 8.
161. Freund, "The Supreme Court and Civil Liberties," in **Selected Essays of Constitutional Law** 462 (1963) quoting **Siepmann, Radio, Television and Society** 203 (1950).
162. **Fried, Right and Wrong** 109 (1978).
163. **Nonet and Selznick, Law and Society in Transition: Toward Responsive Law** 83 (1978).
164. Eule, *supra* note 89, at 442.
165. *Id.*
166. *Id.* at 443.
167. **The Federalist No. 80,** at 522. (Hamilton) (Earle, ed. 1937).
168. Cohens v. Virginia, 19 U.S. (6 Wheat.) 264 (1821) (Marshall, Ch. J.).
169. Eule, *supra* note 89, at442.
170. **Vile, Constitutionalism and the Separation of Powers** 306 (reprinted 1969).
171. *Id.*
172. **Ely,** *supra* note 82, at 90.
173. *Id.* at 92.
174. **The Federalist No. 84** at 559 (Hamilton) (Earle, ed. 1937).
175. *Id.*
176. *Id.*
177. **The Federalist No. 78** at 506 (Hamilton) (Earle, ed. 1937).
178. *Id.*
179. **Jackson,** *supra* note 133, at 323.
180. *See generally* **Vile,** *supra* note 170, at 294–314 (a discussion of political theory, constitutionalism, and the behavioral approach to politics).
181. Schochet, *Introduction: Constitutionalism, and the Study of Politics,* in **Constitutionalism: Nomos XX,** 1, 11.
182. Freund, "The Supreme Court and Civil Liberties," in **Selected Essays in Constitutional Law** 461 (1963).
183. **Berlin, Four Essays on Liberty** 131 (1970).
184. *Id.*
185. *Id.* at 162.
186. *Id.*
187. *Id.* at 163.

188. *Id.* at 165.
189. *Id.*

Footnotes for Part III, Chapter 8

1. See pp. 205-10 *infra.*
2. See pp. 211-17 *infra.*
3. See pp. 217-30 *infra.*
4. See pp. 230-40 *infra.*
5. See pp. 240-44 *infra.*
6. 3 U.S. (3 Dall.) 386, 387-88 (1798).
7. Justice Chase added, "[t]here are certain vital principles in our free republican governments, which will determine and overrule an apparent and flagrant abuse of legislative power; [that authorizes] manifest injustice by positive law; or [which takes] away that security for personal liberty, or private property, for the protection whereof the government was established." *Id.* at 388.
8. 2 U.S. (2 Dall.) 304 (1795).
9. *Id.* at 310.
10. Corwin, *The Basic Doctrine of American Constitutional Law,* 12 **Mich. L. Rev.** 247, 256 (1914).
11. 10 U.S. (6 Cranch) 87 (1810).
12. The exact quote is as follows: "How far the power of giving the law may involve every other power, in cases where the Constitution is silent, never has been, and perhaps never can be, definitely stated." *Id.* at 136.
13. 59 U.S. (18 How.) 272 (1855).
14. *Id.* at 276.
15. 13 N.Y. 378 (1856).
16. 60 U.S. (19 How.) 393 (1856).
17. *Id.* at 450.
18. Not all commentators agree with this proposition. *See e.g.,* Brest, *The Fundamental Rights Controversy: The Essential Contradictions of Normative Constitutional Scholarship,* 90 **Yale L. J.** 1063 (1981).
19. Freund, "Social Justice and the Law," in **Social Justice** 93-95 (Brandt, Ed. 1962). In referring to the development of English common law, Freund writes: "[C]ontract is seen as the progeny of property and tort: The elements of both *quid pro quo* and reliance entered into its inheritance, and its ancestry may flow back to the unifying idea of the satisfaction of reasonable expectations." *Id.* at 96 (footnotes omitted).
20. However, judges may not do as they please; as Professor Tushnet notes, "a substantive due process right should be established only to the extent [it is] supported by the weight of responsible opinion. Tushnet, *The Newer Property; Suggestion for the Revival of Substantive Due Process,* 1975 **Sup. Ct. Rev.** 261, 279.
21. Freund notes that the reasonable expectation standard "is, to be sure a protean concept, but its vagueness has boundaries: It is to be differentiated, on the one hand, from generosity or mercy; on the other, from will or power. Moreover, it connotes rational principles of measure and order." *See* Freund, *supra* note 19, at 96.
22. Richards, *Sexual Autonomy and the Constitutional Right to Privacy: A Case Study in Human Rights and the Unwritten Constitution,* 30 **Hastings L. J.** 957, 961 (1979).
23. **Berlin,** "Two Concepts of Liberty," in **Four Essays on Liberty** 145-54 (1970). As Berlin writes, "[t]his is the argument used by every dictator, inquisitor, and bully who seeks some moral justification for his conduct." *Id.* at 150-51. The technique of the bully is hardly the way to avoid the countermajoritarian difficulty.
24. *See* **Pennock, Democratic Political Theory** 16-50, 58 (1979).
25. *See id.* at 17.
26. Anderson writes:

The basic problem is where to draw the line, or how to maintain a proper balance between individual liberty and legal control. Even those who prize their freedom most highly should be prepared to accept such restrictions as can be seen to be both necessary and just. But there can be no synthesis of liberty and law without justice; for in the last resort it is only justice that can be the arbiter of the circumstances and extent to which law may encroach on liberty, particularly in an era characterized by a widespread demand that everyone should be free to go his own way, on the one hand, and by an unprecedented spate of legislative regulations, on the other. **Anderson, Liberty, Law and Justice** 7 (1978).

27. Freund, *supra* note 19, at 109-10.
28. Berlin notes: " 'Freedom for the pike is death for the minnows'; the liberty of some must depend on the restraint of others." **Berlin**, *supra* note 23, at 124.
29. **Hart, The Concept of Law** 141 (1961). Hart adds:

   [J]udges, even those of a supreme court, are parts of a system the rules of which are determinate enough at the center to supply standards of correct judicial decision. These are regarded by courts as something which they are not free to disregard in the exercise of the authority to make those decisions which cannot be challenged within the system. *Id.* at 141-42.

30. Greenawalt, *Conflicts of Law and Morality — Institutions of Amelioration,* 67 **Va. L. Rev.** 177, 210 (1981).
31. If the Court unjustifiably defies Congress by insisting dogmatically on its own erroneous findings of fact, further remedial legislation will be appropriate. Congress acting in good faith can supplement its remedial legislation with a provision that strips the Supreme Court of appellate jurisdiction to substitute its judgment for congressional findings of empirical facts. *See* **U.S. Constitution,** art. III, § 2. Many commentators have questioned the legitimacy of this approach. *See e.g.,* Auerbach, *The Unconstitutionality of Congressional Proposals to Limit the Jurisdiction of Federal Courts,* 47 **Mo. L. Rev.** 47 (1982); Estreicher, *Congressional Power and Constitutional Rights: Reflections on Proposed "Human Life" Legislation,* 68 **Va. L. Rev.** 333 (1982); Sager, *The Supreme Court, 1980 Term — Foreword: Constitutional Limitations on Congress' Authority to Regulate the Jurisdiction of the Federal Courts,* 95 **Harv. L. Rev.** 17 (1981).
32. Cox, *Congress v. The Supreme Court,* 33 **Mercer L. Rev.** 710-12 (1982); Leedes, *State Action Limitations on Courts and Congressional Power,* 60 **N.C. L. Rev.** 747, 779-82 (1982).
33. *See, e.g.,* Paul v. Davis, 424 U.S. 693, 710-12 (1976).
34. *See* Mashaw, *Administrative Due Process: The Quest for a Dignitary Theory,* 61 **B.U. L. Rev.** 885, 888 (1981). (Mashaw develops the concept of the "positive law trap".)
35. **The American Heritage Dictionary of the English Language** 753 (1969).
36. **Pennock,** *supra* note 24, at 19.
37. Allgeyer v. Louisiana, 165 U.S. 578 (1897). (The Court invalidated a state statute which infringed upon the liberty to contract for insurance.)
38. Lochner v. New York, 198 U.S. 45 (1905). (The Court relied on liberty of contract premises to invalidate legislation restricting hours worked by bakers.)
39. Meyer v. Nebraska, 262 U.S. 390, 399 (1923). (The Court equated liberties having constitutional significance with "privileges long recognized at common law as essential to the orderly pursuit of happiness by free men".)
40. Griswold v. Connecticut, 381 U.S. 479 (1965). (The Court held that a state statute violated the liberty to use contraceptives in the privacy of the marital bedroom.)
41. Roe v. Wade, 410 U.S. 113, 153 (1973). (The Court held that the right of privacy recognized in prior cases was "broad enough to encompass a woman's decision whether or not to terminate her pregnancy.")
42. Monaghan, *Of "Liberty" and "Property",* 62 **Cornell L. Rev.** 405, 409 (1977).
43. **Gunther, Cases and Materials on Constitutional Law** 647 (10th rev. ed. 1980).

44. **Berlin,** *supra* note 23, at 155.
45. *See generally* Leedes, *The Rationality Requirement of the Equal Protection Clause,* 42 **Ohio St. L. J.** 639 (1981).
46. This notion of an individual's substantive due process rights is not at war with man's basic sociability, but reinforces the eighteenth-century tradition that "the concept of an individual is coherent only in the context of social existence." Mashaw, *supra* note 34, at 930.
47. *See* Ackerman, **Social Justice in the Liberal State** 353–57 (1980).
48. However, "there are certain personal matters in which each person should be free to decide what should happen, and in choices over these things whatever he or she thinks is better must be taken to be *better for the society* as a whole, no matter what others think." **Berlin,** Introduction, **Four Essays on Liberty** iii(1970).
49. Palko v. Connecticut, 302 U.S. 319, 325 (1937).
50. **Berlin,** *supra* note 48, at iv.
51. "The only purpose for which power can be rightfully exercised over any member of a civilized community against his will is to prevent harm to others." **Hart, Law, Liberty, and Morality** 4 (1962) [quoting **Mill, On Liberty** (1859)].
52. **Berlin,** "John Stuart Mill and the Ends of Life," in **Four Essays on Liberty** 196 (1970).
53. *Id.* at 191.
54. *See* Karst, *The Freedom of Intimate Association,* 89 **Yale L. J.** 624, 690 (1980). Professor Karst writes:

> Conventional morality influences the judicial process in constitutional cases in two different but related ways. First . . . it is taken into account in developing doctrine — that is, in determining the weights to be assigned in a process of constitutional interest balancing, and particularly those on the state's interest side of the balance. Second, the judiciary is influenced by conventional morality in assessing the relevance to a particular case of its own position in a system of separation of powers. *Id.*

55. **Nozick, Philosophical Explanations** 471 (1981). Nozick writes: "It is not part of our view that all the modulations of moral responsiveness are captured by or are best produced by following formulatable principles." *Id.*
56. **Pennock,** *supra* note 24, at 116.
57. Berlin writes:

> [T]he problem of how an overall increase of liberty in particular circumstances is to be secured, and how it is to be distributed . . . in situations . . . in which the opening of one door leads to the lifting of other barriers . . . how, in a word the maximization of opportunities is in any concrete case to be achieved, can be an agonizing problem, not to be solved by any hard-and-fast rule. **Berlin,** *supra* note 48, at xviii–xix.

58. Mashaw, *supra* note 34, at 909.
59. **Berlin,** *supra* note 23, at 161.
60. *Id.* at 183.
61. 410 U.S. 113 (1973).
62. West Va. State Bd. of Educ. v. Barnette, 319 U.S. 624, 649 (1943) (Frankfurter, J., dissenting).
63. Missouri, Kan. & Tex. Ry. Co. of Tex. v. May, 194 U.S. 267, 270 (1904) (Holmes, J.,) ("[I]t must be remembered that legislatures are ultimate guardians of the liberties and welfare of the people in quite as great a degree as the courts.")
64. **Ellis, The Jeffersonian Crisis: Courts and Politics in the Young Republic** 8 (1970).
65. Kurland, *Government by Judiciary,* 2 U. **Ark. L. Rev.** 307, 320 (1979).
66. *See* Parker, *The Past of Constitutional Theory — And its Future,* 42 **Ohio St. L. J.** 223, 243 (1981).
67. **Unger, Law in Modern Society** 199 (1976).
68. *Id.* Purposive legal reasoning tends to be "characterized by the predominance of instrumental rationality over other modes of thought." *Id.*
69. Letter from Stone to Hughes (Apr. 19, 1938), *quoted in* **Mason, Harlan Fiske Stone: Pillar of the Law** 514 (1956).

70. MacCormick, Legal Reasoning and Legal Theory at 227–28 (1978).
71. Fried, Right and Wrong 8–9 (1978).
72. Rawls, A Theory of Justice 24 (1971).
73. *Id*. at 25.
74. *Id*. at 27.
75. *See* Smart, "An Outline of a System of Utilitarian Ethics," in Utilitarianism For & Against 69–73 (1973).
76. Mackie, Ethics: Inventing Right and Wrong 156 (1977). Mackie notes, "[w]e are rightly skeptical about a man of principle who has a new principle for every case. His decisions are likely to show just that undue deference to what is immediately vivid or pressing which it is one function of principles to counteract." *Id*.
77. Unger, Knowledge and Politics 90 (1975).
78. Fried, *supra* note 71, at 7–8.
79. *See* Ely, Democracy and Distrust: A Theory of Judicial Review 60–69 (1980).
80. Raz, The Concept of a Legal System: An Introduction to the Theory of Legal System 115 (2d rev. ed. 1980). Raz believes:

> An adequate explanation of law is the best starting point for the explanation of the common-sense conception of law. The common-sense conception is made clear by explaining its deviation from the theoretical concept. This approach makes it a desideratum of the theoretical concept of a law that it approximate to the common-sense concept.

81. For an excellent elaboration of the concept of tradition from the standpoint of a sociologist, see Shils, Tradition (1981). Some samples follow: "Tradition acquired the bad name which had become attached to dogma." *Id*. at 5. "Traditionality no more requires intolerance and dogmatism than do scientism, rationalism, and secularism." *Id*. "Tradition . . . is anything which is transmitted or handed down from the past to the present. It makes no statement about what is handed down. . . ." *Id*. at 12. ". . . [T]wo transmissions over three generations are required for a pattern of belief or action to be considered a tradition." *Id*. at 15.
82. *See* Fuller, The Morality of Law 130 (rev. ed. 1969).
83. Formal justice is one of the major steadying factors in our appellate courts. One may not predict with certainty the outcome of a particular appeal; one might know, however, whether to take an appeal or not by calculating the outcome beforehand with some degree of accuracy. In other words, a lawyer advising a client can explain the nature of the business risk that is involved if an appeal were to be taken. *See, e.g.*, Llewellyn, The Common Law Tradition: Deciding Appeals 13–19 (1960); Llewellyn, "My Philosophy of Law," in My Philosophy of Law: Credos of Sixteen American Scholars 184–86 (1941). For critiques of formal justice, *see, e.g.*, Nonet and Selznick, Law and Society in Transition: Toward Responsive Law 103 (1978); Unger, *supra* note 77, at 87–88, 103, 184–85, 261; Unger, *supra* note 67, at 175–77; Lyons, *The Weakness of Formal Equality*, 76 Ethics 146–48 (1966). There is no difficulty in disparaging formal justice, or any other legal standard. It has been said, "If we presume that universal idiocy is conjoined with the standard." Therefore, a theorist should hesitate before he ridicules formal justice. The Court that adheres to formal justice "says. . . in effect, [t]hese are the rules we expect you to follow. If you follow them, you our assurance that they are the rules that will be applied to your conduct." Fuller, *supra* note 82, at 40.
84. Griswold v. Connecticut, 381 U.S. 479, 499–502 (1965) (Harlan, J., concurring); Poe v. Ullman, 367 U.S. 497, 522–55 (1961) (Harlan, J., dissenting).
85. 367 U.S. *at* 548 (Harlan, J., dissenting).
86. 367 U.S. 497 (1961).
87. *Id*. at 548.
88. *Id*. at 552.
89. *Id*. at 551.
90. This general principle of constitutional law explains and justifies both the Court's previous ruling in Skinner v. Oklahoma *ex rel*. Williamson, 316 U.S. 535, 546 (1942)

(Jackson, J., concurring), and Justice Harlan's proposed case rulings in the birth control cases *viz.*, the state's intolerable intrusion into a married couple's intimate sexual life abridged the kind of liberties "that require particularly careful scrutiny of the state needs asserted to justify their abridgement. . . ." 367 U.S. at 543.

91. MacCormick has described the process with characteristic clarity:

> [W]hen we ask what gives a principle [constitutional] quality we must give the answer in terms of its actual or potential explanatory and justificatory function in relation to [constitutional] law as already established, that is in relation to established rules of law. . . .
>
> Does this involve drawing a sharp disjunction between the principles of law and moral and political principles? Yes and no. It involves asserting that there really is a difference between principles which are and those which are not legal, subject to an intermediate *terra incognita* of [inchoate] principles struggling for legal recognition, [such as the constitutional right recognized in *Griswold*]. . . . It does not involve the assertion that a principle which is a legal principle thereby stops being a moral or political principle. . . ." *See* **MacCormick,** *supra* note 70, at 238. It may take a novel case for an inchoate principle, bubbling just beneath the surface of the law, to erupt into plain view.

92. 381 U.S. 479 (1965).
93. *Id.* at 510 (Black, J., dissenting).
94. *Id.* at 513 n. 5 [quoting **Hand, The Bill of Rights** 70 (1958)].
95. 381 U.S. 479, 501 (1965) (Harlan, J., concurring).
96. *Id.*
97. **Hand, The Bill of Rights** 15 (1958).
98. 410 U.S. 113 (1973).
99. 405 U.S. 438 (1972). Justice Brennan referred to "the right of the *individual,* married or single, to be free from unwarranted governmental intrusion into matters so fundamentally affecting a person as the decision whether to bear or beget a chlid." *Id.* at 453.
100. **Woodward and Armstrong, The Brethren** 175-76 (1979).
101. *See* Ely, *The Wages of Crying Wolf: A Comment on Roe v. Wade,* 82 **Yale L. J.** 928-30 (1973).
102. Skinner v. Oklahoma *ex rel.* Williamson, 316 U.S. 535 (1942), was decided on the principle that "'[m]arriage and procreation are fundamental to the very existence and survival of the race," *id.* at 541, and that once a human being is sterilized, it is "to his irreparable injury." *See id.* Griswold v. Connecticut, 381 U.S. 479 (1965). *Griswold* was a very controversial decision which emphasized the marital relationship rather than the birth control aspects of the case. *Id.* at 484-86. Yet, in Eisenstadt v. Baird, 405 U.S. 438 (1972), Justice Brennan made the gratuitous statement that the *"individual"* has a right, "married or single to be free from unwarranted governmental intrusion into matters so fundamentally affecting a person as the decision whether to bear or beget a child." *Id.* at 453 (emphasis in original). This dictum wnet beyond *Griswold,* and paved the way for Roe v. Wade, 410 U.S. 113 (1978), and Justice Blackmun's addendum that the heavy responsibilities and burdens of parenthood make parental control over the timing and size of the family important. *Id.* at 153. Thus, the *Skinner* principle was unpacked for a new and different journey in *Roe,* one which certainly justifies Dworkin's statement that principles are not "a fixed set of standards." **Dworkin, Taking Rights Seriously** 76 (1978).
103. United States v. Carolene Prods. Co., 304 U.S. 144, 152 n. 4 (1938).
104. *Developments in the Law — Equal Protection,* 82 **Harv. L. Rev.** 1065 (1969).
105. *See generally* Gunther, *The Supreme Court, 1971 Term — Foreword: In Search of Evolving Doctrine on a Changing Court: A Model for a Newer Equal Protection,* 86 **Harv. L. Rev.** 1 (1972).
106. Williams v. Illinois, 399 U.S. 235, 259 (1970) (Harlan, J., concurring in result).
107. *Id.* at 260.
108. *Id.*
109. *Id.*

110. *Id.*
111. *Id.*
112. *See* Mills v. Rogers, 457 U.S. 291, 102 S. Ct. 2442 (1982). (The Court granted review "to determine whether involuntarily committed mental patients have a constitutional right to refuse treatment with antipsychotic drugs," but did not reach the merits.)
113. *See* Leedes, *The Revival of Interest in Justice Harlan's Flexible Due Process Balancing Approach,* 19 **San Diego L. Rev.** 737, 761-62 (1982).
114. 457 U.S. 307, 102 S. Ct. 2452 (1982).
115. *See* Fiss, *The Supreme Court, 1978 Term — Foreword: The Forms of Justice,* 93 **Harv. L. Rev.** 27-28 (1979).
116. *Compare* Nebbia v. New York, 291 U.S. 502 (1934) *with* Williamson v. Lee Optical Co., 348 U.S. 483 (1955).
117. Romeo v. Youngberg, 644 F.2d 147, 182 (3d Cir. 1981) (Aldisert, J., concurring), *vacated and remanded,* 102 S. Ct. 2452 (1982).
118. *Id.* [quoting **Smith, Jurisprudence** 21 (1909)].
119. In Cabell v. Chavez-Salido, 454 U.S. 432 (1982), Justice White attempted to justify the Court's inability to adhere to a consistent line of growth in the cases dealing with alienage restrictions in public employment. He wrote, "But to say that the decisions do not fall into a neat pattern is not to say that they fall into no pattern. In fact," he added, "they illustrate a not unusual characteristic of legal development: Broad principles are articulated, narrowed when applied to new contexts, and finally replaced when the distinctions they rely upon are no longer tenable." *Id.* at 436.
120. 644 F.2d 147, 182 (3d Cir. 1980) (Aldisert, J., concurring), *quoting* Ely, *The Supreme Court, 1977 Term. Foreword: On Discovering Fundamental Values,* 92 **Harv. L. Rev.** 5, 32 (1978) [citing Amsterdam, *Perspectives on the Fourth Amendment,* 58 **Minn. L. Rev.** 349, 351-52 (1974)].
121. 644 F.2d at 182.
122. *Id.*
123. Gunther, *supra* note 105, at 8.
124. 457 U.S. 307, 102 S. Ct. 2452 (1982).
125. For example, although Justice Harlan often applied a compelling interest test in First-Amendment cases, "his balancing typically entailed a fair and careful evaluation of the asserted state justifications for impinging upon First-Amendment interests." Gunther, *In Search of Judicial Quality on a Changing Court: The Case of Justice Powell,* 24 **Stan. L. Rev.** 1001, 1006 (1972). Perhaps Harlan's balancing was not always principled, but it was always disciplined.
126. *Compare* Planned Parenthood of Missouri v. Danforth, 428 U.S. 52 (1976) *with* H.L. v. Matheson, 450 U.S. 398 (1981).
127. *See* Scheinberg v. Smith, 659 F.2d 476, 483-85 (5th Cir. 1981).
128. 410 U.S. 113 (1973).
129. The reasonable expectations standard, often transcending the judge's volition, illustrates that pure legal reasoning is often inadequate to dispose of hard cases; although theories of legal reasoning and constitutional law are usually mutually reinforcing, one is incomplete without the other. *See* **MacCormick,** *supra* note 4, at 265.
130. *See, e.g.,* Maher v. Roe, 432 U.S. 464 (1977); Harris v. McRae, 448 U.S. 292 (1980). (The Court upheld funding discrimination, which comparatively disadvantaged females who desired abortions.)
131. Gunther, *supra* note 105, at 1.
132. Zablocki v. Redhail, 434 U.S. 374, 399 (Powell, J., concurring).
133. *See* **Hand,** *supra* note 97, at 69.
134. *Id.* at 68-73.
135. 347 U.S. 483 (1954).
136. The reasonable expectation standard is not always easily applied. For example, assume that a statute prohibits mutilation of the American flag. Mutilation of the flag in order to express hatred of the United States is an act presumably unacceptable to the controlling

majorities in virtually all American communities. On the other hand, it is arguable that the same controlling majorities strongly support the concept of freedom of speech. In this situation, the Court has substantial discretion to balance the competing interests and resolve the ambivalence.

137. Poe v. Ullman, 367 U.S. 497, 542 (1961) (Harlan, J., dissenting).

138. Leedes, *The Supreme Court Mess,* 57 **Tex. L. Rev.** 1361 (1979).

139. As Gunther writes, "[A] Supreme Court opinion should strive for more than "fair balancing" in the individual case before the Court. It should also provide the maximum guidance possible for lower courts and litigants. An excessively particularized opinion lacks that quality." Gunther, *supra* note 125, at 1026 (footnote omitted).

140. *Id.* at 1026–27.

141. *See, e.g.,* New York Times Co. v. Sullivan, 376 U.S. 254 (1964) ("actual malice" rule in libel cases).

142. In the Pentagon Papers case, New York Times Co. v. United States, 403 U.S. 713 (1971), Justice Harlan argued that the First-Amendment protection afforded by courts must take into account "the proper compass of the President's foreign relations power." *Id.* at 757. Thus, he would not presume in all cases that a prior restraint is unconstitutional.

143. The Court's incitement test in subversive advocacy cases is not clearly designed to take into account the gravity of the harm that is advocated. Thus, in some cases, this cryptic test might provide too little or too much first amendment protection. *See* Brandenburg v. Ohio, 395 U.S. 444 (1969).

144. *See, e.g.,* Cohen v. California, 403 U.S. 15 (1971). (Justice Harlan appears to have combined *ad hoc* balancing with First Amendment definitional balancing tests.) In Globe Newsletter Co. v. Superior Court, 457 U.S. 596, 102 S. Ct. 2613 (1982), the Supreme Court noted that case by case balancing is required to determine whether a closure of acriminal trial to the press is justified. Even though the state's interest in protecting the physical an professional well-being of a teenage rape victim is ordinarily compelling, the trial judge must in each case take into account "the minor victim's age, psychological maturity, and understanding, the nature of the crime, the desires of the victim, and the interests of parents and relatives." *Id.* at 2621.

145. The cases that deal with barriers to a candidate's substantive due process right of access to the ballot illustrate the frequent need to adopt a case by case approach. In Clements v. Fashing, 457 U.S. 957, 102 S. Ct. 2836 (1982), the plurality opinion indicated that an extremely deferential level of review is sometimes applicable. Even Justice Brennan, dissenting in *Fashing,* conceded that strict scrutiny may be imprroper when public employees are adversely affected by ballot access requirements. *Id. at 2850. In short, generalizations about levels of scrutiny in these cases are hazardous if not worthless. As Justice Stevens noted in Fashing,* "as in so many areas of the law, it is important to consider each case individually." *Id. See also* Anderson v. Celebreeze, 460 U.S. *780,* 103 S. Ct. 1564 (1983).

146. Williams v. Illinois, 399 U.S. 235, 260 (1970) (Harlan, J., concurring).

147. Poe v. Ullman, 367 U.S. 497, 542 (1961) (Harlan, J., dissenting).

148. **Ely,** *supra* note 79, at 18.

149. *Id.* at 41.

150. Judge Aldisert writes: "The common law 'creeps from point to point, testing each step' and grows slowly by gradual accretion from the resolution of specific problems." Romeo v. Youngberg, 644 F.2d 147, 182 (3rd Cir. 1980) (Aldisert, J., concurring) [quoting **Whitehead, Adventures of Ideas,** ch. 2, § 6 (1967)].

151. Cohens v. Virginia, 19 U.S. (6 Wheat.) 264, 404 (1821).

Footnotes for Part III, Chapter 9

152. Bickel, The Morality of Consent 24–26 (1975).
153. Ayer, The Central Questions of Philosophy 63 (1973).
154. *Id.* at 64.
155. *See* chap. 4, *supra* (a discussion of Reid's common sense doctrine and its influence on the framers.)
156. Bickel, *supra* note 152, at 26.
157. Berlin, Four Essays on Liberty 97 (1970).
158. *Id.*
159. Bickel, *supra* note 152, at 26.
160. Berlin, *supra* note 157.
161. Bickel, *supra* note 152, at 26.
162. Berlin, *supra* note 157, at 100–01.
163. *Id.* at 103.
164. *Id.* at 119.
165. Freund, "Social Justice and the Law" in Social Justice 110 (Brandt,
166. Holmes, The Common Lae 35 (1881). Holmes added, "Most generally to be sure, under our practices and traditions, the unconscious result of instictive preferences and inarticulate convictions, but nonetheless traceable to views of public policy in the last analysis." *Id.* at 35-36.
167. Berlin, *supra* note 157, at 20.
168. Bickel, *supra* note 152, at 142.
169. Fullilove v. Klutznick, 448 U.S. 448, 532 (Stewart, J., dissenting).

INDEX

H. L. v. Matheson, 152n126
Hamilton, Alexander, 18, 26, 54, 62, 64,
    82, 88, 89, 129n152, 134n262, 134
    n264-268
Hamilton, Walton, 45, 46
Hamilton, Sir W., 134, 138n403
Hand, Judge Learned, 16, 19, 102, 106,
    140n14, 145n135, 151n94
Harlan, Justice John, 81-83, 101-103,
    153n142, 153n144
    due process formula, 103
Harrington, James, 36, 128n128
Hart, H. L. A., 5, 93, 95-96, 118n79,
    139n423, 148n29-30
Hayek, F. A., 35, 131n198
Hegel, 74, 141n29
Heidegger, Martin, 21, 141-142n39
Helvering v. Gerhardt, 153n138
Hermeneutics, 74, 140n2, 140n13, 141
    n32
    describes courts' methodoloyg, 67
    explains extraction of textual mean-
        ing, 113
    extended discussion of legal hermen-
        eutics and judge with hermeneutic
        perspective, 18
    legal hermeneutics and judges' prac-
        tical task, 25
Hill, 124n247
Historicism, 73-77, 140n10, 142n42,
    143n56, 143n67
History, 109
    theory of judicial intervention, 100,
        102
    professors of law uninterested in, 21
    pseudo history, 20
    reference to by interpreters, 11
    relevant to court, 17
Hobbes, Thomas, 42, 46
    depiction of state of nature, 42
    Hobbesian psychology, 43
Holmes, Justice Oliver Wendell, 34, 79,
    111, 149n63, 154n166
Hughes, Charles Evans, 85, 145n141-
    143, 149n69

Human rights, 13, 24, 29, 94, 140n18
Hume, David, 36, 38, 40, 44, 46, 50,
    55-58, 62, 125n272, 127n70, 135
    n279, 136n341, 137n362
Huttado v. California, 144n97
Hutcheson, Francis, intro, 33-34, 35, 36,
    37-38, 39, 40, 41, 42, 43, 44, 45, 46,
    47-48, 49, 50, 51, 52, 53-54, 57, 60,
    63-64, 111, 128n107, 128-129n139-
    141, 129, 130, 131

Idea of law, 21, 77
Idea of progress, 4, 77
Impartiality, 113
    Hutcheson's sense of, 41-42, 49, 52
    nourished by Reid's ideas, 65
Impartial judge, 101, 110-111, 113, 128
    n122
    approves of certain actions, 60
    discountenances absurdity, 63
    expected to justify decisions, 54
    need for, 54
Inchoate principles, intro, 26, 68, 75,
    76, 101-102, 139n424, 139n429,
    151n91
Interpreting the Constitution
    difficulties in generalizing, intro
    methods, disagreement over, 9
    preferred mode, 7
    responsibility of authorized interpre-
        ters, intro
    textual ambiguity, intro
    theory of ultimate interpretation, 9-11
Interpretivists and interpretivism, 10-13,
    140n19, 142n40
    debate with non-interpretivists, 11, 67
    extremists among, 71
    inadequacies of, 69
    noninterpretivism, see separate head-
        ing
    ultimate interpretivism, 11, 14, 24

Jefferson, Thomas, 38, 44, 45, 54,
    117n43, 130n43, 130n163, 131